Stress Between Work and Family

The Plenum Series on Stress and Coping

Series Editor:
Donald Meichenbaum, *University of Waterloo, Waterloo, Ontario, Canada*

Editorial Board: Bruce P. Dohrenwend, *Columbia University*
Marianne Frankenhaeuser, *University of Stockholm*
Norman Garmezy, *University of Minnesota*
Mardi J. Horowitz, *University of California Medical School,*
San Francisco
Richard S. Lazarus, *University of California, Berkeley*
Michael Rutter, *University of London*
Dennis C. Turk, *University of Pittsburgh*
John P. Wilson, *Cleveland State University*
Camille Wortman, *University of Michigan*

A CLINICAL GUIDE TO THE TREATMENT OF THE
HUMAN STRESS RESPONSE
George S. Everly, Jr.

COPING WITH LIFE CRISES
An Integrated Approach
Edited by Rudolf H. Moos

COPING WITH NEGATIVE LIFE EVENTS
Clinical and Social Psychological Perspectives
Edited by C. R. Snyder and Carol E. Ford

DYNAMICS OF STRESS
Physiological, Psychological, and Social Perspectives
Edited by Mortimer H. Appley and Richard Trumbull

HUMAN ADAPTATION TO EXTREME STRESS
From the Holocaust to Vietnam
Edited by John P. Wilson, Zev Harel, and Boaz Kahana

STRESS BETWEEN WORK AND FAMILY
Edited by John Eckenrode and Susan Gore

Stress Between Work and Family

Edited by
JOHN ECKENRODE
Cornell University
Ithaca, New York

and
SUSAN GORE
University of Massachusetts
Boston, Massachusetts

WITHDRAWN

PLENUM PRESS • NEW YORK AND LONDON

Library of Congress Cataloging-in-Publication Data

Stress between work and family / edited by John Eckenrode and Susan
Gore.
        p.   cm. -- (The Plenum series on stress and coping)
     Includes bibliographical references.
     ISBN 0-306-43318-4
     1. Work and family. 2. Stress (Psychology)   I. Eckenrode, John.
II. Gore, Susan.   III. Series.
HD4904.25.S86   1990
158.7--dc20
                                                          89-26468
                                                              CIP

© 1990 Plenum Press, New York
A Division of Plenum Publishing Corporation
233 Spring Street, New York, N.Y. 10013

Printed in the United States of America

To Cathy and Josh

To Neil and Zachary

Contributors

Monica Biernat, Department of Psychology, University of Florida, Gainesville, Florida 32611

Niall Bolger, Department of Psychology, University of Denver, Denver, Colorado 80208

Evelyn J. Bromet, Department of Psychiatry and Behavioral Science, SUNY at Stony Brook, Stony Brook, New York 11794-8790

Judith S. Brook, Mount Sinai School of Medicine, New York, New York 10029

Patricia Cohen, School of Public Health, Columbia University, New York, New York 10032

Anita DeLongis, Department of Psychology, University of British Columbia, Vancouver V6T 1Y7, British Columbia, Canada

Mary Amanda Dew, Department of Psychiatry, University of Pittsburgh, Pittsburgh, Pennsylvania 15213

John Eckenrode, Department of Human Development and Family Studies, Cornell University, Ithaca, New York 14853

Carol-Ann Emmons, National Opinion Research Center, 1155 East 60th Street, Chicago, Illinois 60637

Susan Gore, Department of Sociology, University of Massachusetts–Boston, Boston, Massachusetts 02115

Jim Johnson, New York State Psychiatric Institute, 722 West 168th Street, New York, New York 10032

Ronald C. Kessler, Survey Research Center/ISR, University of Michigan, Ann Arbor, Michigan 48109

Eric L. Lang, American Institute for Research, Palo Alto, California 94302

Selma A. Lewis, Committee of Special Education, District 10, 5500 Broadway, Bronx, New York 10463

G. Ramsay Liem, Department of Psychology, Boston College, Chestnut Hill, Massachusetts 02167

Joan Huser Liem, Department of Psychology, University of Massachusetts–Boston, Boston, Massachusetts 02115

Mary E. McCall, Human Development and Aging Program, University of California, San Francisco, San Francisco, California 94143

David K. Parkinson, Department of Preventive Medicine, SUNY at Stony Brook, Stony Brook, New York 11794-8790

Leonard I. Pearlin, Human Development and Aging Program, University of California, San Francisco, San Francisco, California 94143

Linda Beth Tiedje, College of Nursing, Michigan State University, East Lansing, Michigan 48824

Robert S. Weiss, Work and Family Research Unit, University of Massachusetts–Boston, Boston, Massachusetts 02125

Elaine Wethington, Department of Human Development and Family Studies, Cornell University, Ithaca, New York 14853

Blair Wheaton, Department of Sociology, University of Toronto, Toronto M5S 1A1, Ontario, Canada

Camille B. Wortman, Institute for Social Research, University of Michigan, Ann Arbor, Michigan 48106-1248

Foreword

Work, family, and community are the social environments with which we all interact. Most of us experience some sort of "stress" at various times as we interact in these environments, and there is increasing evidence that stress can be dysfunctional for some. This volume organizes and presents some of the rapidly growing body of knowledge regarding stress that stems from interactions between the environments of work and family. Several of the chapters point out the complexity of the interactions between events that are perceived by some as stressful, whether they are due to work, unemployment, or marital conflict over work. But it is clear that the event (stressor) is not the most important issue. Rather, it is how the various actors perceive the stressful event that determines whether or not such events are dysfunctional. Indeed, the differing conclusions drawn in this book in the different chapters that study working mothers demonstrate the complexity of this interaction. Depending on what populations and what measures are used, the conclusion might be that a working mother causes stress in the family or that family demands make working especially stressful for mothers.

Given such different findings, one then wonders if the concept of stress itself has not become outmoded or lost its usefulness, at least as a context within which to plan a research strategy. The term retains its allure for the public: Indeed, everyone seems to know what stress is, until one tries to measure it! The contributors to this volume have advanced the field to the point that researchers no longer should be content to measure an event, call it stressful, and attempt to correlate it with various outcomes but rather must measure the context in which it occurs, the response to the stimulus, and the multiple relationships involved. For instance, in the early 1980s, social supports were widely seen as a mechanism to cope effectively with stress. It is now apparent that the effectiveness of social supports depends on what kinds are available and employed. Some are harmful, some are helpful, many are neutral. We should not let the complexities deter research on stress, however. It has proven to be a very effective umbrella term under which to organize broadly based, multidisciplinary research. Research in the behavioral sciences must use several methods on the same population simultaneously, employ multiple disciplines, and include personal, family, and environmental variables if we are to advance our understanding of these complex interrelations. This collection of chapters by members of the Consortium for Research Involving Stress Processes is a good example of such breadth.

Several years ago, the William T. Grant Foundation initiated a program of "consortia." We have supplied small amounts of funds to bring together talented investigators who are interested in a particular field. There are now seven such consortia, working in different areas. They meet two or three times a year, exchange research ideas, present data at an early stage of their projects, and in some instances, as in this volume, produce one or more monographs or books. We believe this process is one way to advance a research field, and I am pleased to see the creative and stimulating chapters that have resulted from this group.

ROBERT J. HAGGERTY, M.D.
President
William T. Grant Foundation
Clinical Professor of Pediatrics
New York Hospital/Cornell Medical Center
New York, New York

Preface

Since the early studies that documented the influence that life situation has on health status, stress researchers have been trying to refine our understanding of this basic relationship. It has not been easy, and in his foreword Dr. Robert Haggerty appropriately asks whether the concept of stress has lost its usefulness as a research tool. This concern in large part reflects a fundamental and difficult problem: Given the variable nature of stress and responses to it, how do we conceptualize and design research projects that capture the underlying processes in diverse populations and which are critically significant to the health of individuals, families, and communities?

This is the challenge we faced in establishing a consortium to study the stress process 6 years ago with the support of Dr. Haggerty and the W. T. Grant Foundation. In this volume we focus on the work–family interface for two reasons. First, as we see in the chapters to follow, the fit or lack of fit among the activities, obligations, and rewards in these two institutional arenas is currently a personal problem for millions of Americans, and it is the root of major public policy initiatives. Because we know from existing data that these problems affect the health and well-being of adults and children of all ages, we think that this is an important empirical problem for stress researchers—and we believe that we can make a difference. Second, stress research has a rich body of theory and a stock of analytic tools for studying the linkages among environment, group, and individual. Although there are long-standing traditions of research both on the family and on worker health, the meeting of these two arenas cannot be wholly understood from the perspectives of either field. Stress research can add significantly to an understanding both of the characteristic features of the work/family nexus, and of the health-related dynamics that follow from these. In our introductory chapter we identify a general framework for such investigations, and the authors take us still further. In sum, this volume gives us a view of the scope of the investigations that are possible, as well as lessons about the specific concepts and methods that are required for such research.

This volume is a group project of the consortium we call CRISP (Consortium for Research Involving Stress Processes). Many of the studies reported on were initiated during our years together and have been fostered and shaped with the input and support of consortium members. The chapters themselves were presented, circulated, and revised on the basis of group ideas. And we as editors have relied upon and benefited from the group's guidance. We wish to thank all of the consortium members for their contributions and to give a special acknowledgment here to the members whose names do not appear on these chapters. These individuals are: Carol Aneshensel, David Dooley, Susan Folkman, Benjamin Gottlieb, Nan Lin, Peggy Thoits, and Donald Wertlieb. We would also like to thank Eliot Werner, Executive Editor at Plenum Press, and Donald Meichenbaum, editor of this series, for their support and guidance throughout this project.

Contents

Chapter 4. Stress, Support, and Coping among Women

Carol-Ann Emmons, Monica Biernat, Linda Beth Tiedje, Eric L. Lang, and Camille B. Wortman

Chapter 5. The Microstructure of Daily Role-Related Stress in

Niall Bolger, Anita DeLongis, Ronald C. Kessler, and Elaine Wethington

Chapter 6. Single Parenthood and Employment: Double

Patricia Cohen, Jim Johnson, Selma A. Lewis, and Judith S. Brook

Chapter 7. Spillover between Work and Family: A Study of Blue-Collar Working Wives 133

Evelyn J. Bromet, Mary Amanda Dew, and David K. Parkinson

Stress Between
Work and Family

1

Stress and Coping at the Boundary of Work and Family

JOHN ECKENRODE and SUSAN GORE

INTRODUCTION

In this volume we bring together a series of chapters that focus on the nature and management of stress that crosses work and family roles. For some time, researchers and practicioners have recognized the fluid boundaries between work and family life, an idea more recently expressed in the concept of spillover. This concept has been most frequently used to characterize the domestic strains of workers in high stress occupations (e.g., police work) that result from an inability to dissipate the tensions that accumulate over the workday. Alternatively, stress may flow from the family to the work setting, as in the inability of working mothers to keep family responsibilities from impinging upon their workday. A critical and less often researched problem of role boundaries concerns the spread of stress across several members of the family, an observation often made in clinical studies, but less compatible with most large-scale and individualistic research strategies. The spillover concept therefore includes stress and coping processes flowing across individuals as well as social roles. The chapters in this volume reflect this dual concern.

Although intuitively sensible, interesting, and relevant to an increas-

JOHN ECKENRODE • Department of Human Development and Family Studies, Cornell University, Ithaca, New York 14853.   **SUSAN GORE** • Department of Sociology, University of Massachusetts–Boston, Boston, Massachusetts 02115.

ing share of the population, the extent and quality of the research base focused on the work–family interface and its mental health impact lags behind this appeal. The chapters in this volume seek to provide new insights into our conceptual understanding of stress characteristic of work–family linkages and to provide the basis for improving the methodological approaches to this research area.

This volume stands alongside and has clearly been informed by previous books more generally focused on the work–family interface. The pioneering work on dual-career families by Rhona and Robert Rapoport (1971, 1976) helped draw scholarly attention to this increasingly prevalent family form. A monograph by Rosabeth Moss Kanter (1977) provided the field with an important review of the work and family literature to that date and gave us the framework for a research agenda that could no longer assume the "myth of separate worlds." Chaya Piotrowski's (1979) important volume, *Work and the Family System,* followed soon afterwards and provided the field with a ground-breaking qualitative study of the meaning of work for the emotional and family lives of 13 working and lower-middle-class families. Complementing this microscopic examination of family life, Graham Staines and Joseph Pleck (Pleck, 1985; Staines & Pleck, 1983) have produced books that employ the power of a large national data set (the 1977 Quality of Employment Survey) to explore the impact of work schedules on family life and employed wives' role overload. Recent edited volumes have also served to bring together important contributions in this general area. Two examples are *Two Paychecks: Life in Dual Earner Families,* by Joan Aldous (1982), and *Work and Family: Changing Roles of Men and Women,* by Patricia Voydanoff (1984).

The present volume complements these earlier works by similarly addressing linkages between work and family, but it also can be contrasted with them in a number of ways. First, it explicitly focuses on the concept of stress, with these chapters employing conceptual models and methodologies characteristic of the field of stress research. The chapters are authored by researchers who have made important contributions to the field of stress research and who bring these insights to the study of work–family linkages. Second, this volume places an emphasis on the mechanisms or underlying processes that reflect stress transmission across role domains and individuals and the factors that can moderate or buffer these processes. Data of this nature both strengthen the inferences that can be made about stress and its effects and suggest key junctures for intervention. Finally, all the chapters derive from the current research efforts of these investigators and, as such, represent new and previously unpublished information with regard to stress processes that characterize the interconnectedness of work and family arenas.

NEW DIRECTIONS IN STRESS RESEARCH

An important development in the field of stress research has been a movement away from static approaches of conceptualizing and studying stress and its effects to a fuller appreciation of the dynamic processes linking stress exposure to health outcomes. In an earlier work that assessed the status of research on stressful life events and social supports (Eckenrode & Gore, 1981), we challenged the usual approaches taken to the study of the stress process. We characterized the prevailing paradigms as being acontextual in that they failed to take into account the embeddedness of stressors in daily life and the social contexts in which individuals found themselves. In the end we called for research that would bridge the individual and social levels of analysis, in addition to recognizing the inherent links that exist between experiences defined as stressful and the personal and social resources thought to protect or buffer the individual against the traumatic effects of such occurrences.

In sum, we felt at that time that the field of stress research needed to make more explicit the connections between the key junctures in the stress process. Specifically, life events could no longer be viewed as purely external environmental assaults on individuals, unconnected to the structure of people's daily lives. Likewise, stress buffers like social support could no longer be seen as unchanging features of a person's repertoire of resources that in some unspecified way act to neutralize the impact of stressful experiences.

Clearly these old approaches were too shallow and mechanistic. The chapters represented here exemplify research strategies inherent in a new generation of stress research. They seek to place the individual in a meaningful social context and ask not only about exposure to stressful experiences but also consider individual differences in the interpretation and reaction to them. In the final section of this introduction, we introduce these papers in more detail, but we first will present a conceptual framework for the investigation of stress between work and family.

A MODEL OF STRESS BETWEEN WORK AND FAMILY

We propose a working model for the study of stress processes that cross the boundary between work and family in order to provide a framework for the chapters to follow. Our model is also intended to offer a perspective on problems of stress transmission that were beyond the scope of this collection or much of the current research literature. We start with the proposition that stress in the workplace affects the family and vice versa, the extent of which varies as a function of multiple factors related to the structure of the family and workplace in question, the nature of the stressors, and those situational factors that moderate the stress transmission process.

In keeping with our focus on stress across social roles, we must consider the nature of the boundaries that exist across diverse workplace and the family structures and their joint configurations. It is clear, for example, that the boundary between work and family is much more permeable when considering a family-owned business than with work involving paid labor outside of the home. Moreover, the work–family boundary of a single parent may be challenged more frequently than occurs in two adult households. Clearly, the nature of the workplace and the characteristics of the family will determine the structure of the boundary that exists between these two worlds.

Another concept of relevance to our discussion is that of boundary maintenance, a term encompassing those activities initiated by family members or persons in the workplace (at the individual or organizational level) designed to foster or maintain a given type of boundary between these roles. Work–family boundaries are therefore important to us not only in terms of their structural properties but also because concrete activities may be necessary to maintain them. For example, organizations may develop policies concerning the use of the phones for personal (i.e., family-related) calls, just as an individual may maintain an unlisted phone number at home to prevent work-related calls from interrupting official time off from work. Conversely, the trend toward work-site day care facilities may be viewed as permitting a controlled degree of overlap between work and family spheres.

Figure 1 depicts the major sets of variables that will be considered in the papers in this volume. In this model we incorporate four major sets of variables: (1) stressors, both ongoing and eventful; (2) coping resources and strategies; (3) health-related outcomes; and (4) characteristics of the participants that may modify the stress and coping process (e.g., gender), family structure variables as well as variables defining the structure of the workplace.

Three sets of related, but conceptually distinct, processes will also concern us: (1) *transmission processes* that involve the carryover of stressors or coping resources from one role to the other or one person to the other; (2) *stress-mediating processes* within the family and workplace that involve the pathways through which stress impacts on a family member's or worker's well-being; and (3) *stress-moderating processes* that reflect the presence of conditions that may prevent stress from crossing over from one role to the next, from one person to the next, or in determining reactivity to stress within a given role or a given role.

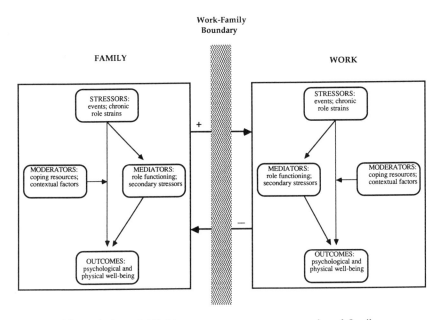

Figure 1. A model linking stress processes across work and family.

As this figure makes clear, stress may flow across the work–family boundary in both directions and have a net positive as well as negative influence in terms of the well-being of the worker and his/her family. This is in keeping with a general understanding of the stress process as involving stressors and negative outcomes on the one hand but also positive resources and experiences that may buffer the adverse effects of stressful situations. For example, stress in the workplace may cross over into the family through a basic stress contagion process, that is, the distress caused by work events or conditions is brought home and displayed in the family setting by the worker being fatigued, anxious, distracted, depressed, or otherwise unavailable emotionally or physically to other family members. This is evidenced by data that show work-related stressors experienced by one family member having an effect on the family/household functioning or well-being of a spouse or a child.

On the other hand, stress in the workplace may serve to mobilize family resources and, through the initiation of positive forms of social interactions aimed at an outside threat, lead to more cohesiveness among family members. Here stress in one setting results in positive outcomes in another setting, even if the original source of stress in not directly modified. Processes of this nature are increasingly documented in stress research, contradicting earlier thinking that multiple roles necessarily lead to more role conflict and distress.

At the level of coping with stress, it is also clear that effective coping behavior and processes in one role setting may be dysfunctional in another and that the effects of coping in one domain may display positive or negative spillover into another. For example, negative transmission may occur if coping skills relevant to a particular set of work-related stressors are inappropriate to coping with stressors in the family or other role settings. Kohn's research (Kohn, 1969; Kohn & Schooler, 1982) is an example of this process at the level of personality and values. He and his colleagues have demonstrated that workplace conditions that entail close supervision, work that is not substantively complex, and that is excessively routinized can undermine a sense of self-direction and reinforce conformity to external authority. Likewise, Pearlin and Schooler (1978) showed that cognitive disengagement was an effective coping strategy for work-related stressors, but not for family-based stressors. Therefore, survival skills adequate to cope with chronic stressors in the workplace may not serve individuals or their children well in terms of coping with family-related stressors that require a sense of self-efficacy and control for the initiation of effective problem-focused or emotion-focused coping responses.

In addition to learned coping responses failing to effectively generalize to other role settings, other forms of negative transmission can occur. One such process may involve what has been called *resource drain*. The vigilance and mobilization of resources required to cope effectively with stressors in the family or at the workplace may leave the individual with diminished resources to cope with stressors in the other setting.

Positive transmission involving coping could occur in several ways. The individual, having successfully mastered problems at work, may experience a renewed sense of mastery or self-esteem, these being resources at the individual level that are generally helpful in coping with a variety of stressors outside of work. Second, specific skills learned at work may be transferable to the family setting and vice versa. The physician should be well prepared to cope with medical emergencies in the home, and the plumber can prevent a small home maintenance hassle from evolving into a major headache. Third, family role relationships and support structures may be altered in positive ways in response to work stress. This could benefit the children as well as adults if they are developmentally at a stage where increased autonomy and responsibility are facilitative of psychological growth, as demonstrated in the research of Elder and his colleagues with children of the great depression (e.g., Elder, 1974). Fourth, extended social networks that are built and maintained in one role area may be mobilized when coping with stressors arising in the other setting. For example, family-based social relationships may be called upon to assist a laid-off worker find alternative employment. Finally, formal coping resources in the work setting may assist the individual in coping with family-based stressors. An example here would be employee assistance programs that may help a worker not only with work-based problems but also problems involving substance abuse, marital conflict, or other family stressors. Employer-based day care centers provide support to families and may serve to prevent the occurrence of chronic family stressors arising from inadequate day care, and basic health insurance benefits can clearly buffer the impact of medical problems for the family.

It is clear therefore that coping resources and strategies also move across the work–family boundary in both a positive and negative direction. Previous research has recognized certain of these linkages, as is the case of studies in occupational stress that have explored the role of social supports as stress buffers. For example, House and his colleagues (House, 1981; LaRocco, House, & French, 1980) explored the relative effectiveness of spouse, co-worker, or supervisor support in buffering the effects of chronic work stress, whereas Gore (1978) explored some of these effects for men who lost their jobs. Such studies have provided the field with critical baseline information about the importance of diverse social relationships in buffering occupational stressors.

The distinguishing feature of the present collection is the attention given to the processes by which such buffering mechanisms are facilitated or inhibited. What these chapters make very clear is that stress transmission and stress-buffering processes are by no means simple or automatic. Rather, they are quite sensitive to the characteristics of the people involved (e.g., personality characteristics that favor or discourage disclosure of stress experiences and their emotional consequences), characteristics of the relationships in question (e.g., the degree of preexisting conflict, disclosure, and support in a marital relationship), the combination of work and family roles assumed by members of a particular household (e.g., whether the wife or mother is working or whether children are present), and the nature of the stresses involved. As with stress research in general, the chapters in this volume share a common concern with identifying those contextual variables that help explain why some individuals or families are more resistant than others to having stress in one role negatively affect relationships or functioning in another role area.

Beyond stress transmission and buffering processes, a third set of issues our model emphasizes concerns the mechanisms by which stress in one role setting is transmitted to the other. Here we are concerned with mediating processes, that is, identifying the pathways through which stress exerts its effects across the work–family boundary. If the work-related stressors of one family member appear to influence the health and functioning of other family members, it is important to identify the ways in which such an effect occurs. For example, if level of work stress experienced by one marital partner is found to be associated with the quality of the family life or emotional well-being of the spouse (cf. Staines & Pleck, 1983), is this a direct effect of the spouse's knowledge of and reaction to the work conditions, or is this effect mediated through the worker's own level of psychological well-being that in turn may alter the relationship itself? Previous research (e.g., Atkinson, Liem, & Liem, 1986; Dew, Bromet, & Shulberg, 1987) has indeed suggested that this latter pathway may be the most the feasible one linking job loss of husbands to psychological outcomes among their spouses.

Other pathways linking stressors to adaptive outcomes are likely but as yet have received little attention in the research literature. We know very little, for example, of the way in which family-based stressors enter the workplace and are reflected in worker turnover, absenteeism, or low productivity. Stressors originating in the family may influence such workplace outcomes directly via the employee's mental or physical health or that of other family members. For both men and women, high levels of work–family interference also lead to a desire to work fewer hours (Moen & Dempster-McClain, 1987), which may lead to lower levels of motivation and productivity on the job. Stress at home may also influence work-related outcomes by altering the balance of social relationships on the job, for example, increasing or decreasing their supportiveness. Understanding such pathways not only would help us better appreciate the ways stress may influence work, it would also help us focus on workplace interventions that are more social, and less individualistic, in nature.

Another mediating pathway involves stress in one domain increasing the likelihood of stressful experiences in the other. The employee experiencing stress in the workplace may arrive home fatigued and in a bad mood, with such emotional outcomes affecting the spouse or the children through the production of family-based stressors (e.g., conflicts). A more subtle, and less easily studied, mediational process involves stressors in one role producing negative outcomes in other domains through the erosion of the reserve of coping resources in the latter area. For example, the spouse who must continually act as a source of support for his/her partner's work stress may be unable to respond to family obligations as well as his/her own work problems and may perceive the distressed spouse (accurately or inaccurately) as being unavailable in turn to help solve family problems. This in turn lessens the family's overall problem-solving capacity.

The distinction we have made between mediating and moderating processes will prove useful in the context of the chapters to follow, but it is also clear that a given variable may act as both a mediator and moderator of stress effects. A case in point is marital conflict. Research dating from at least the 1930s has documented the negative impact that work-related stressors such as unemployment may have on the marital relationship and in turn on the psychological well-being of both spouses. This represents one fundamental pathway by which work stress may enter the family and has an impact on the well-being of other family members, that is, stress in one role area increases stress in the other.

However, we could also consider marital conflict as a moderator of work stress, and two of the present chapters (by Bolger *et al.* (Chapter 5) and Wheaton (Chapter 8) consider this possibility. Low levels of conflict with corresponding high levels of social support from the spouse may act to buffer the mental health effects of work stress. But an equally important moderating process may occur when marital conflict is high, in this case centered on the transmission of stress across the work–family boundary. Some evidence is beginning to emerge suggesting that when marital conflict is high, the work stress of one spouse may have a lesser effect on the well-being of this spouse's partner than when conflict is low. This may be because conflicted couples are not sharing work experiences, positive or negative, with each other. The negative implications of such a situation, however, may not be apparent in these findings. As can be seen in the chapter by Weiss (Chapter 2), the costs of short-circuiting the stress transmission process incurred by providing fewer opportunities to offer and receive positive support between couples may outweigh the benefits derived from being shielded from important stressors occurring to a significant other. The chapters represented here at least begin to address such complex questions.

GENDER

A final set of factors represented in Figure 1 (labeled *contextual factors*) concerns individual, social, or organizational variables that are likely to interact with stressful events or chronically stressful conditions to influence the stress transmission or stress-buffering processes discussed before. These factors are to be distinguished from personal and social resources thought to directly buffer stress such as social support, although they would fall into the category of conditioning factors and may well be correlated with the presence or absence of buffering variables.

We will consider only one example here—gender. We chose gender (1) because several of the chapters in this volume present results which highlight the sensitivity of these stress processes to the effects of gender; (2) because the number of single-parent, female-headed families is increasing dramatically; and (3) because the work–family literature has long recognized that combining work and family roles is not the same issue for men and women. This is not to say that other variables, such as social class or ethnicity, do not exert equally powerful effects on the processes we are considering, only that the literature generally, as well as the present works have less to say about these concerns.

A rich research literature has taken the field beyond the simplistic notion that for men unemployment is the critical work-related issue having a negative impact on the family, whereas for women, employment is problematic (cf. Spitze, 1988). Recent research on women's employment considers not only the employment status of the woman but also the employment conditions she encounters and the processes by which employment-related stress enters the home environment (Repetti, 1987; Voydanoff, 1987). This has led to a recognition that having positive work-related experiences may have beneficial effects on the psychological well-being of large numbers of women and carryover to other family members (Piotrkowski & Crits-Christoph, 1981). There is also evidence that being employed can buffer the effects of marital stress for women (Kandel, Davies, & Raveis, 1985) and that the employment of wives can buffer the work stress experienced by their husbands (Billings & Moos, 1982).

This current trend in research on women's employment does not, however, attempt to romanticize the benefits of women's employment, for it also identifies certain conditions under which employment may interact with family conditions to produce adverse outcomes for the woman and her family. There is evidence that work–job interference is experienced as a greater problem for women than men (e.g., Pleck & Staines, 1985; Voydanoff & Kelly, 1984). The positive benefits of work may also not be realized for those women lacking the supportiveness of their husbands, especially for women in low prestige jobs (Baruch, Biener, & Barnett, 1987). Women with children at home also appear to gain less psychologically from employment than other working women, are more reactive to work stress, and have more difficulties in their relationships with their husbands than do mothers who are not parents (Cleary & Mechanic, 1983; Kandel et al., 1985; Thomas, Albrecht, & White, 1984). Finally, the work of Miller, Schooler, Kohn, and Miller

(1979) reveals that some of the same job conditions Kohn and his colleagues earlier reported for men as negatively influencing parental values and attitudes also hold true for working women.

All these studies serve to remind us that, although the precise processes that transmit stress across the work–family boundary may vary for men and women, they are equally pertinent to both sexes. Stressful job conditions, including job overload, conflict, and ambiguity, clearly influence the transmission of stress from work to family for women as well as men. Likewise, juggling work and family responsibilities is becoming an issue for an increasing number of men, even if the rate of men assuming instrumental roles in the family has not kept pace with the increasing rate of labor force participation among women.

In considering the moderating effects of gender, our concern must not be limited to the adults occupying work and family roles, because gender differences may also be evident for children as well. There is some evidence that employment of mothers has a greater impact in male children (Hoffman, 1979). A similar gender difference has been observed for children exposed to family stressors, such as divorce. We have barely begun, however, to determine the robustness of these gender effects, let alone isolate the mechanisms for them.

OVERVIEW OF CHAPTERS

This volume begins with two chapters that examine microprocesses that define the nature and functions of marriage as a source of social support for persons experiencing job stress. The chapter by Robert Weiss (Chapter 2) eloquently details the process by which work stress finds its way into the family among a sample of middle-aged men in demanding administrative and managerial positions. This contribution adds significant new insights into the nature of gender role differentiations as it affects stress transmission and stress-buffering processes in families. His vivid case desriptions of how these men set about asking for help, or contain these inclinations, and of what they wanted in the way of social support from their wives, trust and loyalty above all else, contributes to our understanding of the complexity of the support-seeking and support-giving processes that studies employing less intensive data collection methods often miss.

These themes are further elaborated in the chapter by Leonard Pearlin and Mary McCall (Chapter 3). As with the Weiss chapter, the focus is on the marital relationship. The sample, however, is quite different from the one interviewed by Weiss, including a broader age range, more diverse occupations, multiple social and ethnic groups, and working women as well as men. Pearlin and McCall define for us the steps that take place in the process leading from stress on the job to a response in the marital relationship. At each step we are reminded of the truly interactive nature of social support, its reciprocal character, and the multiple ways in which efforts to give and receive support may succeed or fail. Interestingly, like Weiss, these authors note the chilling effect advice giving may have on outcomes of these support encounters. They further characterize a key support function as "meaning shaping," that is, helping to establish a perspective on a problem. Future research on support mobilization will clearly benefit from the richly detailed accounts given by these authors.

Chapter 4, by Carol-Ann Emmons, Monica Biernat, Linda Beth Tiedje, Eric L. Lang, and Camille B. Wortman considers how married, career-orientated professional women with preschool children manage stress at the interface of work and family. This chapter helps fill the gap in the current research literature on coping with the role conflicts experienced by many working women. The data reported here are drawn from the first wave of an impressive four-wave longitudinal study of 135 women and their husbands. Specific coping strategies used at home by these women are explored as they relate to perceived levels of stress and satisfaction in the work, marital, and parenting domains. Planning emerged as the coping strategy most likely to be associated with positive outcomes, although it was not the most frequently used strategy. This chapter also explores how these women's perceptions of role conflict and its effects on their family may differ significantly from the perceptions of their husbands, providing an important point of comparison to the chapters by Weiss and Pearlin and McCall.

The next two chapters shed new light on long-standing questions about the psychological costs and benefits of multiple role occupancy. Both represent more sophisticated methodological approaches to these questions than are typically seen in cross-sectional survey studies contrasting role statuses. These chapters not only provide a test of the effect of combining work and family on the well-being of women, men, and their children but also are able to explore alternative mechanisms for these effects as well as rule out competing hypotheses.

The chapter by Niall Bolger, Anita DeLongis, Ronald C. Kessler, and Elaine Wethington (Chapter 5) explores the link between multiple roles and stress processes using diary data recorded on a daily basis with a sample of married couples. This methodology provides us with a unique description of the ways in which work and family stresses are expressed in the daily lives of these men and women, while at the same time enabling these researchers to bring methodologically powerful techniques to bear on theoretically important issues in this field. This chapter skillfully tells us that the processes linking stress and coping processes at the boundary of work and family roles are much more complex than reflected in the literature to date. In fact, some widely held beliefs about gender specific processes are refuted.

The chapter (6) by Patricia Cohen, Jim Johnson, Selma A. Lewis, and Judith S. Brook also provides a fresh look at the issue of multiple role occupancy. In an important departure from most research in this area, these authors are able to contrast the effects of maternal employment for a group of single mothers as well as mothers who are married. Data from this large longitudinal study point to possible harm to both mothers and their children associated with maternal employment. These authors probe for possible mediating mechanisms for these overall effects and carefully seek to rule out the influence of confounding variables. These data will raise new questions about how working women can be supported in such a way to short-circuit these negative outcomes.

Most studies of occupational stress have concentrated on male samples, whereas most studies of marital conflict and stress have been conducted with female samples. In a striking contrast to this predominant trend, the chapter by Evelyn J. Bromet, Mary Amanda Dew, and David K. Parkinson (Chapter 7) explores the mental health effects of spillover with a large sample of blue-collar women working in an electronics plant. Aside from the uniqueness of the sample, this chapter is also distinctive for its attention to spillover from family to work as well as from work to family. Because of the care in which other known risk factors for poor mental health outcomes were examined, this chapter also serves to demonstrate the unique effects of spillover for the well-being of these female workers. It also reminds us that, for women, spillover from work to family may be as important a pathway as is the transmission of stress from family to work.

Stress in the work or family domains may eventually express itself in terms of discrete life events such as divorce or unemployment. Chapters 8 and 9 of this volume seek to define contextual variables that may determine the impact of such events both within the role area in which the event occurs and across the work–family boundary.

The chapter by Blair Wheaton (8) brings the analytic power achieved with a large national sample to bear on an issue that has considerable theoretical and clinical importance. In criticizing the often simplistic conceptions of the stress process inherent to much of the research on life events, many observers have pointed out that even in the seemingly tragic case of the death of a loved one, the event of death may bring relief to one individual and devastation to another. Wheaton has developed these insights in this study of the effects of divorce and unemployment, showing that the mental health effects of these events are dependent on whether they occur in the context of chronic strains within the same role (i.e., marital stress for divorce, chronic job stress for unemployment) or outside that role. Such work–family interactions have rarely been addressed by stress researchers, but the data presented here may well provide an antidote to the common practice of segmenting role domains and focusing only on chronic starins or acute life events when investigating stress processes.

The chapter by Joan Huser Liem and G. Ramsay Liem (9) serves to pull together a number of themes addressed throughout this volume in the context of a study of the effects of unemployment on family and individual functioning. As with the Wheaton chapter, this one also explores critical contextual factors that may help explain the impact of this discrete event across time and across individuals. It also directly considers several mechanisms through which the stress of a husband's unemployment may be transmitted into the family and explores these issues through the eyes of both the husbands and their wives. The strength of the longitudinal design and the sensitivity of these researchers to the dynamics of the stress process as it unfolded in these families makes this study a continuing source of new insights into the impact of unemployment and the nature of work–family linkages.

Together, the chapters in this volume represent a diverse array of methodological approaches to investigating stress and coping processes between work and family. As we noted earlier, however, we believe that they also reflect themes common to some of the best research now being conducted in the stress field. Although the "myth of separate worlds" may no longer characterize the starting point for most research on work and family, there is still much work yet to be done to arrive at a more complete understanding of the precise ways in which these worlds intersect. We hope that researchers, practicioners, and policymakers concerned with the stresses facing the contemporary family will gain new insights and rethink old questions after reading this volume.

REFERENCES

Aldous, J. (1982). *Two paychecks: Life in dual earner families*. Beverly Hills: Sage.
Atkinson, T., Liem, R., & Liem, J. (1986). The social costs of unemployment: Implications for social support. *Journal of Health and Social Behavior, 27,* 317–331.

Billings, A. G., & Moos, R. H. (1982). Work stress and the stress-buffering roles of work and family resources. *Journal of Occupational Behavior, 3,* 215–232.

Baruch, G. K., Biener, L., & Barnett, R. C. (1987). Women and gender in research on work and family stress. *American Psychologist, 42,* 130–136.

Cleary, P. D., & Mechanic, D. (1983). Sex differences in psychological distress among married people. *Journal of Health and Social Behavior, 24,* 111–121.

Dew, M., Bromet, E., & Schulberg, H. (1987). A comparative analysis of two community stressors' long term mental health effects. *American Journal of Community Psychology, 15,* 167–184.

Eckenrode, J., & Gore, S. (1981). Stressful events and social supports: The significance of context. In B. Gottlieb (Ed.), *Social networks and social support* (pp. 43–68). Beverly Hills: Sage.

Elder, G. (1974). *Children of the Great Depression: Social change in life experience.* Chicago: University of Chicago Press.

Gore, S. (1978). The effect of social support in moderating the health consequences of unemployment. *Journal of Health and Social Behavior, 19,* 157–165.

Hoffman, L. (1979). Maternal employment: 1979. *American Psychologist, 34,* 859–865.

House, J. (1981). *Work stress and social support.* Reading, MA: Addison-Wesley.

Kandel, D. B., Davies, M., & Raveis, V. H. (1985). The stressfulness of daily social roles for women: Marital, occupational, and household roles. *Journal of Health and Social Behavior, 26,* 64–78.

Kantor, R. M. (1977). *Work and the family in the United States: A critical review and agenda for research and policy.* New York Russell Sage.

Kohn, M. (1969). *Class and conformity: A study in values.* Homewood, IL: Dorsey Press.

Kohn, M., & Schooler, C. (1982). Job conditions and personality: A longitudinal assessment of their reciprocal effects. *American Journal of Sociology, 87,* 1257–1286.

LaRocco, J. M., House, J., & French, Jr., J. R. P. (1980). Social support, occupational stress, and health. *Journal of Health and Social Behavior, 21,* 202–218.

Miller, J., Schooler, C., Kohn, M., & Miller, K. (1979). Women and work: The psychological effects of occupational conditions. *American Journal of Sociology, 85,* 66–94.

Moen, P., & Dempster-McClain, D. I. (1987). Employed parents: Role strain, work time, and preferences for working less. *Journal of Marriage and the Family, 49,* 579–590.

Pearlin, L., & Schooler, C. (1978). The structure of coping. *Journal of Health and Social Behavior, 19,* 2–21.

Piotrkowski, C. (1979). *Work and the family system.* New York: The Free Press.

Piotrkowski, C., & Crits-Christoph, P. (1981). Women's jobs and family adjustment. *Journal of Family Issues, 2,* 126–147.

Pleck, J. H. (1985). *Working wives/working husbands.* Beverly Hills: Sage.

Pleck, J. H., & Staines, G. L. (1985). Work schedules and family life in two-earner couples. *Journal of Family Issues, 6,* 61–82.

Repetti, R. (1987). Linkages between work and family roles. In S. Oskamp (Ed.), *Family processes and problems: Social psychological aspects.* Newbury Park: Sage.

Rapoport, R., & Rapoport, R. (1971). *Dual-career families.* Baltimore: Penguin Books, 1971.

Rapoport, R., & Rapoport, R. (1976). *Dual-career families re-examined.* New York: Harper & Row.

Spitze, G. (1988). Women's employment and family relations: A review. *Journal of Marriage and the Family, 50,* 595–618.

Staines, G. L., & Pleck, J. (1983). *The impact of work schedules on the family.* Ann Arbor, MI: Institute for Social Research.

Thomas, S., Albrecht, K., & White, P. (1984). Determinants of marital quality in dual-earner couples. *Family Relations, 33,* 513–521.

Voydanoff, P. (1984). *Work and family: Changing roles of men and women.* Palo Alto: Mayfield Publishing Co.

Voydanoff, P. (1987). *Work and family life.* Beverly Hills: Sage.

Voydanoff, P., & Kelly, R. F. (1984). Determinants of work-related family problems among employed parents. *Journal of Marriage and the Family, 46,* 881–892.

2

Bringing Work Stress Home

ROBERT S. WEISS

Work is the sector of life most productive of stress for middle-aged men in administrative and managerial occupations. Although marital problems and troubles with children can produce stress as intense as any stress produced at work, marriage and parenthood only infrequently give rise to stress at all. Administrative and managerial work, in contrast, foster stress so regularly that most men doing such work report at least one experience at work within the preceding month that led to persisting preoccupation and irritability, and many report at least one in the preceding year that resulted in difficulties in sleeping.

Whereas work, for middle-aged managers and administrators, is the sector most productive of stress, home and family is the sector (other than work itself) in which support is most likely to be sought. In this chapter, I report on the way in which men's marriages function as supportive relationships when men experience work-based stress.

The chapter is based on a study of 75 men aged 35 to 55 who are occupationally successful as managers or administrators. We chose names randomly from the residential lists of four upper-income suburbs. In these lists every address is followed by the names of people residing there, together with their ages and occupations. (Some suburbs also give the heights of adults, presumably to insure identifications at voting sites.) We sent potential respondents a letter describing our study

ROBERT S. WEISS • Work and Family Research Unit, University of Massachusetts–Boston, Boston, Massachusetts 02125. This chapter is modified from a chapter in the forthcoming Free Press publication, *Staying the Course*, by Robert S. Weiss. Used with permission of the Free Press, a division of Macmillan, Inc.

and followed with a telephone call in which we confirmed their eligibility for the study and requested their participation. We were able to achieve nearly a 75% rate of acceptance.

Each of our respondents was interviewed at least three times, at intervals of about 2 weeks, with each interview lasting about 2 hours. We also interviewed the wives of twenty of our respondents, again three 2-hour interviews plus a single interview in which we talked with the couple together. Respondents were asked to describe the nature of their emotional investments in the various sectors of their lives, including the aims, gratifications, stresses, and supports there to be found. Interviewers were instructed to obtain detailed and concrete description of incidents that appeared exemplary or critical.

WORK STRESS BROUGHT HOME

Our concept of stress is that it is mobilization of energy and attention that persists despite efforts at relaxation. In an active office or manufacturing plant, this emotional state might not be very different from mobilizations produced by challenge in work. It is when men return home from work and they would more appropriately attend to the life of the household, that their work-based stress becomes evident.

Most men believe that they should not bring stress home with them. Doing so suggests that they have not been able to meet the challenges of their job. And, because work is their domain of responsibility in the marital partnership, they are failing the partnership by not having it under their control. Mr. Grant, head of an accounting firm, explained in this way limiting his discussions of his work problems with his wife.

> I have this client who is in financial trouble that I didn't know was going to be in financial trouble. He owes me a lot of money. And I can't get it straightened out. I told my wife what the problem is, but there really isn't anything she can do. This is a business matter, and that's the way it is.
>
> I suppose it helped to talk about it. I was probably looking to vent a little steam. Sally was sympathetic. Understanding. But it's not her job. It's my job.
>
> I try not to burden Sally with too many problems. If I have something that's really bothering me, I'll say, "This is a pain in the neck," or something like that. She'll say, "What re you going to do about it?" And I'll say, "Well, this is what I think I'm going to do about it." Period. That's all. I don't think a wife should be too concerned about what's going on. A wife has her own problems to worry about.

Men would lose self-respect if they regularly had to ask their wives' help with work problems. This is suggested by Dr. Bartlett, business administrator of an academic institution. Dr. Bartlett, though he prides himself on the closeness of his relationship with his wife, does not want to be the sort of man who would "run home" with problems.

> I don't tend to share small problems, like a problem at work. If it's something that troubles me a little bit, I had an argument with somebody or I did something that wasn't high quality or I was criticized, or whatever that might take me a little while to come to grips with, I don't run home and start talking about it.

Furthermore, displaying stress at home can be seen by men as failing their responsibilities to their families. Men tend to include among their family responsibilities the protection of their families from the tensions they experience in making a living. Mr. Dennis, head of an advertising firm, said:

> I take home the positive aspects of the job and leave the negative aspects at the office. Because there is absolutely nothing my wife can do about the negative aspects of the work. All she can do is worry. So why have her worry about things that she can't do anything about.

Some men say that their wives are constitutionally unable to deal with problems without getting upset. If they were to share their worries with their wives they would only create more problems for themselves. Mr. Fitzgerald, head of buildings and grounds for a large university, said:

> Occasionally I will talk to my wife about what I am doing. But she doesn't handle problems very well. She gets all upset if the Mastercard gets too high. That's not even on my list of what to think is a problem. So because I can handle problems and she can't, I generally don't get involved in explaining a problem.

There are still other reasons men are reluctant to seek their wives' help or advice or solicitude or indulgence. They not only take a dim view of asking for help with activities they believe to be their responsibilities, but they attempt to manage their stress by compartmentalizing it—by keeping it out of the focus of their attention. Mr. Cox, owner of a typewriter store, said:

> Whenever I get upset in my work, one way or another I put it on the shelf where it belongs. I tend to forget about it. Nobody likes to remember all the bad things. They like to remember the good things.
>
> Usually, between the store and the house, a 10-minute drive, I try to put problems on a shelf. I'll arrive home and instead of coming clean and saying, "Look, I had a bitch of a day," I'll feel that involves more explanation than I care to give.

The rationale for compartmentalization is: If you cannot do anything about it, do not worry about it. At the end of the day, leave your worries behind you when you close the office door. To be sure, an event that carries genuine threat—a warning from a boss, for example—may resist compartmentalization. So may a problem that must be dealt with or it will become a threat. But ordinary work worries, and some threats as well, may be seen as best dealt with by "putting them out of your mind."

Some men seem to have a knack of being able to compartmentalize almost anything that happens. Mr. Turner, co-owner of an industrial janitorial service, seems to be like this.

> I always leave the business at the office when I go home. Always. When I leave the office, that's it. It really is. I don't know how I do it, but I do it. In the 15 minutes it takes me to get from office to home, that's it. I just put it out of my mind. I don't even think about it.

Actually, it is the more painful aspects of the work that Mr. Turner puts out of his mind. There is no need to compartmentalize events that carry no charge of distress.

> I talk about work at home, to a degree. It's something to converse about. I'll say, "Well, this secretary quit today." Or, "We got a new account today." Or, "Someone went bankrupt," but I don't like to relive my business life blow by blow when I go home and say, "This person did this to me," or, "I had to do this to this person." I did it once already. I don't want to relive it. I don't like to relive every day again at night. So I just don't.

Mr. Turner's business at one point came close to bankruptcy. He now says proudly that he never once lost sleep over it. He also said rather little about his business worries, even then, to his wife. (Perhaps relevant here is that Mr. Turner's wife had recently recovered from a life-threatening illness. Mr. Turner had been much more worried about her than about the business.)

Compartmentalization, for most men, is a fragile defense. Merely talking about what happened during the day is likely to be enough to dissipate it. Indeed, only thinking about talking about them may produce painful awareness that the day's incidents have been distressing. Mr. Metzger, a production manager, put the matter neatly:

> Bad enough going through it the first time; why go though it again?

The aim of compartmentalization is to give men relief from what would otherwise be a flooding of consciousness by anxiety. But compartmentalization constricts marital communication; after a bad day it will have been exactly those experiences of the day that had emotional meaning that the man will not discuss. What his wife will hear is bland evasion—or nothing.

Men may therefore react to their wives' wish to hear about their day by insisting that there would be a cost in talking about the day and nothing to be gained. Their wives would be unable to understand enough about their work to give useful advice. Their wives might even make matters worse by reacting emotionally. Mr. DeVries, an independent broker, said:

> I spent a year and a half on a deal that would have paid over $100,000 in fees. And the deal didn't go through. We got to the contract, and they said that's fine, and then if fell apart. You can't afford to spend that kind of time on that kind of deal and have it fall apart. And I felt pretty bad.
>
> I didn't talk to my wife. I often don't even tell her if a deal works or not. Two weeks or so before, one went the other way. I think I mentioned that to my wife. I probably told her something.
>
> My wife is always paranoid about all these things. She's fairly high strung. She wants low-risk, high income. But that's not the way the business works. It's high risk. The whole thing is high risk.
>
> She gets more worked up than I do. So it doesn't help me. It makes it worse. She gets so upset she starts getting at me, "Where will the income come from?" It's better not to say anything.

It would, however, be mistaken to conclude from these reports that men do not talk with their wives about their work at all. It is about their *problems* at work that men are likely to say little at home. *Successes* at work are another matter. When things are going well at work, men want their wives to know. Just as doing badly at work represents failing the marital partnership, so doing well at work is a contribution to the marital partnership they would like recognized.

Mr. Norris, a middle-level executive, says little to his wife about the problems of his work. But he want his wife to know that he is working hard for her and their children as well as for himself. He also wants her to know that he is on the road to promotion and increased income.

> I would like her to know that I'm doing a good job. I'm trying to improve things for her. "Hey, we are not just going to be sitting here for the rest of our lives. I'm trying to do a better job and earn more money so I can give you and the kids a better life."

Mr. Norris is not able as yet to demonstrate his worth by a significant promotion. He has to tell his wife that he is doing well and that the proof of this will come.

Men may also display for their wives their grasp of important or difficult work issues as a way of demonstrating their competence. Dr. Stevenson, a physicist, was among the first to move laser technology from laboratory to factory. He often uses his wife as an interested listener. He had begun doing this before their marriage, when both were in graduate school.

> Sometimes I talk something I'm working on through with Kitty and sometimes I don't. But if there's anybody I talk things out to, it's her. I will try pieces out on Kitty. Especially when I get some neat insight that really works out well, I'll try to bedazzle her with it.

Men are concerned about their presentations of themselves to their wives partly because their wives can significantly affect their feelings of worth. When their wives are respectful and admiring, men more fully believe in themselves. Telling their wives about their successes or displaying for their wives their brilliance is a way of enhancing their wives' image of them. Mr. Layton, a financial officer of an insurance firm, although reluctant to tell his wife about the problems he encountered in his work, unfailingly reported his triumphs.

> Holly knows this new product that I've recommended. I think she is sort of amazed at times because the list of people that are copied on the memo keeps growing. And Holly sees the names on it. The vice president, now. Every time the list comes back, there is somebody else on it. She says, "Oh, my God, this is incredible!" She was sort of watching this whole thing develop. I think she thinks, "Gee, he really has initiative." She has worked with enough people to see people who are just content to come in and work 9 to 5. And she knows that I'm beyond that.

Mr. Abbott, a high-level technician, enjoyed, like Dr. Stevenson, telling his wife how well he was doing. He believed himself to be so excited about his work that he had to share it.

> You're so wound up, you get home, you don't want to go right to bed. Catherine's not sound asleep because I haven't got home. Or I'd get home at 3 in the morning and she's asleep and all of a sudden she wakes up and says, "Thank God you're home."
>
> And I'd start talking to her. I would tell her exactly what's going on, and what we're doing. And the trials and tribulations, the hard parts or the difficult parts of the job. Or how we combat it and how we get out of problems. And, naturally, where we ate or the kind of food they brought in.
>
> Catherine says a lot of times I talk too much about the company. She doesn't want to hear it. She used to tell me, "Everytime we go some place you are always talking about the company." She says, "I'm bored! Talk to *me*." I notice that I've cut down talking about the company quite a bit.

Mrs. Abbott may be mistaken in suggesting that her husband is not talking to her. Mr. Abbott certainly wanted her to hear what he was saying, though he might not have cared as much that she understand it as that she be awed by it—and admiring of him. What Mrs. Abbott objected to was being cast in a role that so limited her ability to react. She wanted to be talked *with* rather than talked *to*.

The predominant policy among men, in relation to discussion of work with their wives would seem to be: Keep your problems to yourself; share your triumphs.

Fatigue tends to be treated differently from stress. Men are willing to permit their fatigue to be visible. Weariness, after all, suggests a long and hard day working for the interests of the family; stress, on the other hand, suggests challenges unmet. Weariness indicates devotion to duty; stress indicates inadequacy. A man who would like to leave his worries at the office is willing on coming home to provide a theatrical demonstration of fatigue; he will slowly, haltingly, open the door to his home, wearily drop his coat and briefcase, collapse into an easy chair. He might not, on the other hand, want his wife to know that he was frightened of failure.

But although men often want to hide their state of stress, they find it difficult to do so. Men under stress give constant evidence at home of their state. They are preoccupied with the problems or incidents that led to the stress. Their preoccupation may cause them to respond only slowly or not at all to others in the family. Men under stress are also easily irritated: They feel themselves already to be dealing with as much as they can manage; they display a sometimes anxious anger when asked to deal with more. If their state of mobilization should continue through the evening and into the night, they are likely to have problems in sleeping: They cannot get to sleep, or they wake in the middle of the night, after which they cannot return to sleep.

Men recognize that despite their best efforts, they bring stress home, and the stress is visible to their wives and children. Their irritability is especially evident. Mr. Orcutt, a middle-level manager, said:

> I'm sure I have brought stress home from work. I don't think that it happens that frequently. I try to lock it in the drawer at night, to maintain some separation. But I'm sure there are times when I come home, and it's because of something that has happened at work that I act differently.
>
> I come home mentally exhausted, just hoping supper's not ready to sit down to. I come in the door and say, "What time is supper going to be ready?" "An hour? Fantastic! I'm going to go to sleep for an hour." And I'll conk out for about half an hour or so. And I'll probably feel better.
>
> I may be a little shorter with the kids. Or I have even said to the kids, "Look, I'm in no mood for any of your horsing around tonight. Just tread lightly. Don't push it tonight." I warn them ahead of time.

Mr. Cox, the owner of a typewriter sales and repair business, said:

> A situation that is perfectly normal and next to nothing—something happens with a kid—I may go into a tailspin over it. I might boil up or boil over. Norma will then fly up and say, "You are not treating them fairly." And then it will come out that at that particular point I was up to my eyebrows with the damned business and I just wasn't relaying that. In fact, I was keeping that in.

Preoccupation is also difficult to hide. Some men believe they have perfected the ability to think about work problems while apparently listening to their wives, but when under stress this ability is likely to fail. The sorts of work problems that provoke stress leave little room in men's thoughts for even minimal attention to their wives and children. Mr. Cox went on to say:

> I would wrestle with a problem to the point of I would be eating supper and interacting with the kids and gradually tune out and disappear. I would be physically there, but I would just be out of it.

The result is that when men are under stress, despite their attempts to hide the state, their wives are apt to recognize it. The experience of Mr. White, an administrator in an insurance firm, is in this respect typical.

Mr. White's firm had embarked on a program of cost cutting. His department was to be disbanded. For a time he had nothing to do, although he had been assured that with reorganization he would have an important position. Meanwhile others in his department were being told to empty their desks and go. Mr. White wanted to protect his wife from anxiety by understanding his own upset.

> I haven't wanted Dolores to worry needlessly so I haven't painted a *totally* dismal picture. I'd say she is aware of the fact that people are leaving. I have no indication that Dolores is thinking about it. She's never indicated to me that she does. She's aware of the fact that X, Y, Z, have left. But I haven't told her point blank that I spend a lot of time thinking about this. I haven't really gotten down to basics with her.

We talked with Mr. White 2 months later. He acknowledged that he had not been able to hide his stress.

> My wife knew. I'd come home, and she could just see me walking up the driveway and she could tell. I tried to shake it off walking from the bus home, a 7-minute walk. I tried to psych myself up, throw everything behind me. But I'd walk in, and she would see right through me.

Quite possibly it had been helpful to Mr. White's wife that he had been unable to hide his stress from her. She may have been prepared for further developments. For, despite the assurances he had been given, Mr. White had been correct to worry. He was only briefly in his new and important position when the position was downgraded. A new position was created and inserted above his. Mr. White remained in the job a few more months and then took early retirement.

Men tend to regret letting their wives know that they are under stress. They wish they could compartmentalize more successfully. Mr. Metzger, the production manager, for example, said:

> I try to isolate my work problems from my family. With mixed results. Once in a while I bring it home, to the real detriment of my family life. Usually I don't. Usually I'm a little happier or a little sadder at night, depending on whether the day went a little better or a little worse. But I can certainly think of some examples, hopefully not more than one a year or two a year, where extreme frustration has

found its way in my doing unnecessary yelling at my family or acting in an extremely crotchety manner to build family stress where it shouldn't have happened.

I would tell Doris what happened, briefly, why it happened, briefly. Not over-elaborating, because she's only mildly interested. And it might have been a really painful thing to happen, and I don't care to elaborate.

In a minority of marriages, men and their wives are too distant from each other enough emotionally for the wives to appear to be unaware when their husbands are under stress. Even in these marriages, it may be that the wives' apparent insensitivity may sometimes be a refusal to care rather than a failure to observe. Mr. Ellis, a business consultant, and his wife, a human service professional, maintained a marriage of edgy separateness. Mr. Ellis's work very often subjected him to stress.

When I'm stressed, she's sympathetic, I guess. Sometimes there's been physical pain or mental pain, and sometimes it gets talked about. And sometimes, I suppose, it's ignored, not talked about. Forgotten. I don't know if she even knows.

She is under stress a lot because she has arthritis. She has some amount of discomfort, a certain amount of limitation. How much pain I don't know.

Stress affects everybody differently. It may be very serious to me, and she may not recognize it. Or I may not recognize it in her. It's the type of thing: "What's bothering you?" "Oh, nothing."

THE REACTIONS OF THE WIVES TO BEING PROTECTED FROM MEN'S WORK-BASED STRESS

It might be noted that men's policy of keeping to themselves their experiences of stress is based largely on the demands of their own emotional economy. What is the effect of this policy on their wives?

Their wives, of course, are aware that the men are under stress. One wife whom we interviewed (married to an insurance executive) told us that she could estimate by dinner time, if not before, how severe was her husband's tension. In addition, she would sometimes overhear his telephone conversation with colleagues and, very occasionally, be the recipient of his comments about one of the firm's programs. She felt that by evening she had a pretty good idea not only of the extent to which her husband was under pressure at work but what had led to the pressure. But she felt this to be a thoroughly inadequate method of partnership communication. Nor did she like being asked to provide her husband with unquestioning support, as though she were a subordinate rather than a partner.

We interviewed Mr. and Mrs. Cox together before scheduling separate interviews with each. At the time of our interviews, Mr. Cox was worried about his business. His sales of new equipment had been reduced by competition from computers, and his repair work had been reduced by the appearance of inexpensive electronic typewriters. Mr. Cox did not share his worries with his wife.

> I thought my business was so secure that I actually went out and borrowed money for expansion. And then all of a sudden it fell off. And I got very concerned about that. So I'm saying to Norma, "Don't spend any extra money this week," or "try and cut down this month." And my feeling is that she can help me more by dealing with those things than she can by crawling into all the details of my business. Which I judge from time to time she would like to know more about, and I basically don't feel that it is necessary for her to.
>
> I don't find that working out my problem with somebody else is my most successful way. I can't explain a damned thing to myself, let alone explain it to somebody else. And somebody else will pick up on something that I don't want to spend time on, and I get very frustrated. I might not discuss the situation with Norma until I'm really looking for a double check on what my final resolution is. If we are talking ten stages in resolving the problem, I'm almost at the ninth stage.
>
> Norma gets angry as hell over this. She doesn't feel I'm sharing my life with her. I like to think I'm doing her a favor, that she really wouldn't want to have this to wrestle with.

But few wives are likely to be pleased by the patronization of husbands who will not burden them with reports of their troubles at work. And it can only be diminishing to their self-esteem for their husbands to suggest that if they were aware of the stresses the husbands faced daily they would get upset and make things worse. Mrs. Cox listened quietly to her husband and then said:

> He is so proud, telling people that he works things out himself and he doesn't worry his family. If he's got a difficulty, he sits and ponders, and he works it out and then when he has it all worked out, then he shares it with us. Well, that really isn't the case. Because what happens is, he has a problem, whatever it is, whether it is a difficult supplier or an individual customer or whatever, and he just is a *bear*. He is a bear to live with until he has it worked out.
>
> And if we say, "What is the problem?" He will say, "What do you mean, what is the problem: The hose was left out." Well, that isn't the problem. And it would be nice if he could say, "I'm so fried over this supplier because he is not cooperating." "All right, would you like to talk about it?" "No." "Well, fine, but if you do, fine, I'll listen."
>
> I can be supportive by shutting up and playing music or by not playing music or by staying home or leaving home or whatever. But it is very difficult when something is going on in his head, where he is really trying to work something out, but if that process is interrupted, then he can be very infuriated. He doesn't have much patience. And I guess one of the hardest things for him to understand is why everybody doesn't march to the beat of his drum.

Some wives insist that their husbands tell them about their workday, despite their husbands' reluctance to do so. They may discover that talking can be as distancing as not talking. Mr. Draper, marketing director of a manufacturing firm, said:

> When I come home, Muriel asks how the day went or how the office was or whatever. I have now discovered that when I have answered the question by saying, "Okay," I usually get a challenge from Muriel, "Is that all? Just okay?" And I've got to come forward with more explanation because that doesn't satisfy her curiosity.
>
> I'm so used to Muriel asking how the day went I almost expect that there is that compassion where earlier in our marriage we tended to ask each other how our days went. How fully she listens I don't think I can answer. She may or may not, or may or may not fully. I guess at this point if all of a sudden she stopped asking I'd get made because it would show a lack of interest and support and love. So I don't rebel at it and I don't resent it. Even though it's an annoying kind of prying in a sense.
>
> I almost enjoy telling her that a day was crummy. Because my last year really has been kind of a disappointing crummy one. You like to share your misery. And I've had a lot of misery.
>
> I can ramble on for quite some minutes on a series of usually petty incidents, at least to the layperson or the wife. Usually she ends up sorry she asked. Because I'll get into a long dissertation. It will be boring, repetitive. It is the same old stuff. We failed to deliver, or the quality was bad, or whatever my headaches or my problems of the day might have been.

THE KINDS OF SUPPORT MEN SEEK

We might specify our concept of support as help in the achievement of goals, whatever these might be, and help in the maintenance of the morale necessary to the achievement of goals. The very structure of marriage, the opportunity it provides men to perform as husbands and householders, provides support. That men are doing well in their roles is validated by the acknowledgment of how much they are doing by their wives and children. For none of these benefits do men need to talk with their wives about their situations. Men's wives are supportive just by managing the homes they share with the men, caring for their children and, not least important, looking after the men themselves. One point of the marital partnership is that its existence establishes that at least one other person is committed to what has become a shared enterprise. For men, their wives' shopping and cooking and cleaning not only are logistic services that free the men's time for work but are also reminders that although the men are the figures out front, there are others who care about them, are invested in them and whom they represent. They can count on their wives, and they can feel that their wives count on them, and each of these is sustaining.

Especially when men experience work-based stress and feel their sense of worth endangered, they want to be assured that they retain their wives' support. Their wives can demonstrate this by unquestioning acceptance of their performance as husbands and householders. And so men would like their wives to recognize that they are burdened, to tolerate their withdrawal and preoccupation, and to understand them well enough and trust them enough not to burden them with questions or themselves become anxious or irritated. They would like their wives to accept that whatever the men are worrying about is theirs to worry about and to let it go at that, without objection, without intrusion. They would like to feel that their wives accept that when the men are ready to tell them what is happening, they will.

In all these ways men's marriages, augmented by their children, are supportive to men quite apart from any special requests men might make for help.

Mr. Leverett, vice president of an electronics firm, regularly worked late in the evening and sometimes around the clock. Mr. Leverett's marriage had times of tension because of his commitment to his work. Nevertheless, his wife provided him with a home and tolerated, more or less well, his schedule.

> Depending on how late I get home, home may just be a place to come to and go to bed after everybody else has gone to bed and is asleep. But the family is supportive. I'm home and I'm tired and everybody understands it and so, while they are not happy or delighted about my not having been there for dinner, I don't get beat up about it either.
>
> The family would like more time. I count on their understanding the problems that I'm struggling with. My wife says, "When are you going to get unburied?" It's a problem for her, the lack of the husband and father. There are questions, particularly if it's on a weekend, "Where were you?" Or, "What were we going to do over the weekend that got scrubbed?" There are hard feelings. I guess if there weren't, I would be disappointed in that I'd feel nobody cares whether I'm around or not.

This kind of support is provided to all men who are married and have families. It is, to be sure, provided more or less well, more or less grudgingly, with different levels of friction. And yet, even in the most unhappy of marriages, men can find confirmation in having a home and in meeting the responsibilities of husbands and fathers.

Men do sometimes actively seek their wives' counsel. Ordinarily this will happen only if the men are absolutely assured that their adequacy as husbands is unquestionable, or if they are becoming hopeless about maintaining that adequacy. Or—a third alternative—if the issue about which they seek counsel is one they are able to define as irrelevant to their competence in their work.

Mr. Andrade was someone who was entirely confident of his adequacy in the workplace. Nevertheless, he had several reasons for seeking his wife's counsel. He headed a now successful high-technology firm. He had consulted his wife extensively during the early tense days before the company became established. He did so, he now says, for the ulterior motive of wanting to strengthen their relationship. But he also did so because his wife was the one person he could trust to be entirely identified with him.

> My wife, Evelyn, is my most important relationship. We've been married 14 years, almost 15. We are very close. She is someone I can always turn to. You can always trust she will be there no matter what the situation is. It helps you through situations. I share with her a lot of things that go on in the company. She's a confidante.
>
> When I left my former company to go and launch this one, the biggest risk I had was losing my wife and family. If you look at all the people who have gone and become entrepreneurs, the divorce rate is very high. They end up devoting a lot of their time to the company. And their priorities change. Some of them move from one economic stratum to another. Through a whole course of reasons it results in a divorce.
>
> So I've tried to involve Evelyn. Her involvement makes her feel good. She can sort of see what's going on. And her involvement tends to make her feel a part of the firm as opposed to it or in competition, like a mistress or something.

But even with his wife the one person he entirely trusted, Mr. Andrade tended to discuss especially "human relations" issues with his wife. These can be extremely troubling issues, to be sure. And they are issues about which it is extraordinarily difficult to achieve objectivity, and another perspective is most valuable. But these are also issues for which Mr. Andrade—and other men—are able to disclaim responsibility; getting things done are men's issues, human relations are women's.

> I share stuff which I can sense she can be helpful on: more in the people area than the technology area. I am more of an engineer, and she's more of a human-type person. She is more interpersonally sensitive, where I'm analytic. And so she tries to give me her views, and it helps me in that side of the operation. Occasionally we'll have people conflicts, and I can share with her what's going on and she can share with me, "Gee, you could do this, make the person feel better, as opposed to if you do that, it is probably going to aggravate them." Little things. Although I try to be sensitive to people, in fact in many areas I'm blind to what other people might feel.

Is Mrs. Andrade actually superior in her grasp of human relations? Are women, in general, superior to their husbands? Men very often say that they are.

Dr. Braden is a nuclear engineer. His wife of 26 years is a pharmaceutical chemist. Dr. Braden said that she often helped him with the human issues of his work.

> When we were first married I thought it would be impossible to describe my work because my work was engineering and Grace was not an engineer. And I forced myself to describe something that had happened and how I felt about it, putting the

engineering aspects of it into laymen's terms. And I was amazed to find that I could do it, and I could always do it. That helped me, because I could talk about things with somebody I really trusted, my wife. And she's fairly bright. She's a Ph.D. pharmaceutical chemist.

If you can talk to your spouse, it's good because you can always trust your spouse. If you can't, then you might as well pack it in. That's the one person that's been with me all this time. All of my friends have come and gone.

Once in a while somebody will get under your skin at work. I would tell my wife what was going on, and she would understand. She is pretty supportive in that way. I would describe the problem and say, "This fellow said this." And she would say, "Well, he's really telling you that he just doesn't accept you as a person, let alone your opinion." And I would think about that and say, "Gee, you might be right." And that would help me to deal with that individual in the future.

Men believe that their wives are good on feelings and meanings and motivations: on the emotional elements in relationships. They rely on their wives to interpret for them what could have been the layers of meanings in an employee's complaint or what might account for an employee's intransigence. Their frequent reference to their wives as more sensitive, more knowledgeable in issues of human relations, suggests that the men believe themselves to be insensitive sorts, their attention more on money and machines than on people. But most of these men are successful managers and administrators. And it is difficult to imagine someone being successful in business without adequate human relations skills.

How then can we account for men deferring to their wives' human relations skills? It does seem the case that men's human relations skills are differently focused from those of their wives. Men are alert to aspects of personality that affect collegial relationships: competence, loyalty, trustworthiness as subordinate and peer and supervisor. And they are alert to aspects of personality that affect ability to respond to challenge: persistence and ability to function under pressure and all the other issues that will affect ability in the man's particular line of work. Indeed, when men talk with each other they will sometimes offer assessments, perhaps guardedly, perhaps not, about men with whom they work: that they come through on projects or do not, that they are helpful to colleagues, or that because of competitiveness they want the people they work with to fail, that their judgment is good, or that they are given to impulsive decisions and have a tendency to make a fool of themselves. Men who function as managers and administrators—and very likely other men as well—have a repertoire of empirically based, fine-grained theories about how people work. The men are not, to be sure, interested in the issues that interest their wives; but they know a good deal about "human relations."

But it can nevertheless be easy for men to grant their wives greater competence in human relations than they have themselves because human relations is understood by them as their wives' domain. They are interested in getting things done; their wives in the feelings of the people involved in the doing. Their wives may, indeed, be better on these feelings than they are, because their wives have been more concerned with them. And their wives are much more likely to take them seriously.

For quite different reasons, men will consult their wives should they be considering a job change that would require changing residence. And they will also consult their wives should their current job be in danger, especially should they be considering resignation or planning a confrontation that might lead to the loss of their job. Mr. Metzger, who makes a principle of not talking with his wife about his work, said:

> It's not to say I've never talked to Doris about my work. I have, on occasion. It probably happened, in 11 years, on two or three occasions where I got in a severe argument with my boss where I felt my pride was attacked. I would talk it over with Doris, and she always gave me the same advice, that we could get by, no matter what I make. I appreciated that type of advice. Even though it may not have been the right decision, it was very supportive.
>
> I wouldn't have it any other way, anyway. I wouldn't even listen to any other type of advice. I know that careerwise I can do anything I want and Doris will support it. And that is extremely important to me. I don't think I would be able to exist in the household otherwise.

It was not his wife's counsel that Mr. Metzger wanted. Rather, he wanted her respect and the assurance that her respect would continue whatever he did on the job. He wanted a vote of confidence.

Other men may indeed want counsel. Mr. Ryder, a scientific administrator, was among these. He had been offered a job in an attractive field but worried about the risks of going with a new company. His current position was thoroughly safe, although unchallenging. But now his children were grown and no longer needed his attention, and he wanted a chance to do more than his current job permitted. And yet he was reluctant to relinquish his current job's security. He and his wife gave a good deal of time to talking about the decision.

> We talked about it all the time. One of our favorite things is, we have a block here that is, from my house around the block and back, almost a mile. And we usually take a walk after dinner, and we talk about different things. This is something that we hashed over many times.

When we last saw Ryder he had taken the new job. He said that he was working harder than he had at his previous job but enjoying the work more. He did worry, at times, about his competence in the new field. Still, the job was developing the way he and his wife had expected.

And having talked over with his wife all the risks of the new job before he had taken it, Ryder felt less vulnerable now to disappointing his wife should the job not work out.

SEVERE STRESS AND NEED FOR HELP

Many men have times, perhaps only one or two in their adult lives, when things go very badly for them. They fear not only failing in some respect but losing their grip, their ability to function. They are regularly preoccupied. They are irritable and distant with their children. At night their sleep is interrupted, when they finally do achieve sleep.

At such times, under such severe stress, men may talk to their wives about their situations. One man who was in continuous conflict with a supervisor and thought he was being forced to quit could barely contain his anger; he talked regularly to his wife to maintain his balance. Another man, unemployed for a time, could not specify exactly how it was that his wife had helped, but said that her support had been indispensable. Apparently she had been unflagging in her belief that he would find a place for himself. A third man had seen his business sinking into bankruptcy and said he would always be grateful to his wife because she never complained, recognized he was doing his best, and tried to help him as much as she could. They were at the time planning to divorce and separated not long after the business actually failed.

Mr. Stavros is a man who had been extraordinarily successful. He began with nothing except energy and intelligence and developed a firm whose gross was in the hundreds of millions. In the belief that his company's financial situation was secure, he began giving his attention to the development of a radically new product. Soon the company was in financial trouble. He dropped what he had been doing and resumed direction of the company. For a time, though, he seemed to have lost the knack of making things work.

> I was working to finish a project, and there was a swing in the economy and the down risk became enormous. And things that I did were wrong. It created one of the worst stress situations I have faced in the last twenty years.
>
> It manifested itself in my not being able to sleep. I usually can sleep very easily. And I can sleep at odd hours. If I have 15 minutes I can fall asleep. I also sleep more than average for my age group: I sleep 8 hours; the average is 7. And I need that. Sleep is for me a tremendous release of tension.
>
> When I get to the point where I go to bed and I start thinking, and it is 2 o'clock and then 3 o'clock, I know I'm in trouble. That happened twice to me in the last 4 months. There were two periods that lasted for about 5 or 6 days when I couldn't sleep. My wife was very helpful, very supportive.

> In the last twenty years every time I couldn't sleep at night, I'd tiptoe out of the room at 3 o'clock in the morning and try to have a warm drink. And my wife would get up and we'd start discussing other things. Tennis. She knows how to change the subject. She doesn't ask me what's wrong with me, because she knows. And so we change the topic of conversation. She's done that every time that I'm having a psychological problem.

We can infer that Mr. Stavros and his wife had an unstated understanding. When he became so stressed that he could not sleep and, at 3 in the morning, had finally given up trying, he would leave the bed quietly enough so that his wife could resist being awakened but not so quietly that she would not know he had left. His wife would then rouse herself and join him in the kitchen. There she would provide not discussion of his problems, but companionship and, with it, reassurance of her affiliation.

A still more persisting level of stress was described by Mr. Morse, a vice president of an industrial consulting organization. He had entered a depression for what seemed to him to have been no reason at all.

> I was depressed. I don't know whether it was a midlife crisis or what. I just felt as though I didn't have much command over my life. I didn't sleep well. I got very anxious. And my wife was really available and supportive. I really never forget that. That's when I *really* needed her. When I'm feeling fine and capable and basically able to run my life, I wouldn't want to be without her, but I don't *need* her. At that time I really needed her. And she was available. And that really is worth a lot.
>
> I'd wake up at 2 o'clock in the morning. I couldn't sleep. And Andrea had said to me, "If you want to talk to me, you can wake me up. It's all right, you can wake me up." And I did. And she was responsive. And I know how much she likes to sleep. And I know she doesn't like her sleep disturbed under ordinary circumstances. And all of those things were not issues.
>
> As a matter of fact, it was during that time that our last child was conceived. She wasn't planned. But it was really because we were closer and she was much more available and so on.

One outcome of that earlier time was that Mr. Morse began taking night classes in the law. When we talked with him, he had obtained his law degree but had not yet taken the bar examination. He was now worried about the security of his job. He felt that younger people in the firm were indifferent to him and at times ignored him. He suspected that the agency head wanted him out. His workload had become extremely heavy, and his requests for additional staff had been denied.

We talked with him again some months later and were told that his anxieties had been justified. He had for some time been marked as someone to be let go should there be a reduction in workload. His wife, he said, had been immensely helpful to him.

> I have been complaining about the fact that I am overwhelmed. I come home and I say, "I really don't know if I can keep this job. I just can't stand it. It is just too much."

And instead of saying, "Well, don't worry, dear," or "It's only temporary," Andrea says, "Well, maybe you really should give that thought. Take another job." That's a totally new approach. Because I'm not really ready to quit my job. But she's honest. This is not a ploy. She really means it. She says, "Well, if the job is that terrible. . . ." That is her attitude about life.

What happens to me then is, I feel supported. Because I have that option. And then I say, "Oh, no, I can't do that." I mean, this is absolutely one of the best jobs that anybody could have and still live in this area and be in my field. And it's an interesting job basically. So I end up saying to her, "Look, I may not be able to keep the job, but I certainly will never quit it." And so that takes care of that.

When we last talked with Mr. Morse he had been told that he would be asked to leave the firm at the end of the contract on which he was working. He would then have retirement income but not much. Rather than search for another position in the field of his present job he had decided he would begin a career in the law. He was worried that he would not earn nearly what he was now earning. Again his wife was supportive.

The possibility that I shouldn't be earning adequately bothers me a great deal. We do have a couple of dependent children. It is not only putting away money for our own retirement, which we have been trying to do, but also giving our children as much as possible and trying to get some money for *their* education.

If I go into the legal profession I will probably not earn as much. And all of the benefits are gone. If there is a snowstorm, then you don't get paid. If you have a sore throat, you don't get paid. And there is no vacation, no sick leave, no holidays and no retirement. And no Blue Cross. None of that. I keep telling my wife that. And she says, "Don't worry about it. You'll be all right."

She is quite supportive along these lines. I don't have the additional burden of having her worry about what is going to happen. She says, "Look, we can get along on less, and I'm still working, and you'll do as much as you can. And you'll build up, maybe."

Mr. Morse has the reassurance that so far as his wife is concerned, he is doing fine as a partner. She still respects him; and he can continue to respect himself.

TWO CASES

Two executives had quite similar problems with their bosses. One of the executives reviewed his situation with his wife and was heartened by her response. The other executive did not tell his wife what had happened because when he had done so in the past her response had been dismaying.

Mr. Reynolds is head of the research and development department of a very large manufacturing firm. As an engineer he reports to the vice president in charge of engineering in the home office, distant from the plant in which he works. His immediate superior is the plant manager who assigns him projects and whose department he is required to assist.

> Lorimer is the top engineering boss, and I work administratively for him. But I work operationally for Cal, the vice president in charge of operations. And sometimes when Cal is stressed and under a lot of pressure, he'll beat me around the ears a little bit. Threats. "I don't need you any more, I need somebody here who is going to do what I want." "Why the hell don't you do what I want you to do? Why the hell do you do it your own way?" Once it reached the point of him going to Lorimer and saying, "I want this guy off the job." That happened about 6 months ago. And I was greatly stressed and angry because I'm doing a good job. I knew that, and I knew that he was wrong. But he went to Lorimer, and he told him that he wanted me off the job. Lorimer told me pretty much verbatim what Cal had said. And Lorimer said, "Don't worry about it." He said, "No one could do the job you're doing better than you are doing it." But I was deeply hurt. And I was angry. I offered to move off this job into some other job. And Lorimer said, "Don't take it seriously. It will work itself out."
>
> I went through a period of about 2 or 3 days of feeling stressed. Beat up. I knew that because of the way I felt and also my gastric juices started to work. I was telling myself on the one side that who I am is more important than what I do. And on the other side I was forgetting that wisdom and wondering if I was really worth anything at all.
>
> I talked a lot to my wife during that time. And what she said was, "I know you and I know how valuable you are, how good you are. And I also know that we can make it no matter what you do." And that just really made me feel good. There was less at stake then after she said that.

Worth considering is that phrase, *less at stake*. Mr. Reynolds's wife's reaction in no way changed the situation on the job. But more was at stake for him initially than simply holding the job and retaining his integrity. In addition he was responsible for protecting his family from distress. When his wife said that she would feel he was meeting his responsibility to the family so far as she was concerned no matter what he did, he was, at least, relieved of that particular concern. *That* was what was now less at stake.

The outcome of the story was happy. Mr. Reynolds's manufacturing plan proved successful. The departmental vice president called him in to tell him so and added that he thought that he and Mr. Reynolds made a good team.

The second executive, Mr. Davis, is head of quality control in a firm almost as large as Mr. Reynolds's. He, too, came under attack from a superior. In contrast to Mr. Reynolds, he said nothing about the attack because he was convinced his wife would not come through for him.

> My boss has a staff meeting Monday mornings at 8 o'clock and that is when we get together and he tells us about things that have been going on. There may be six or eight people at the meeting, maybe something like that. And this particular staff

meeting we had a discussion of quality control. And he said that quality control costs were just completely getting out of hand. Costs were about 50% over original estimates.

We knew this problem had been boiling up. It was just a question of time before it got to the point where people would want to know what happened. So it was mostly making sure that our story was clear. Manufacturing always has the feeling that we are protecting our ass by identifying problems. But we've been doing this job for quite some time, and we do have a track record.

The minute I understood what was being said I said, "Look, the reason quality control is so expensive is because you've introduced changes. Let's see if we can't redesign to improve reliability."

Davis said that he had not told his wife what had happened. He was sure that if he had, her reaction would have been unhelpful.

Sue's reaction is to rail at how can my boss be so goddamned stupid. And she would want to get in and try to problem-solve. And so I don't, quite often, tell her that much about work. Because what happens is, I'll tell her about a particular situation, and she will jump in and want to solve it without really knowing enough about the problem to solve it. And I'll find myself in a position of having to comment on it in some way.

Her expectations from me would be, "Sue, that is a good idea; we can do it." And I can't find the right way to say, "Sue, I don't think it is going to work because there is another factor that I haven't told you about." And what will generally happen is that she'll be angry because she is feeling that I'm being negative to her solutions. And so I just find myself not telling her that much about work.

There is a part of me that would like to have tea and sympathy and more mothering and whatever. And I don't feel that I get much of that.

Davis respects his wife's intelligence and acknowledges that she knows enough about his work to make constructive suggestions. But his need from her is reassurance that he is meeting his responsibilities to her and to the family and, furthermore, that he is adequate enough, competent enough, to have her confidence that he will meet whatever challenges arise. When his wife offers him help in solving his problems not only is she missing the point of what he wants and needs, but she is implying that he may not be all that capable after all.

Sometimes husbands and wives are aware that helping each other by problem solving can be no help at all. Mrs. Cox, wife of the owner of the typewriter store, contrasted how she and her husband had once behaved toward each other, in the early days of their marriage, and how they behaved toward each other now.

I think back when we were both working, we both had such different jobs. I would tell him some things that were happening. But he wasn't then turning around and telling me what to do about it. He was listening. And I certainly couldn't tell him what to do because I didn't understand his work. But now we tend to tell each other how to handle it. "Rather than such and such, why don't you try such and such." So now there is sort of a wall there.

Dismissive problem solving seems to be practiced more often by husbands than by wives. A man, asked by his wife to listen to an interpersonal problem, a dilemma, may analyze the problem quickly, list the options, suggest advantages of one or another, urge his wife to choose. The analysis can be entirely correct and yet leave the wife with the feeling that she has not been understood. But dismissive problem solving can be practiced by either sex, with the same consequences for the partner.

CONCLUSION

The marital partner is indeed men's primary source of support, but this sometimes gives rise to paradoxical behaviors. To protect their wives as supportive figures, men may attempt to dissimulate the extent to which they are under stress. Asking for help—which men may do under situations of extreme stress—is itself injurious. But to gain help while not asking for help can require from their wives a high level of understanding and forbearance.

ACKNOWLEDGMENTS

The work reported on in this chapter was supported by grant 5-R01 MH36708 from the Prevention Center of the National Institute of Mental Health.

3

Occupational Stress and Marital Support
A Description of Microprocesses

LEONARD I. PEARLIN and MARY E. McCALL

INTRODUCTION

In this chapter we examine the support that married couples provide when one of them is confronted by a stressful job problem. Social support has emerged in recent years as a very useful concept but one whose study is still notably incomplete. It is useful because it helps to explain why some people are damaged by the life problems to which they are exposed and others, faced with similar problems, are able to resist threat to their psychological and physical well-being. Of course, social support is not alone in its capacity to shield people from the deleterious effects of difficult life circumstances. Other conditions have similar mediating functions, such as coping behavior, self-esteem, and mastery. However, whereas other mediators are essentially intrapsychic in character, social support is distinctively and inherently a social construct.

Paradoxically, it is its social character that has not received the attention it deserves. As we have observed elsewhere (Pearlin, 1985), the social and interactional character of support have either been ignored altogether or largely taken for granted. Specifically, the study of social

LEONARD I. PEARLIN and MARY E. McCALL • Human Development and Aging Program, University of California, San Francisco, San Francisco, California 94143.

support has tended to focus exclusively on the *recipient* of assistance, overlooking the *donor* and the interactions between the two. As a consequence, we have assumed that whether or not people succeed in getting support depends, first, on their good luck in having it available and, second, on their skill in activating it. Obviously, however, one does not succeed by oneself in obtaining effective support; success also requires that there be others willing and able to provide the support.

The social and interactional character of support may be observed in virtually all relationships in which individuals are engaged. Nevertheless, for several reasons the support process is revealed with particular clarity in marriage, the relationship that is of exclusive concern here. Marriage is usually a more continuous relationship than most others, despite its brittleness. And it is usually more inclusive than most, encompassing over time a vast array of shared experiences that enhance sensitivity and understanding between the marital pair. Moreover, it is characteristically marked by intimacy and trust, attributes that can make it a bountiful source of emotional support. However, despite its distinctiveness, the processes of support found in the exchanges of husbands and wives are still fundamentally the same as those existing in other primary relationships. Indeed, we would argue that because of the range of problems faced by married couples and the range of their potential responses to them, marriage is strategically well suited to the identification of processes found in any relationship marked by stability, caring, knowledge, and trust. Much of what we learn of the social nature of support in marriage is directly generalizable to processes of expressive support as it is exchanged in other informal relationships. This will be increasingly evident as our analysis progresses.

By looking at married couples and the interactions between them, therefore, we hope to take a step toward the social study of social support. It needs to be recognized, however, that there is a level of social analysis that lies beyond that which is attained when we examine the individuals making up a relationship. That level entails the relationship itself, its properties, and its functioning as a system. Indeed, some scholars suggest that the proper unit for the study of stress and its ameliorative processes, particularly as it involves family relations, is at a social system level (La Gaipa, 1981; Reiss & Oliveri, 1980). By and large, however, even where stress and support are conceptualized within a family system framework (Boss, 1986; McCubbin *et al.*, 1980), the actual data are at the individual level. As Fisher (1982) aptly points out, we have system theories but individual data. The unit of analysis that is employed here falls between the individual and the supportive system and can be thought of as involving transactions.

The perspectives of this volume and this chapter underscore an emerging fundamental tenet of stress research: The stresses that people experience and their efforts to deal with these stresses are likely to involve multiple institutional roles. As Walker (1985) points out in the study of family, stress necessarily implicates the large contexts in which family is enfolded. One of the important contexts with which family relations are interconnected is occupation. Although job and home are usually segregated in time and space, the experiences in one sphere can have a profound effect on experiences in the other. Thus there is good evidence that job stresses can negatively impact on relationships in the family domain (Pearlin, 1983; Pearlin & Turner, 1987). Severe, chronic job problems can come to infect marital and parent–child relations with chronic anger and hostility. When these kinds of emotions become embedded in family relationships, they become sources of stress in their own right. But there is another side to this coin: Family relations do not merely fall victim to job stress; they may also stand as forces that mediate and ameliorate the stresses that occur outside its boundaries (House, 1981; Pearlin & Turner, 1987). It is the part played by the family as a mediating force that will be described in this chapter.

The interconnections between job and family should underscore the fact that the stress process does not occur as scattered fragments of people's lives. Instead, stress influences and is influenced by the significant contexts within which individuals' lives and their social relationships are organized. Outstanding among these contexts, of course, are family and occupation. The study of marital support for occupational problems illustrates both the structured integration of people's multiple roles and the pivotal part played by family relations in social support.

SAMPLE

The observations in this chapter are drawn from qualitative interviews with 25 couples. Because the interviews were conducted separately, there is a total of 50 interviews, half with wives and half with their husbands. The selection of couples was largely by convenience. Nevertheless, we were careful to recruit subjects who together possessed a useful mix of key social and economic characteristics. Thus, approximately 25% of the sample is in their 20s, with similar percentages distributed across the succeeding decades through 50 and older. There is also a range of occupational statuses represented, including professional, technical, clinical, skilled and semiskilled workers, as well as several unemployed and retired people. Finally, multiple social and ethnic minorities are represented. Despite the blend of participants, the size of the sample precludes any suggestion that it is representative of the San Francisco Bay Area from which it was drawn. This does not hinder us in accurately describing the interactive aspects of support in marriage or in discerning the microprocesses involved in such support. However, as with any small-scale qualitative study, we cannot capture here the nuances and variations that may occur within small social and economic subsamples, nor are we able to specify the conditions under which different patterns of support are likely to be present. That kind of analysis must await a larger and more systematic study.

A CONCEPTUAL OVERVIEW OF MARITAL SUPPORT

The qualitative interviews covered a broad conceptual terrain and produced a very substantial body of data. We sought in our general questioning to learn about the kinds of life strains people experience, both in and outside of the family domain, the effects of these strains on marriage, the ways in which individuals attempt to cope with the strains that confront them, and—the concern of this chapter—how the marriage provides or fails to provide support for the partners.

Information about support is drawn from a series of interrelated questions. When respondents reported a problem—it could be about work, family finances, child rearing, conflicts with other family members, health, and so on—they were then queried as to whether their spouse knew about the problem, how the spouse felt about it, what the spouse did, and how the respondent felt about the spouse's recognition of and responses to the problem. A parallel set of questions inquired into respondents' awareness of and responses to spouses' problems. Together, the interviews provide a complex body of qualitative data enabling us to discern some of the salient features of the interactive aspects of social support.

To harness and give some clarity to the rich data that were produced by the 50 interviews, we shall organize the material around a description of stages that can be discerned in the process of giving and receiving of support in marriage. It needs to be recognized, however, that the treatment of support in terms of stages is an abstraction. That is, it does not present the shades of difference that distinguish the patterns of support of one couple from others but, instead, gives a composite picture of the entire group of participants.

The four stages are (1) revelation–recognition, (2) appraisal, (3) selection of forms of support, and (4) support outcomes. As we shall describe later, activation of the support process depends on the first stage, that of *revelation–recognition*. Unless the donor of support is aware that his/her partner is experiencing a stressful problem on the job, support for dealing with that problem cannot be mobilized. However, people differ in whether or not they are aware of their partners' job problems and, if they are, how and when awareness surfaces. Underlying these differences are differences in workers' willingness to reveal their problems to their spouses and in the mode and timing of their revelations. The second stage, *appraisal*, is one at which the donor makes a number of key judgments, including the legitimacy of the problem and its amenability to amelioration. Once the donor appraises the problem as meriting support, decisions are made regarding the *forms of support* and their sequencing. The forms of support, in turn, are instrumental to the *outcome* of the support, whether the donor's actions are indeed supportive or, as occasionally happens, inadvertently contribute to conflict between the partners. We turn now to a detailed discussion of each of the stages.

Stage I: Revelation and Recognition of the Problem

It will be remembered that we are particularly interested in knowing about support given by one spouse in response to a problem that the other has faced in his/her occupational sphere. As could be expected, the range of distressing job events and problems that people reported was quite wide: overload, the lack of challenging work, being passed over for advancement, dissatisfaction with the rewards, lack of recognition for one's contributions, an unkind word from one's supervisor, conflicts with fellow workers, and so on. Because the job is separated from the home, the potential donor of support cannot be a direct witness to these kinds of problems. How then, does the donor come to recognize or gain knowledge of the difficulty and the distress it is causing the worker? Recognition, of course, is essential to support, for the partner cannot supportively respond to a troubled spouse if the trouble is not recognized. Because the job problem is beyond the direct vision of the partner, the donor's recognition of the problem ultimately depends on the worker's revelation of it. However, there is considerable variation in the manner and timing of revelation.

There are three distinctly different ways in which donors of support come to recognize that their partners have encountered stressful job problems. The first is also the simplest and most direct: something distressful occurs on the job and the worker comes home at the end of the day and tells his/her partner about it. Once the partner comes to recognize the problem in this fashion, the remaining stages of the support process are set in motion.

A second scenario is similar to the preceding but in one respect is quite different. Here, as in the first, the workers verbally communicate information about their stressful job problem; however, they delay this communication. That is, the worker lets an interval of time lapse between the occurrence of the problem and the time that he/she is ready to reveal the problem. We find in some cases that the withholding of information about problems lasts for but a brief period, such that the interval between the emergence of distress and verbalization of it is minimal. However, there are some who need a larger period between the surfacing of the stressful problem and the time when they are prepared to talk about it to their spouses. There seem to be at least two functions to this interval of silence. One, simply, is to give the problem a chance to crystallize in the mind of the worker or, as one respondent put it, to have time to figure out "what's really bugging me." It is during this interim gestation period that people, in effect, form the definitions of the problem and find the language to describe it to themselves and their spouses. Second, some people use it to "cool off," to get control over their distress so that when they are ready to talk about it, they can do so without overflowing with rage or fear. Such people, usually men, do not want to discuss their difficulties with their wives until they can convey a measure of control over the problem and over their emotional reactions to it. They are open to revealing the problems in their work lives, but they are less open to revealing that the problems undermine their sense of control. Consequently, they use the interval of silence in an attempt to gain some management over their feelings so that when they finally decide to talk about them, they will not appear to their spouses as vulnerable or out of control.

Finally, some donors come to recognize that the worker is troubled not through direct verbal communication, immediate or delayed, but through indirect behavioral cues. This happens, of course, in instances where the worker attempts to withhold any information about his/her job problem and to mask the resultant distress. Although this happens only in a minority of cases, it is potentially very disruptive of the support process and, therefore, merits close attention.

Whenever respondents told us that they did not discuss job problems with their spouses, they were asked why they did this. A variety of reasons were given. One, seemingly rooted in personality, is an inhibition that disposes people to hold large areas of their inner selves as private preserves. A male in his 50s speaks for such respondents when, in reflecting upon himself, he states that

I think there are certain things at the core of an individual that you can never share with anybody else. I couldn't name exactly what they are, but I think at the bottom line people keep themselves to themselves. They can't really open up to anybody else, no matter how close they may get to other people.

Occasionally privacy is interpreted as taking responsibility for oneself, without help from one's spouse. In the words of one man: "When we were first married, I just expected me to take care of my own problems most of the time and her to take care of her's."

However, although some people attempt to conceal job distress from their spouses as a result of a deep-seated aversion to any kind of self-revelation, most people disposed to privacy gave different reasons. Thus, several respondents report that they attempt to remain private not because of reluctance to be self-revealing but out of a desire to protect a spouse who is already emotionally burdened by his or her own work or household problems. One wife states that her husband is often depressed anyway, and she does not want to exacerbate it by telling him her worries or problems. Ostensibly, at least, the silence of these workers is testimony to their benevolent desire to shield their already emotionally overloaded partners from more concerns.

Although some people withhold information because they do not want to tell their spouses about their job problems, others withhold information because they feel their *spouses* do not want to hear about their problems. To reveal one's distress to an unreceptive spouse can evoke a response that is far from supportive. This is reflected in the experience of a director of a child care center whose job is very demanding, involving one crisis after another. She reports that she is very reluctant to speak to her husband about these job stresses because he is already somewhat resentful of her consuming involvement in her job and of the fact that she must do much of her work at home in the evenings. To speak to her husband about difficulties at work would, in her view, only heighten his existing sensitivity to the intrusion of her work on their relationship. Under these conditions, she prefers to keep things to herself. This person, then, withholds information simply because her husband's resentment of her work would stand in the way of his supporting her and would very likely lead to conflict between them.

Other respondents report that they avoid discussions of job problems not because they anticipate that support will be withheld but because they fear the attempt at support will be inappropriate. One person, for example, is deeply troubled because he feels he is not able to contribute to a law practice as much as the other lawyers in his office, yet this is not something he discusses with his wife. He states that he is afraid that because she does not have an understanding of what the problems are, she is likely to give him inappropriate advice: "She is very quick when she detects a problem to offer a solution to it." This places him, in turn, of having to reject her advice, thus risking conflict with her. (We shall have more to say about inappropriate attempts at support later.)

Whereas some avoid revelation because they anticipate unwanted advice, others withhold information because the worker anticipates an unwanted emotional response. Thus they speak of their spouses' emotional volatility that erupts with the revelation of job problems, placing the worker in the position of having to deal not only with the job problem and his/her own distress but also having to assuage the spouse's distress. As one man describes it, he gets quieter and quieter when something is bothering him, partly in response to his wife's tendency to blow up quickly, which forces him into the position of dealing with her distress instead of his own. In effect, the person who should be the donor of support preempts the recipient's role, an action that inhibits the direct reporting of job problems.

Finally, there are instances in which individuals feel that if they reveal their job problems, they will be judged badly by their spouses. Fear of losing the esteem of the spouse is particularly likely to arise when job holders judge themselves as being responsible for their problems or for failing to find a solution. If the worker suffers a loss of self-esteem as a result of encountering job problems, he/she is also apt to fear the loss of the spouse's esteem.

It should not be inferred that because people do not give verbal expression to distressful problems, or because they delay their expression, their spouses do not recognize their distress or are unresponsive to it. On the contrary, most respondents tell us that they are very sensitive to the emotional distress of their partners, even when the distress is not directly verbalized. Although they cannot be sure what might be amiss, they do know that something is not right. The sensitivity is not magical; it is in response to numerous behavioral and mood changes that are "read" as cues of inner turmoil. One may be less talkative, watch television more, bang the pots and pans louder, assume a different facial expression, be more distant and less reachable, be less patient, and so on. As has been observed elsewhere (Sade & Notarius, 1985), distress is usually powerful enough to break through masking efforts.

Some spouses, alert to the distress of the worker, are willing and able to wait calmly until their mate is ready to talk. From repeated experience, they are able to function with certain knowledge that whatever is bothering the other person will eventually come out in the open. But some spouses are unable or unwilling to bear the burden of ambiguity about the source of the distress, and this can lead to conflict. First, the distress and the ambiguity surrounding it can lead to a contagion of mood. The spouse, experiencing withdrawal, distance, and bad humor on the part of the worker can herself/himself begin to experience an anger nurtured by resentment. Soon the couple may be separated by a wall of irascibility that is buttressed from both sides although, perhaps, with neither understanding clearly how the wall came to be erected in the first place.

In this highly charged atmosphere, it takes little to trigger an overt confrontation. The confrontation, of course, is usually very remote from the problems that initially contributed to the emotional climate. In some cases, the confrontations and arguments over these remote issues may lead back to the real problems in a positive way. One respondent tells us, for example, that it is almost as though she and her husband need a blowup about something irrelevant and trivial before they can address what is really bothering them. Reconciliation around something trivial enables them to lower the barriers to communication over issues that are more important and bothersome. For some, an emotional rapprochement is set in motion through a peripheral conflict that then leads to recognition of the real issues underlying the argument. For others, the climate of hostility is not dispelled but lingers on, only adding to the difficulties that led up to it.

In addition to the charged emotional climate that is created, there is a second channel through which silence and ambiguity can impact on spouses and the support process. For one reason or another, there are spouses who are unable to tolerate a situation of uncertainty about their mates' distress and its cause. To dispel the ambiguity, they will make verbal observations about the others' bad moods or aberrant behavior, or they might importunately press the worker to explain the reasons for his/her ill humor. Utterances such as "you're certainly in a bad mood" or "you're acting strangely tonight" or "what's eating you" may occasionally loosen constraints on the exchange of information. More often, however, this kind of probing can boomerang by precipitating defensiveness and resentment, thus reinforcing the withholding of information and furthering exacerbating conflict. Indeed, one wife reports that when she asks her husband what's bothering him, he takes the position that she should know without having to ask; for him, the asking comes to stand as evidence of her insensitivity to him. Although the prodding and probing by the spouse may result in revelation, in some instances it may also result in an even more determined effort at concealment.

There is a final untoward consequence of silence in a situation of recognized distress. Two of our respondents—both wives—report that when they are uncertain about the nature and source of their husbands' distress, they begin to think that the cause lies with themselves. That is, they come to wonder if it was something they did—or failed to do—that is responsible for the anguish of their husbands. For these women, then, silence leads them to interpret their husbands' distress as a result of their own putative failings, thus provoking self-recrimination. In the midst of silence, these spouses are quick to blame themselves for distress that in fact was precipitated outside the home. In this manner, an unwillingness by one person to reveal the nature of his or her stressful problem produces guilt and self-blame in an innocent other.

It should be quite evident that the first stage of the support process, recognition, cannot necessarily be taken for granted because revelation is not always direct and immediate. For a variety of reasons, troubled workers may not want to discuss their job problems with their spouses, at least not right away. However, because of changes in behaviors and affect, the partner nevertheless is likely to be aware of the worker's distress. But while the spouse may know that something is wrong he/she may not know what it is. Such ambiguity not only acts as a barrier to support but may, indeed, come to constitute an additional source of conflict. Through it all, in most instances, both the presence and nature of the job problem come into recognition. As recognition emerges into clear view, a second phase of the support process is set in motion. This is the process of appraisal, which essentially involves the donor deciding *if* he/she should do something and *what* that something should be.

Stage II: Appraisal

Whereas the recognition of a problem for which support may be given depends largely on the behavior of the potential recipient of support, the appraisal of the problem depends largely on the perceptions of the potential donor. Although the appraisal process can involve a number of distinct judgments, it is fundamentally organized around a single issue, that of legitimation. Once the donor recognizes the presence of distress in the spouse, the donor must decide—consciously or not—whether to respond. This decision is based on assessments of the worthiness of the distress and its presumed underlying cause. Simply put, the donor implicitly asks if the recipient indeed merits support, if there is legitimate reason for it.

The answer to this question will depend in part on the perceived fit between the problem and the distress it is creating. In most cases, the donor will judge that the intensity of the distress is entirely consistent with the gravity of the perceived problem, thus advancing the chances of a supportive response. But occasionally a donor might have trouble acknowledging that an appreciable problem really *does* exist or that the distress it evokes is in reasonable proportion to its seriousness. Thus the potential donor might tell the distressed person that "it's all in your head," "don't be so bothered," or "don't make a mountain out of a molehill." When the very existence of the underlying problem is challenged or when its importance is demeaned or trivialized, the legitimacy of the distress is in effect being denied.

It cannot be assumed that the donor will invariably withhold support if she or he is unable to legitimate the source or magnitude of the distress. Even in instances where the donor is unable to validate the reasons for the worker's distress, support still might be forthcoming. In effect, support in such instances is given to one's partner unconditionally, regardless of the perceived legitimacy of the problem or the intensity of the emotional reaction to the problem. It essentially does not matter *why* or *how much* one is distressed, only that she/he *is* distressed. One working wife describes her husband's attitude like this: "He understands my concerns because he understands my personality. He never thinks I'm unnecessarily concerned." The donor, in this kind of relationship, is responding only to the spouse's distress and that support might be needed. The presence of distress alone constitutes sufficient legitimation of support; the merits of the problem are either taken for granted or ignored. Thus there can be an underlying concern for one's spouse that transcends the appraisal of specific problematic situations. In these kinds of relationships, legitimacy is assumed without perceptual weighing and balancing of the problem. As could be surmised, these relationships are marked by unquestioned respect and caring.

Just as there are instances where support is accorded in the absence of legitimation, there are instances in which support for the worker is withheld despite the spouse's judging the distress to be warranted and valid. There are several reasons for this. One concerns reciprocity. In marriage, the roles of donor and recipient are normally very fluid, with an exchange of roles occurring quite rapidly and frequently. There are marriages, however, in which people tend to become frozen in one role or the other, and this can breed both a sense of exploitation and, from the donor's perspective, stand as a cause for rationing or refusing support. This is reflected in the words of a woman who said:

> He takes a lot of crap [at his job]. He gets very few rewards for what he does, and people are not very facilitating there. So it's up to me when he comes home to try and fill that need and make him feel good about himself. And yet, I am not getting any reverse back.

Here is a person, then, who is sensitive to the difficulties her husband faces at his work and is understanding of his distress. However, because of the lack of reciprocity that she wants, she responds to his job problems only reluctantly and with obvious resentment.

In several households the activation or inhibition of support was regulated not by issues of reciprocity but by judgments of the seriousness of the problem when compared to other problems the family was confronting at the same time. The seriousness of one problem is not gauged in isolation from other problems that challenge the marital partners; instead, it is weighed and assessed as being more or less important than other difficulties they are simultaneously facing. The importance of this weighing process derives from what appears to be an *economy of concern* that operates in families. That is, there may not be sufficient emotional energy to focus on all problems that enter the family domain. Consequently, problems are ordered according to their importance; those that are deemed less serious than others may be dismissed because they seem trivial by comparison. Obviously, these judgments are in the eye of the beholder and something judged as ignorable by a potential donor might not be experienced as such by the potential recipient. Moreover, there is a tendency to elevate one's own problems to a level of considerable importance, with the result that the spouse's problems may be placed in disadvantaged competition with one's own. If scarce support energies need to be mobilized and allocated, therefore, problems judged as less imperative may be passed over. This is illustrated by the words of a man who was asked if there were times he would rather not hear about his wife's problems:

> Yup. When I'm worried about my own problems. No specific times but mostly when I'm worried about [his work], seeing that I don't have many problems besides that. I'm not worried about my bowling score or whether or not I'm going to get to go on so and so vacation this year.

It is the hypothetical trouble-free spouse who is most likely to give support, no matter how insignificant the problem for which it is given.

Finally, the withholding of support for a problem of recognized legitimacy can also result from what might be called support burnout. In such instances, the donor acknowledges the presence of a work problem and validates the distress it causes the worker, at least initially. However, if it is a problem that either resurfaces frequently or otherwise has a chronic history, the donor may become increasingly reluctant to muster support for it. The very persistence of the problem bespeaks the donor's failure to have made a substantial or lasting difference to the spouse's distress. Understandably, this can generate frustration on the part of the donor and give rise to the suspicion either that the spouse is not fully open to the support that is provided or that in some way the spouse is contributing to the perpetuation of the difficulty. For example, a woman described the problems of her husband who worked only intermittently on marginal construction jobs for which he was paid little and late. She had been urging him to seek other work, which he had not done. Recently he was again complaining to her of not being paid for work he had done, and she described her reaction as her husband related his latest woes:

> He doesn't want to work on a [steady] job where he knows he's going to get his money. I don't even care [any longer] if he doesn't get paid. He doesn't want the sure thing; he likes the hassle. He likes all this confusion he's in; he likes that garbage. So there's no need of me bothering him any more.

Obviously, support that is repeatedly given for a problem will eventually be withheld if the donor sees no evidence of its effective use. The withdrawing of support because of burnout, moreover, can itself lead to conflict and further distress.

Although we have been emphasizing conditions that limit the exchange of support in marriage, it needs to be understood that in the majority of cases people report that both they and their spouses have supportive reactions to a recognized problem and that there are no conditions constraining the support. What this bespeaks, of course, is that the partners have no difficulty in validating the problems that the other confronts in the workplace, that there is likely to be some reciprocity in support exchange, and that the problem for which support is given is not a fixed, unending travail. Knowing that people usually do react supportively, however, does not inform us as to what kind of support is given. Because people are alike in recognizing and legitimating problems does not mean that their supportive responses will be alike. There is, in fact, a good deal of variation in the forms of support that marital partners extend, variation that stems both from the nature of peoples' problems and from established patterns of interaction that go on in marriages. We now turn to a description of the forms of support that donors give to their spouses.

Stage III: The Forms and Functions of Support

Are there forms of behavior that by their very nature can be assumed to be supportive? Although this is a straightforward question, for several reasons it defies a simple answer. One reason is that the range of acts that have the potential of being supportive is bewilderingly varied. On top of this, support is laden with symbolism, such that an act that is perceived as supportive by one person may not be by another, or an act that is supportive at one time or for one problem may not be when it occurs at another time or for another problem. It is not surprising, therefore, that it is difficult to prejudge whether or not a given act is supportive. As Jacobson (1987) points out, the "meaning context" of support can vary considerably among people, including marital partners. These kinds of complexities notwithstanding, it is possible to discern in the interviews a number of forms and functions of support. It might be useful to underscore once more that in describing these patterns of support, we are speaking only of marital support given in response to problems one of the partners faces in the occupational realm. Other forms and functions of support would undoubtedly be identified were we examining other types of social relationships and other life problems.

A major consequence of social support is its contributions to individual coping. In earlier work (Pearlin & Schooler, 1978), we found that one of the most important functions of coping is to construct a meaning of the difficult situation such that its threatening properties are neutralized. This management of meaning can be performed by a number of cognitive and perceptual devices and is similar to, although not the same as, what Lazarus and Folkman (1984) refer to as an appraisal process.

Our interviews repeatedly suggest that the meaning of job problems is shaped and influenced by marital interactions. There appears to be two aspects of the meaning-shaping functions of support. One involves the sheer definition of the problem and the language to describe it. It quite commonly happens that people know that they have a job problem before they know what the nature of the problem is. They harbor feelings of anxiety or distress knowing that something is not right but not knowing precisely what is wrong. As described earlier, this is a circumstance that leads some workers to delay discussion of the problem with their spouse. Such feelings of distress might be triggered, for example, by an impatient or sarcastic word from a supervisor or by being passed over for promotion, or by some other perceived affront that suggests that something ominous and threatening may be going on. Repeatedly, respondents told us that when the nature and dimensions of the job problem are not clear, the opportunity to talk with their spouses can be very helpful in bringing the difficulty into focus. As one worker describes it, talking to his wife helps to "put into words the feelings I'm having." Thus, support can provide the very language needed to talk about problems and, in so doing, it also influences the meaning of the problems. Occasionally, we might note, the clarification of a problem that results from support involves a major redefinition of the problem. Thus one woman reports that she now views her involuntary unemployment as an opportunity for exploration rather than as a loss, due to her husband's offering a different perspective of the situation.

Along with its meaning-shaping function, marital support also provides coping assistance. It does so by helping to identify for the distressed worker options for coping strategies within the work situation. Respondents report that talking with their spouses about job problems can lead to the recognition of coping alternatives that the worker did not initially discern. What we see, then, is that support can help both to give definition and meaning to a problem and bring into view optional strategies for coping with the problem. Once such functions of support are fulfilled, the individual worker is presumably better able to cope within the context of the workplace. In these ways, social support does, indeed, involve coping assistance as Thoits (1986) describes it.

Marital support may also have vital consequences for the self. Stressful problems are often damaging to people's self-esteem and their view of themselves as meriting the respect of others. The very nature of many job problems is interpreted as representing either the absence or the withdrawal of esteem and, as has been previously demonstrated (Pearlin, Lieberman, Menaghan, & Mullen, 1981), this kind of assault on the self leaves one open to depressive symptoms. What had been observed in our earlier research is certainly confirmed within the present interviews. The self is commonly a casualty of exposure to job problems, especially those that are repeated or prolonged. How does support protect one from the diminution of self-esteem? In part, the self-concept of the worker is protected when the problem is defined in a way that places its cause outside of his/her responsibility. For example, problems with a supervisor at work may be reinterpreted as a "difficult supervisor" rather than the worker's inability to perform well under rigorous supervision. There are other mechanisms that function to shield the self. Sometimes the spouse will simply remind the worker of his/her strengths and virtues. One woman, for example, tells us that occasionally she feels that her work is beyond her capabilities but her husband says, "Oh, no, you're great, you're smart, you can do it." When asked how words like that make her feel, she said simply, "That's nice to hear." Other times the buttressing of self-esteem does not involve words but, instead, physical contact and the exchange of affection. Affection appears to stand as reaffirmation of one's worthwhileness and attractiveness at a time where one otherwise can feel quite worthless and unattractive.

Still another function of support, one that may involve no direct communication, is what might be called protection against stress overload. This essentially represents a conscious effort to keep additional pressures from the worker while she or he is grappling with a job problem. It is an indirect form of support in the sense that the spouse may be doing nothing to assist the worker directly in dealing with the job problem. Instead, it is an effort to keep the worker as unencumbered as possible with other problems so that his/her attention and energy can be focused on the job. Sometimes this protection may simply take the form of controlling one's own ill humor. One woman, for example, describes what she does when her husband is troubled by something at his work: "I back off, like instead of being bitchy or complaining or something, I'll try to maintain a little more peace for him to be able to handle his problems." Or occasionally the protection involves the management of children. Thus, one woman, when she sees that her husband has come home troubled, describes that she will tell the children that "Dad has a lot on his mind. If you want to ask him for something, wait until later." Whatever the specific measure that is taken to head off overload, they all represent an attempt to make the home a temporarily stress-free zone. These indirect supports have a basis in reality, for it is easier to deal with one problem at a time than to be confronted with a pileup of problems, even trivial ones.

A final form of marital support involves diversion. In earlier work (Pearlin & Schooler, 1978), we observed that one of the major functions of individual coping involves the management of the symptoms of stress. We think that this is also a function of marital support. That is, spousal support can help the worker keep symptoms of stress under manageable control, primarily through diversion. Spouses can be quite conscious of what they are doing when they try to get the workers' "minds" off their problems. It entails virtually any activity that succeeds in providing some temporary escape or a relief of tension: taking a talk together, going to the movies, making love, seeing other people, and so on. This kind of support, at its best, enables the worker to avoid being overwhelmed and immobilized by internal emotional distress.

In sum, several forms and functions of support have been identified. These include meaning-shaping functions, where the interactions with the spouse help the worker to clarify the nature of the problem and to identify problem-solving strategies and options. Self-esteem can also be reaffirmed or bolstered through support, specifically where the spouse helps the troubled worker to maintain a sense of self-worth and mastery. The protection against stress overload is still another function of marital support. Here the spouse, primarily through the management of the household environment, attempts to shield the worker from problems off the job. In this manner, a conscious effort is made to keep one from being overwhelmed by multiple problems. A similar function is represented by deliberate efforts to divert the worker in a way that reduces or contains tensions and other symptoms of stress. As in the case of shielding, this support does not directly assist the worker in dealing with his job problems but, instead, prevents these problems from becoming excessively stressful.

We have been emphasizing modes of support, both conscious and unconscious, that seem to work. However, a number of our respondents report either that their spouses make no effort to support or fail to support them effectively. Good intentions do not always lead to good consequences, and support does not always support. We turn now to consider some of the conditions that seem to lead to failure.

Stage IV: Successful and Unsuccessful Support

In discussing other aspects of the support process, we have alluded to a few of the conditions that result in people not giving support. For various reasons, for example, the presence of a problem might not be recognized. Or, as we saw, the problem might be recognized but support nevertheless withheld because there was no basis for legitimating the problem. Asymmetry in the exchange of spousal support may also dampen one's willingness to extend support, as will support burnout. In these cases, the troubled worker may expect and seek support but be unsuccessful in evoking it. There are other instances, however, where the donor attempts to provide support for the distressed worker but the worker, nevertheless, does not perceive himself/herself as being the recipient of support. It cannot be taken for granted that if one gives support the other receives it. It is the occasional disparity between giving and receiving that we shall address here.

Where support fails, it is usually because the support that is given is not that which is wanted. To understand unwanted support, it needs to be recognized that there is really but a limited number of ways support is conveyed. Specifically, it can be given merely by listening to the troubled worker, by asking questions, by giving guidance and advice, by demonstrating esteem and affection, and, more indirectly, by shielding the stressed person from additional stress buildup and by providing stress-reducing diversions. The skilled donor probably utilizes each of these mechanisms to convey support. However, one of these mechanisms sometimes interferes with or disrupts the effectiveness of the others. The culprit is *advice giving*. In most instances where respondents report dissatisfaction with the support given by their spouses, they point to unwanted or untimely advice as the reason. Why is advice unwanted? In answering this query, we shall limit ourselves to the manifest reasons that respondents give us, ignoring the latent dispositions to defensiveness that in some instances might be surmised.

One explanation that we repeatedly heard from respondents is that the substance of advice is not appropriate to the nature of their problem. There is, of course, a structural separation between the work setting, where the problem arose, and the household, where the support process unfolds. This separation, in turn, can lead to a gap between what is actually going on in the workplace that is stressful and the spouse's understanding of what is going on. Such gaps are particularly likely to occur where the problem involves complex work relationships or job duties. When the worker perceives that the advice is given without the benefit of an understanding by the spouse of the nature of the problem, its complexities and its implications, it will probably be rejected with resentment and with heightened resistance to further supportive efforts.

Sometimes advice is unwanted because it is perceived to be more in the service of the donor's own inner needs than those of the recipient. One poignant example (this one not involving job problems) was given by a woman whose son was killed in an automobile accident about a year prior to the interview. She looked to her husband as the one person in whose company she could cry and express her grief without constraint. But on the occasions that she would turn to him for emotional support, he would lecture her on the importance of putting her sadness aside and getting on with her life. According to his wife, his tendency to fall back upon advice giving reflected his own need to avoid intense and threatening emotions. In responding in a way that catered to his own needs and dispositions rather than those of his wife, he inadvertently created a situation of disappointment and conflict.

In still other instances, advice fails because it is experienced by the worker as an attempt by the donor to take over the management and control of the problem. Thus, one man, who was very anxious because his work was being closely evaluated, describes his wife's failed support efforts in this way:

> She has a very mothering quality about her when she wants to take control and do something. I think she feels like she's not there for me unless (she can do this). Whereas a lot of times I feel just like telling her and having her listen.

This quote suggests a very interesting explanation of why unwanted advice so often fails to be supportive. It is that advice giving by itself may be less important than the sequential order in which it is given. It is our impression that advice is likely to be more accepted and more effective if it is offered *last* in a sequence of supportive acts rather than *first*. If we were to abstract from the interviews to an ideal sequence of supportive acts, it would begin with listening, followed by an expression of affection, after which there would be an exchange organized around questions that were in the service of gathering relevant information, and, last, the offering of advice. Advice is not inherently ineffective; it is ineffective when it is separated from the other modes of support delivery and placed as the first and primary channel of support.

DISCUSSION

This chapter has sought to call attention to the interactional character of social support. The social aspects of support need to be emphasized because they are typically ignored in research. Support, of course, is inherently social because it necessarily involves people who have a relationship with one another. In the case of informal support, with which we have been concerned in this chapter, the supportive relationships and the role sets from which they are derived may be overarching and stable through time. The social and interactional features of informal support also should be studied in other types of relationships, such as those involving friends, work associates, and relatives. However, they are perhaps nowhere more clearly observed than in marriage. The intimacy, knowledge, emotional stakes, range of shared experience, and the modal continuity of this relationship make it ideal for examining interactional aspects of social support and its exchange that have a general relevance.

Individuals, of course, have multiple roles, and the integration among them is more often a fact taken for granted than a dynamic process taken for investigation. Thus, despite their spacial and temporal separation, we know that what transpires in the workplace affects transactions in the family and vice versa. In this chapter we have seen that the marital support that is initiated in response to stressful job problems represents one bridge that joins the occupational and family contexts. The facilitating effects of family relations in dealing with work and its problems have serious implications for the conceptualization and study of the stress process. Too often our research fails to capture full both the range of stressors to which people are exposed and the resources they are able to draw upon in dealing with the stressors. By taking into account the family when studying occupational stress and by being cognizant of occupation when studying the family, we are able to develop a more comprehensive picture of the stress process and its organization in people's lives. In examining stress as it is intertwined with individuals' roles and their social relationships, as is being done in this volume, it becomes clear that stress and its amelioration by support is clearly joined to social life itself.

As we described the various stages that can be discerned in marital support for occupational stress, we have tended to highlight the conditions within each stage that can interfere with successful support. Thus there may be considerable ambiguity on the part of the spouse concerning the nature of the problem; support may be withheld because the spouse is unable to legitimate the problem; the form or function of support may be ineffective; or the mode of support—the means by which it is conveyed—is unwanted. At each step, failed support can lead to conflict between the partners. We believe that the focus on failed support helps to illuminate support processes. This focus, however, should not obscure the fact that in the majority of the couples we interviewed, marital support for stressful job problems does go on, and it seems to go on in a most effective manner. It is by looking closely at instances where there is a disruption in marital support that the key elements in the process may be more clearly revealed. The deviant case can often tell us a great deal about the norm. However, among our limited sample of married people, the norm for the exchange of support, although not trouble free, is one that bespeaks caring, sensitivity, appropriateness, reciprocity, and effectiveness.

It should be noted in this regard that small-scale, intensive qualitative studies often enable the researcher to observe phenomena in depth. There is no doubt that the flexibility and probing character of such research allows one to pursue the hint of something important and to amplify it in a manner not permitted by more structured inquiries. But although it may lead to some riches, it leads away from others. Specifically, it is very difficult to conduct a comparative analysis of these data. Thus we cannot be sure what kinds of people under what kinds of conditions are likely to engage in what kinds of supportive behaviors. By way of example, we are unable to analyze how occupational status, family size, and the employment of wives may interact in shaping support processes.

These factors could and should be examined in larger, more systematic investigations. Despite these limitations, we do have clear impression of certain *gender differences*. These differences are not discrete: There are men who "act" like women and vice versa. This overlap notwithstanding, there are pronounced dispositional differences. As might be guessed, for example, men are more likely than women to attempt to withhold information about distress on the job, and they are also more likely to complain about their wives' advice giving. Women, on the other hand, are more ready to be unconditionally supportive, they are more disposed to shield their husbands from household stresses and irritants, and they are more active in providing diversions for their distressed husbands. Men and women appear to be similar in according greater importance (and support) to the occupational life of the husband than to that of the working wife or to the trials and tribulations of the homemaker. In addition to gender differences, there appear also to be differences corresponding to class status and age. The systematic evaluation of such differences awaits a larger study. What we can understand at this time, however, is that differences in patterns of support are not merely reflections of individual differences in personality dispositions but, instead, correspond to their status in the larger social order.

We also need to emphasize that the most powerful ingredients of informal social support do not involve special behaviors or acts that carry the label of "supportive". Much of what we observe as part of a support process is essentially built into the ordinary interactions that go on in social relationships, regardless of whether one is stressed or not. Thus people in continuing and intimate role sets usually are aware of each other's changes in emotional states; they often make judgments and appraisals of others' behavior; they commonly exchange words and gestures that indicate encouragement and approval; and, similarly, ordinary interactions are made up of acts of listening, asking, and telling. It is because support is a built-in feature of ongoing social relationships that support may often be received without a deliberate effort either to seek it or to give it.

The construct of informal social support, then, is to a large extent an abstraction from the give-and-take of ordinary social relations. As such, it raises certain questions: Is it possible to have effective support from those with whom we share difficult and conflictual relations; is it possible that ineffective support will be derived from relationships that in other respects are good? It is our judgment that neither of these contingencies is likely. Support is not apt to be drawn from relationships in which people do not matter to each other, in which actions reflect an absorbing preoccupation with self, and in which there is considerable interpersonal awkwardness and uncertainty. Social support does not grow out of people being masters of technique; instead, it is the result of their being masters of their social relationships.

Obviously, much more needs to be done to understand more completely the social nature of social support. We believe that as this understanding grows, so will our understanding of the powerful place of social support as a mediator in the stress process.

REFERENCES

Boss, P. (1986). Family stress. In M. Sussman & S. Steinmetz (Eds.), *Handbook on marriage and the family* (pp. 695–793). New York: Plenum Press.

Fisher, L. (1982). Transactional theories but individual assessment: A frequent discrepancy in family research, *Family Process, 21*, 313–320.

House, J. S. (1981). *Work stress and social support*. Reading, MA: Addison-Wesley Publishing Company.

Jacobson, D. (1987). The cultural context of social support and support networks, *Medical Anthropology Quarterly, 1*, 42–67.

La Gaipa, J. J. (1981). A systems approach to personal relationships. In S. Duck & R. Gilmour (Eds.), *Personal relationships, I: Studying Personal Relationships* (pp. 68–89). London: Academic Press.

Lazarus, R. S., & Folkman, S. (1984). *Stress, appraisal and coping*. New York: Springer Publishing Company.

McCubbin, H. J., Joy, C. B., Cauble, A. E., Comeau, J. K., Patterson, J. M., & Needle, R. H. (1980). Family stress and coping: A decade review, *Journal of Marriage and the Family, 42*, 855–870.

Pearlin, L. I. (1983). Role strains and personal stress. In H. B. Kaplan (Ed.), *Psychosocial stress: Trends in theory and research* (pp. 3–32). New York: Academic Press.

Pearlin, L. I. (1985). Social structure and social supports. In S. Cohen & L. Syme (Eds.), *Social support and health* (pp. 43–60). New York: Academic Press.

Pearlin, L. I., & Schooler, C. (1978). The structure of coping, *Journal of Health and Social Behavior, 19*, 2–21.

Pearlin, L. I., & Turner, H. A. (1987). The family as a context of the stress process. In S. V. Kasl & C. L. Cooper (Eds.), *Stress and health: Issues in research methodology* (pp. 143–165). New York: John Wiley & Sons.

Pearlin, L. I., Lieberman, M. A., Menaghan, E., & Mullan, J. T. (1981). The stress process, *Journal of Health and Social Behavior, 22*, 337–356.

Reiss, D. & Oliveri, M. E. (1980). Family paradigm and family coping: A proposal for linking the families' intrinsic adaptive capacities to its responses to stress, *Family Relations, 29*, 431–444.

Sade, J. E., & Notarius, C. I. (1985). Emotional expression in marital and family relationships. In Luciano L'Abate (Ed.), *The handbook of family psychology and therapy*. (Vol. I, pp. 378–404). Homewood, IL: The Dorsey Press.

Thoits, P. A. (1986). Social support as coping assistance, *Journal of Consulting and Clinical Psychology, 54*(4), 416–423.

Walker, A. J. (1985). Reconceptualizing family stress, *Journal of Marriage and the Family, 47*, 827–837.

4

Stress, Support, and Coping among Women Professionals with Preschool Children

CAROL-ANN EMMONS, MONICA BIERNAT, LINDA BETH TIEDJE, ERIC L. LANG, and CAMILLE B. WORTMAN

One category of workers for whom the transmission of stress between work and home is particularly problematic are those women who are attempting to nurture a young family and a career at the same time. Mothers of pre-school-age children comprise the fastest growing segment of the American work force (Hayghe, 1986). Fifty-two percent of such women are currently employed outside the home, compared with only 12% in 1950 (Bianchi & Spain, 1986). Furthermore, it has been predicted that by 1990, 64% of all families with children will include working mothers responsible for 10.4 million children under the age of 6 (Hofferth & Phillips, 1987).

Many of the difficulties encountered by working mothers stem from the fact that society has yet to catch up with women's employment trends. Only a very small percentage of U.S. employers provide any type of child

CAROL-ANN EMMONS • National Opinion Research Center, 1155 East 60th Street, Chicago, Illinois 60637.   MONICA BIERNAT • Department of Psychology, University of Florida, Gainesville, Florida 32611.   LINDA BETH TIEDJE • College of Nursing, Michigan State University, East Lansing, Michigan 48824.   ERIC L. LANG • American Institute for Research, Palo Alto, California 94302.   CAMILLE B. WORTMAN • Institute for Social Research, University of Michigan, Ann Arbor, Michigan 48106-1248.

care benefits for their employees. Moreover, only this year did the U.S. Supreme court rule that maternity leave be treated the same way as extended sick leave by those employers who provide extended sick leave benefits to their employees. Paid maternity leave, already a reality in over 100 other countries (Fielding, Gerdau, Crichton, Gonzalez, & Stafford, 1986), remains a distant dream for American couples struggling to combine career and family roles.

Even in their own homes, employed married women can expect to find little accommodation to their role accumulation. Although husband participation in household tasks and child care is gradually increasing (Pleck, 1985), recent studies of dual-career couples show that wives still perform a disproportionate share of these duties (Bryson, Bryson, & Johnson, 1978; Pleck, 1978, 1985; Weingarten, 1978; Yogev, 1981). These findings are in accord with those indicating that women experience greater interrole conflict than men (Behrman, 1982; Herman & Gyllstrom, 1977; Sekaran, 1983) and that employed married women report more role conflict (particularly with respect to role overload) than married women who are full-time housewives (Hall & Gordon, 1973). Bolger, DeLongis, Kessler, and Wethington (Chapter 5 this volume) also note that spousal arguments are more prevalent in dual-career families than in those where only one spouse works.

Some investigators have noted, however, that occupying multiple roles enhances feelings of personal worth and security (Sieber, 1974) and promotes psychological well-being by providing a sense of meaning and purpose to one's life (Thoits, 1983). Research also suggests that paid employment is associated with better mental health in married women (Gove & Geerken, 1977; Kessler & McRae, 1981; Welch & Booth, 1977). The evidence is by no means consistent, however (Pearlin, 1975; Radloff, 1975; Wright, 1978). Moreover, even in those studies that do find mental health benefits associated with paid employment, these benefits vary appreciably with the demands of family life and conditions on the job.

A study by Kessler and McRae (1981), using data from a large national survey administered in 1976, found that the positive mental health effects of employment were less for mothers than for working women without children. They also found that lack of assistance with child care and job pressures further modified the relationship between employment and distress. For women whose husbands did not share child care responsibilities, the advantages of employment were negligible. Furthermore, among women at the upper part of the income distribution, who lacked support from their husbands, increases in income were associated with increases in psychological anxiety. The authors attributed this finding to an overload effect produced by high work pressure combined with responsibility for children and housework. Similarly, Cohen, Johnson, Lewis, and Brook (Chapter 6 this volume) found evidence that maternal employment was positively associated with psychopathology, for example, depression, among working mothers and their children.

Although the findings are mixed (D'Arcy & Siddique, 1984; Parry, 1986), women with young children may be even less likely than other mothers to derive the mental health benefits of employment (Gore & Mangione, 1983). Moreover, the presence of small children in the home has been found to reduce the marital satisfaction of employed women (Staines, Pleck, Shepard, & O'Connor, 1978; White, Booth, & Edwards, 1986). These findings, taken together, suggest that the pressures of managing multiple roles are greatest, and the psychological benefits from employment are least, under conditions of heavy family responsibilities.

Understanding how working mothers who choose to remain fully involved in their careers cope with the competing demands of their multiple roles should be considered a research priority. Dropping out of the labor force, for even short periods of time, or cutting back on career involvement to meet growing family demands is likely to have negative effects on a woman's career (Rapoport & Rapoport, 1971), as well as on the career opportunities available to women in general (Fraker, 1984). Moreover, this strategy removes women from the labor market at a time when they are most valuable, that is, after acquiring years of education and training (Behrman, 1982). Thus the stresses associated with organizing and integrating multiple roles are costly, not only in terms of individual mental health but also with respect to the underutilization of human capital in society as a whole.

To date, however, only a handful of studies have looked at the coping behavior of women in dual-career families (cf. Elman & Gilbert, 1984; Gilbert, Holahan, & Manning, 1981; Hall, 1972; Harrison & Minor, 1978), or at the psychological consequences of labor force participation experienced by working women with young children (Bianchi & Spain, 1986). Although the level of role conflict experienced by working mothers has been well documented, far less is known about the actual situations that lead to the experience of conflict in women's lives. Finally, relatively little is known about how the families of working women, particularly their husbands, perceive and react to their situations.[1] Few prior studies focusing on working women have collected data from

---

[1]See the chapter by Weiss (Chapter 2 this volume) for a discussion of how wives react to their husbands' work situations.

these womens' husbands (for exceptions, see Bailyn, 1970; Chassin, Zeiss, Cooper, & Reaven, 1985; Smith, 1985).

The present study focuses on a particular group of working mothers: married women *professionals* with pre-school-age children. Although such women might be expected to possess the financial resources for effectively managing the competing demands of multiple roles, they nonetheless have certain characteristics that make them an interesting target population in which to study the interface between work and home. First, as noted, such women comprise one of the fastest growing segments of the American work force (Hayghe, 1986). Second, such women are likely to possess a high degree of job involvement, causing them to view their work not as a secondary role, but as a second primary role. This, in turn, can lead to greater competition between their work and family lives (Ladewig & McGee, 1986). Finally, professional occupations tend to be quite demanding, and the nature of the work is such that it is not finished when one leaves the office for the day. This also increases the likelihood of conflict between work and home demands.

The findings presented in this chapter are based on the first of four waves of data collected from a sample of women professionals with pre-school-age children. Data were also collected from the women's husbands. The first part of the chapter focuses on how these women view their lives and examines the specific situations that lead to the experience of role conflict. The second part of the chapter presents a comparison of wives' and husbands' perceptions of and reactions to the wife's situation.

METHOD

Subjects

The respondents were 135 women professionals with pre-school-age children and their husbands. The women were selected from two broadly defined occupational fields: university professor and businesswoman. All respondents were identified through their employers. To be eligible for the study, a woman had to be working at least 30 hours per week, be married and currently living with her husband, and have at least one child between the ages of 1 and 5 years old.

University professors were identified from lists of instructional faculty provided by the four largest universities in Michigan and the two largest universities in the Chicago area. Every university contacted agreed to participate. All of the universities, except one, were state institutions. Telephone screening interviews were conducted to determine the eligibility of each female on each list. Using this method, a total of 116 eligible female university professors were identified, of which 108 (93%) agreed to participate.

Businesswomen were selected from companies in geographic proximity to the universities. The target population included all companies with 50 or more employees located within a five-county area in Michigan or in Cook County in Illinois, and having one of four Standard Industrial Classification (SIC) codes. The SIC codes corresponded to four industries that tend to attract female professional-level employees: banking, accounting, law, and advertising. The sampling frame was stratified by size into small, medium, and large companies, and companies were randomly selected from within these strata to obtain an even distribution of participants across the four types of companies. A total of 104 companies were contacted, 72 in Michigan and 32 in Cook County. Sixty-eight of the Michigan companies (94%) and 26 of the Chicago-area companies (81%) agreed to participate.

Because most companies were reluctant to release the names of their employees, businesswomen could not be contacted directly. Instead, the personnel director in each company was relied upon to identify all professional-level women in the company who fit the eligibility criteria for the study. In 70% of the companies, the personnel director was willing and able to identify all such women (in most cases there were only a few). After obtaining their permission to be contacted by the researchers, he or she released their names. In those cases where the personnel director was unable or unwilling to identify eligible respondents, he or she was asked to distribute letters to all professional-level female employees. The letter described the study and contained a reply postcard on which the woman was to indicate her eligibility for and interest in participating in the study. The letter asked that every woman return the postcard, regardless of her eligibility or interest; however, only if a woman was both eligible and interested in participating in the study was she to write her name on the postcard. Follow-up letters and postcards were sent until an acceptable response rate was obtained from each company. Using these procedures, 98 eligible businesswomen were identified, 93 of whom agreed to participate. This yielded an appropriate response rate of 85.5%.[2]

The following analyses are based on a subset of cases for whom data are available from both the woman professional and her husband. This

[2]This figure is only an approximate response rate because there was no way to verify the total number of businesswomen who were eligible to participate in the study.

subsample includes 67 university professors and 68 businesswomen. When compared to the subset of cases whose husbands did not participate, the only demographic variable that differentiated the two groups was job tenure. Women whose husbands refused to participate in the study had been in their current jobs significantly longer ($M = 5.4$ years) than women whose husbands agreed to participate ($M = 4.2$ years), $t(198) = -2.54$, $p < .05$.

Procedure

Each woman was interviewed in person by a trained interviewer. The interview was conducted either in the woman's home or office, depending on her preference. These interviews averaged 2 hours in length. Prior to the interview, each respondent received a questionnaire to be completed and returned to the interviewer at the time of the interview. Along with the preinterview questionnaire, each respondent also received a spouse questionnaire for her husband to complete. The spouse questionnaire contained instructions for the husband to complete the questionnaire on his own and mail it directly back to the study investigators.

Sample Description

Ninety-one percent of the women in this sample were white; 3% were black, and the remaining 6% were of other races. The mean ages of the women and their husbands were 35.0 years and 37.2 years, respectively. These couples had been married an average of 8.0 years. Fifty-six percent of the couples had one child, 33% had two children, 10% had three children, and 1% had four children. The children ranged in age from 13 months to 21 years old. The median age of the children in single-child families was 2.5 years old; in families with two children, the median age was 4.9 years; and in families with three or more children, the median age was 10.5 years. Eighty-four percent of the women and 77% of their husbands had college degrees. Seventy-eight percent of the women and 68% of their husbands also had graduate degrees. Fifty-eight percent of the husbands were employed in professional and technical occupations, 23% were managers, 13% were sales workers, and the remaining 6% were clerical workers, craftsmen, operatives, and service workers. The median total family income, reported by both members of the couple, was in the category $70,000 to $74,999. The median income the women reported for themselves was in the category $30,000 to

$34,999. The median income reported by their husbands was in the category $35,000 to $35,999.

Comparisons between the university professors and businesswomen showed that the professors were significantly older ($M = 37.5$ years) than the businesswomen ($M = 32.6$ years), $t(133) = 7.55$, $p < .01$. Professors had also been in their present jobs significantly longer ($M = 5.0$ versus 3.5 years), $t(132) = 2.90$, $p < .01$ and had been married significantly longer ($M = 9.1$ versus 7.0 years), $t(133) = 3.22$, $p < .01$. Additionally, a significantly greater proportion of the professors had college degrees (100% versus 70.6%, χ^2 (1, $N = 129$) = 21.23, $p < .0001$), and graduate degrees (98.5% versus 27.0%, χ^2 (1, $N = 114$) = 38.16, $p < .0001$). Although personal and spouse incomes were not significantly different for these two groups of women, the mean total family income of the university professors ($M = \$85,000$ to $89,999) was significantly higher than that of the businesswomen ($M = \$70,000$ to 74,999), $t(131)$ = 2.23, $p < .05$.

Measures

The Effect of Womens' Roles on One Another. The effects of women's work and family roles on one another were measured with a series of six questions asking women to assess how much each of their roles suffered or was enhanced by each of their other roles. For example, one question asked, "How much does your performance in your career *suffer* because of your family life or responsibilities?," and another, "How much is your performance in your career *enhanced* by your family life or responsibilities?" The other four questions asked about the effect of the woman's career on her relationship with her husband and on her relationship with her children. Responses were coded on a 5-point scale ranging from "A Great Deal" to "Not at All." Husbands were asked a parallel set of questions about their wives' roles.

Career-Related Support from the Spouse. Women were asked to report how often their husbands provided four different types of support for their careers. These were (1) listening to her talk about work-related problems, (2) encouraging her to take advantage of professional opportunities, (3) being understanding when she has to work extra hours, and (4) performing extra household chores when she needs to devote more time to her work. Responses were coded on a 5-point scale that ranged from "Never or Almost Never" to "Always or Almost Always." Husbands were asked two parallel sets of questions. The first set measured how

marriage.

often their wives provided them with each type of career support, the second, how often they gave each type of support to their wives. Additionally, both husbands and wives were asked to rate how equitable career support giving was in their marriage, and whose career generally took precedence. Each of these was assessed with a single question, and responses were coded on 5-point scales.

Perceived Division of Household Tasks. Women were asked to report the proportion of time they and their husbands spent on each of six household tasks. The six tasks were (1) grocery shopping, (2) cooking, (3) laundry, (4) cleaning the house, (5) managing household finances, and (6) making repairs and doing maintenance work around the house. Unlike most measures of the division of household labor, which are measures of the relative time each spouse spends doing each activity (Staines & Pleck, 1986), these responses were coded on 5-point scales ranging from "Never or Almost Never" to "All or Most of the Time," *for each spouse.* If, for example, the couple hired someone to clean the house, a woman could report that the task was done "never or almost never" by both herself and her spouse. On the other hand, if both partners did their own laundry, the wife could report that the laundry was done "always or almost always" by both herself and her husband. However, the person who physically does a household task is not necessarily the one who has responsibility for it. Therefore, in addition to asking who did particular tasks, women were asked to indicate who had responsibility for making sure that each of the six tasks got done. This was a relative measure, with response options coded on 5-point scale ranging from "Wife Much More than Husband" to "Husband Much More than Wife."

Perceived Division of Child-Care Tasks. Women were also asked to report the proportionate division of labor by both partners on child-care tasks. The eight child-care tasks were (1) caring for the children's physical needs, (2) teaching the child skills or things about the world, (3) getting up at night with the child, (4) playing interactively with the child, (5) staying home with a sick child, (6) responding when a child asks for something, (7) making alternate arrangements for child care, and (8) driving children to day care or activities. The responses were coded on 5-point scales ranging from "Wife Much More than Husband" to "Husband Much More than Wife."

Perceived Role Conflict. The frequency with which a woman experienced role conflict was assessed with the following question: "During the past month, how often would you say you have experienced conflicts between your work and family responsibilities?" Responses were coded on a 7-point scale ranging from "Never" to "Two or Three Times a Day." Husbands were asked an identical question about themselves, and a parallel question about their wives (i.e., to report the frequency with which their wives experienced role conflict). The types of conflicts women experienced were measured with a series of 10 close-ended questions, developed from focus group interviews conducted during the pilot phase of this research. These questions asked women to report how often, during the past month, they had experienced such problems as having to stay home from work with a sick child or having to work during a time they usually spent with their family. Responses were coded on 5-point scales ranging from "Never or Almost Never" to "Almost Every Day."

Perceived Role Overload. Role overload is a type of role conflict that results from expectancies that one perform a variety of tasks, all of which are mutually compatible in the abstract but which are actually impossible to complete within the given time limitations (Kahn, Wolfe, Quinn, & Snoek, 1964). In the present study, role overload was measured separately in the home and work domains. The general form of the question assessing this construct was: "During the past month, to what extent have you felt overwhelmed because of having too much to do at (work/home) and not enough time to do it in?" Responses were coded on 5-point scales ranging from "Not at All" to "A Great Deal." Husbands were also asked to estimate their wives' role overload at work.

Problems at Work and at Home as a Result of Balancing Multiple Roles. In the pilot phase of the study, women were asked the following open-ended question: "As a result of trying to balance these various roles, what problems, if any, does this create for you at work and at home?" Women's responses to these questions were used to construct two series of close-ended questions for the main study. In these, women were asked to indicate how often they experienced each of 10 home-related problems and each of eight work-related problems, as a result of trying to balance the demands of a career, a marriage, and a family. Responses to these questions were coded on five-point scales that ranged from "Never" to "All the Time." Husbands were also asked to rate how often they experienced these problems, "as a result of your wife's trying to balance the demands of career, a marriage and a family."

Coping Strategies Used at Work and at Home. Women's coping strategies were assessed by asking them to rate how characteristic each of a list of strategies was of the way in which they had coped, over the past few months, with having too much to do and not enough time to do it in. Separate, but parallel, lists of coping strategies were generated for the work and home domains, based on information collected from focus group interviews conducted during the pilot phase of this research. Care was also taken to include items representing the three types of coping in Hall's (1972) model of coping with role conflict among college-educated women. These were (1) *structural role redefinition,* or attempts to alter external or structurally imposed expectations of others; (2) *personal role redefinition,* or changing one's own attitudes toward or perceptions of role senders' expectations; and (3) *reactive role behavior,* or attempts to improve the quality of role performance so as to satisfy the expectations of all one's role senders. Response options measured personal endorsement of the coping strategies and were coded on 4-point scales that ranged from "Not at All True" to "Very True." Higher scores indicated the strategy was more characteristic of the way in which a woman coped.

Husbands' Preferences Regarding How Their Wives Allocate Their Time. Women were asked, "Compared to the amount of time you currently spend (on a specific activity), how much time does your husband think you should be spending?" The activities were (1) career-related activities in the evening or on weekends; (2) time with the children; (3) time alone with him; (4) time alone on personal relaxation; and (5) housework, errands, meal preparation, or home maintenance. Responses were coded on 5-point scales ranging from "Much Less Time" to "Much More Time." The husband was asked how much time he actually preferred that his wife spend on these activities, compared to the amount of time she was currently spending.

Quality of Women's Work Role Experience. The quality of women's work role experience was conceptualized as consisting of three variables: (1) job stress, (2) job satisfaction, and (3) job functioning. *Job stress* was measured along seven dimensions frequently encountered in the literature on work stress. These were: flexibility in terms of time and place of work, quality of interpersonal relationships at work, control over one's work, role overload, role ambiguity, intrarole conflict, and the extent to which the work was bounded by time and place. Each dimension was assessed with a two- or three-item scale. The alpha reliability of this scale was .69. Higher scores indicated greater stress.

Job satisfaction was measured with a six-item scale based on Pearlin and Schooler's (1978) measure of occupational stress. Respondents were asked to rate how often they had felt happy, satisfied, frustrated or angry, insecure, and unhappy in their job, and how often they enjoyed themselves in their job during the previous month. Responses were coded on 5-point scales, ranging from "Never or Almost Never" to "Always or Almost Always." Negatively-worded items were reverse scored. The alpha reliability of this scale was .78. Higher scores indicated greater satisfaction.

Job functioning was assessed with six items from the work role subscale of the Weissman and Bothwell (1976) Social Adjustment Scale. These items were selected to tap several distinct dimensions of work functioning, including how many days the respondent had missed from work during the past month, how well she was able to do her work, how productive she had been in her work, how well she got along with other people at work, how often she felt upset while doing her work, and how interesting she had found her work during the past month. Higher scores indicated better functioning.

Quality of Women's Role Experience at Home. The quality of women's role experience at home was conceptualized as consisting of four variables: (1) marital stress, (2) parental stress, (3) marital satisfaction, and (4) parental satisfaction. *Marital stress* was assessed with 20 items measuring emotional support from one's spouse, how dependable the respondent saw her husband as being, the respondent's satisfaction with the amount of self-disclosure in the marital relationship, the respondent's satisfaction with her sexual relationship with her husband, the respondent's self-esteem as a wife, and the amount of affection in the marriage. The alpha reliability of this scale was .80. Higher scores indicated more stress.

Parental stress was assessed with seven items from the DOTS-R (Windle & Lerner, 1986) measuring child temperament. In addition, two items from Connors (1970) and two items from the Parenting Stress Index (Abidin, 1983) were used to measure the respondent's perceptions of her child's well-being. The alpha reliability of the combined scale was .60. Higher scores indicated greater stress.

Marital and parental satisfaction were measured with six-item scales based on Pearlin and Schooler's (1978) measures of marital and parental stress. Respondents were asked to rate how often they had felt happy, satisfied, frustrated or angry, insecure, and unhappy, in their marriage and as parents, and how often they enjoyed themselves in each of these roles during the previous month. Responses were coded on 5-point scales, ranging from "Never or Almost Never" to "Always or Almost Always." Negatively-worded items were reverse-scored. The alpha reliability of these scales were .81 and .77 for marital and parental satisfaction, respectively. Higher scores on each scale indicated greater satisfaction.

Mental Health. Two aspects of women's mental health were assessed: depression and well-being. Depression was measured with the 13-item depression subscale of the SCL-90 (Derogatis, 1977). The alpha reliability of this scale was .85. Higher scores indicated more depression. Well-being was measured with the nine items from the Affect Balance Scale (Bradburn, 1969). The alpha reliability of this scale was .91. Higher scores indicated greater well-being.

RESULTS

This section of the chapter presents descriptive data regarding women's perceptions of their current life circumstances, focusing on the actual situations that lead women to experience role conflict in their lives. The topics examined include (1) how these women think their work and family roles are affecting each other; (2) the extent to which they perceive their husbands as helpful and supportive; (3) the problems they face at work and at home as a function of balancing multiple roles; (4) the frequency and type of conflicts women experience between work and family responsibilities; and (5) their strategies for coping with feeling overwhelmed by having too much to do and not enough time to do it in.

How the Women Viewed Their Lives

Effect of Each Role on the Others. Most women in this sample felt their family lives were having only a mildly detrimental effect on their careers. Only about 10% of respondents thought their performance in their careers suffered "a great deal" or "quite a bit" because of their family responsibilities. This contrasts sharply with the large percentage who said their careers suffered "some" (43.9%), "just a little" (34.2%) or "not at all" (11.4%). When women's perceptions of the net effects of their family lives on their careers were examined, the sample divided into three, roughly even, groups. That is, approximately one third (32.7%) saw their careers as mostly enhanced by their family lives; another third (36.3%) thought their careers suffered more than they were enhanced by their family lives; and the final third (31.0%) rated the positive and negative effects of their family lives on their careers as equal. Women were also asked to view the situation from the opposite direction, that is, the effect their careers were having on their family lives. In general, these women were more positive about the effect their careers were having on their relationships with their *husbands* than they were about how their careers were affecting their relationships with their *children*. In fact, the majority felt that their relationships with their husbands were actually enhanced by their careers to some degree. Paired *t* tests showed that respondents, as a group, felt their relationships with their husbands were enhanced by their careers to a significantly greater degree than these relationships were harmed ($t[112] = 4.45, p < .0001$). Looked at another way, the majority (52.6%) said their relationships with their husbands were enhanced more than harmed by their careers. The remainder of the sample was approximately evenly divided between seeing their relationships with their husbands as primarily hurt by their careers (22.8%) and seeing their relationships as equally enhanced and hurt by their careers (24.6%).

The situation was different, however, regarding women's relationships with their children. Paired *t* tests indicated that these women thought their relationships with their children suffered more because of their careers than did their relationships with their husbands ($t[112] = 3.35, p < .002$), and also more than their careers suffered as a result of their family responsibilities ($t[112] = 2.60, p < .02$). Moreover, a greater proportion (40.4%) saw their relationships with their children as primarily suffering because of their careers than viewed these relationships as primarily enhanced (28.1%), or equally harmed and enhanced (31.6%). Bolger *et al.* (Chapter 5 this volume) suggest that at the *micro*level, stress spillover between work and home is bidirectional in effect. However, these data argue that women perceive work as having a stronger impact on parenting than vice versa.

Perceived Career-Related Support from Their Husbands. The majority of women perceived their husbands as engaging in each type of supportive behavior "much of the time" or "almost always." With regard to how equitable they thought career support giving had been in their marriage, over half (59.3%) felt that they and their spouse supported each other's careers equally. Women who reported some inequity, however, were more likely to say that they supported their husbands' careers more than their husbands supported their careers (23.0%); only 18% felt that they received more support from their husbands than they gave in return. Regarding whose career takes precedence, more women said it was their husbands' than said it was their own (34.1% versus 24.4%). However, the largest group (41.5%) responded "both about the same."

Perceived Sharing of Household Tasks and Child Care. Only about a quarter of the women in this sample (23.9%) said their husbands contributed "too little" to household chores and child care. The majority (62.8%) described their husbands as doing a "satisfactory amount" of these things, and 13.3% said their husbands contributed "too much." Women's perceptions of the proportions of time they and their husbands each did various household tasks agreed with their global evaluation of their husbands' contributions. Specifically, of the six household tasks asked about, women perceived themselves as doing two tasks a significantly greater proportion of the time than their husbands, two tasks the same proportion of the time as their husbands, and two tasks significantly less than their husbands. Those tasks that women perceived themselves as doing a significantly greater proportion of the time than their husbands were cleaning the house ($t[100] = 4.40, p < .0001$) and managing the household finances ($t[95] = 2.61, p < .02$). The two tasks which women reported doing the same proportion of the time as their husbands were grocery shopping and cooking, and the two tasks which women said their husbands did a significantly greater proportion of the time were laundry ($t[86] - 3.64, p < .001$) and household repairs ($t[85] = -7.45, p < .0001$). However, when asked whose responsibility it was to see to it that each of these tasks was accomplished, the majority of women said the responsibility was more their own for every task except household repairs.

On the eight child care activities assessed, the percentage of wives doing more than their husbands was always greater than the percentage of husbands doing more than their wives. On three child care activities, however, the majority of respondents reported that both partners shared equally. These activities were: teaching children skills about the world (78.3% reported parents did this "Both About the Same"); playing interactively with the children (67.2%); and responding to children's requests (58.3%). Finally, it is important to note that on none of the reported child care activities were more than 17% of the husbands doing more than their wives.

Problems at Home as a Result of Balancing Multiple Roles. The problems women encountered at home, as a result of balancing multiple roles, reflected a lack of time to keep up with all the things they wanted to get done. Three problems were reported by 75% or more of the women as occurring "often" or "all the time." These were (1) not having the time to tackle big projects around the house (e.g., cleaning out the garage, attic, basement, or closets) as much as they would like to; (2) not being able to spend as much time alone with their husbands as they would like; and (3) not having enough time for themselves to do such things as relax, exercise, or spend on their appearance. As one pilot respondent remarked in the open-ended precursor to this set of questions, "I'm not in the house enough hours to do everything that needs to be done. . . . By the time I've done all I need to do, I'm too tired for my husband." Another commented, "I'd like to have more time for myself to exercise, to put on makeup, to spend on my hair, to sleep, to be rested."

Over two-thirds of the women also reported not having enough time to keep the house as clean as they would like it to be and not being able to keep up with little projects and errands, like mending, taking clothes to the cleaners, or getting things repaired. According to one pilot respondent, the problem involved failing to live up to her ideal. As she put it, "It's hard to explain. I suppose it's basically not being perfect, and part of it is being very different from what I grew up thinking I would be . . . like having a nice clean house, a house you're proud to invite people in to see, and well-cooked meals. . . . It's all different." Even the least common problems at home were experienced by close to a quarter of the sample "often" or "all the time." The problems women encountered at home as a result of balancing multiple roles were also each significantly correlated with feelings of being overwhelmed in the home domain.

Problems at Work as a Result of Balancing Multiple Roles. As in the home domain, the problems women experienced at work also reflected an acute shortage of time. The problem women experienced most often was having to carefully plan all their time in order to get their work done. The stress this created for these women is captured in excerpts from the open-ended precursor to this series of questions asked of women in pilot interviews. One pilot respondent remarked, "I feel pressured to use every minute of my time constructively at work. There is no "ease" for mistakes or surprises; no "time flexibility." Another said, "There is a greater sense of the need for a payoff when life has to be so organized and planned. If I sacrifice time with my family to work on a grant, I want to be rewarded. I want to get it! It's harder to be satisfied with mediocrity."

Not being able to stay late or work in the evenings or on weekends as much as they would like or thought they should was also reported by almost half of these women as occurring "often" or "all the time." Again responses to one of the open-ended questions asked of pilot respondents illustrate this problem. One such respondent described her feelings as follows, "I feel that I don't have as much flexibility in my time as my colleagues who are single, or who are married and don't have children.

They have more evening time available to them so they have the option to work extra hours." Another women explained, "I would like to be doing more writing and research, but . . . I've made a decision that I'm not going to take time away from my family."

Not being able to put in as much time on their work as they felt they needed to, not having the time to take advantage of professional opportunities that might advance their careers in the long run, and not having the time to develop professional relationships with their colleagues were also frequently encountered problems. One pilot respondent described the situation this way, "I can't spontaneously be available beyond my normal work hours. I have to plan far in advance. I can't socialize with people from work spontaneously." Another women said, "I don't have the energy to look into what I need to do to further my career. Work and kids are all I can handle."

Because so much has been written, anecdotally, about the problems encountered by working mothers, it is also instructive to look at the types of problems *not* often experienced by the women in this sample. More than half said that not being able to travel as much as they should or being unable to concentrate fully on their work because of being preoccupied with family matters were "rarely" or "never" problems for them at work. Similarly, more than 40% "rarely" or "never" felt as though they were cutting corners in their work, and an additional 40% felt this way only "sometimes." As in the home domain, work problems were significantly related to feeling overwhelmed at work. The lack of problems caused by family preoccupations intruding on work time seems particularly intriguing because it is commonly believed that mothers find it difficult to concentrate on work. We found additional evidence, in fact, that children's temperament, age of children, and number of children living with a couple had no influence on a woman's job functioning or job stress levels.

Conflicts between Work and Family Responsibilities. Conflicts between work and family responsibilities were a common phenomenon for most women in this sample. Over 75% reported experiencing such conflicts almost every day. Only three women (2.2%) said they never had such conflicts. The average frequency of role conflict in this sample was "two or three times a week" during the past month.

Four conflict-generating situations were mentioned by over half of the respondents as having occurred at least two or three times during the past month. The most frequently reported situation was having to rush their children to get ready in the morning so that they, themselves, would not be late for work. This "tug-of-war" between work and family time was also reflected in the problems women reported experiencing with the second greatest frequency. These were having to leave work earlier than they would have liked to because of their children and having to work during times usually reserved to spend with the family. Finally, work-related travel often took time away from the family, preventing women from fulfilling their usual household and child care responsibilities.

Again, it is useful to examine the types of problems women said they rarely or never encountered. For example, over 80% said they never had to send a sick child to school or day care because neither they nor their husbands were able to take time off from work to stay home. Over three-quarters of these women reported never having stayed home from work during the past month to take care of a sick child, and nearly as many said they never had to cancel a professional engagement during the past month because of an unexpected situation involving their children. Finally, over half said they had not missed a work-related function they really wanted to attend during the past month because of family responsibilities.

The Relationship between Role Conflict and Perceived Role Overload. From the data presented it appears that most conflicts between work- and home-related responsibilities were not the result of intrinsic incompatibilities between these responsibilities but rather the result of these women having more to do than they could accomplish in the time available to them. One question arising from these findings is whether the feeling of being overwhelmed *within* a particular role (for example, at work) was responsible for the conflicts women encountered *between* their roles. Some notion of the relationship between perceptions of overload in each role and the frequency of role conflict can be obtained by examining the bivariate correlations among these variables. These correlations indicated that both types of perceived role overload were significantly related to the frequency of role conflict ($r = .28, p < .01$ for work; and $r = .18, p < .05$ for home). However, when the relationships between perceived role overload and frequency of role conflict were examined with standardized path analysis, the only significant path coefficient was the one indicating the influence of perceived role overload at work on the frequency of role conflict ($B = -1.10, SE = .37, p < .01$). In other words, greater role overload at work led to greater frequency of inter-role conflict.

Because the home is often characterized as a haven from the stresses of the outside world, the extent to which women felt overwhelmed at home because of having too much to do was compared with the extent to which they felt this way at work. Although role overload at work was more strongly related to role conflict than was overload at home, it is noteworthy that the *level* of overload experienced by these women was quite similar across domains. Specifically, a paired t test showed no significant difference between the mean level of role overload women perceived at work and that which they perceived at home.

Coping Strategies Used at Work and at Home. A major purpose of this study was to examine the coping strategies women employ to deal with the demands facing them at work and at home. Drawing in part from previous work on role conflict among women professionals, particularly that of Hall (1972); in part from the stress and coping literature (see, e.g., Lazarus & Folkman, 1985; Kessler, Price, & Wortman, 1985), and in part from comments made by women who participated in focus groups in a pilot phase of our research, an effort was made to group the coping strategies into four conceptually distinct categories. These were: (1) a "superwoman" strategy, which involved working as hard and efficiently as possible to meet all role expectations; (2) "planning" and time management; (3) "cognitive reinterpretation" of one's role demands; and (4) "divesting" oneself of unimportant activities, which also included being careful not to take on other responsibilities. A representative item from each scale, the number of items in each scale, and alphas for each scale are presented in Tables 1 and 2. Factor analyses of the coping strategies within each domain provided some support for this conceptual grouping.[3]

Our "superwoman" strategy is similar to Hall's (1972) strategy of reactive role behavior and involves trying to meet all role demands experienced through increased effort. Our cognitive reinterpretation strategy is similar to Hall's strategy of personal role redefinition and involves changing one's perceptions of the role demands, rather than the role demands themselves. Items included within this strategy involve viewing the situation in a more positive or less upsetting way. Our "divesting" strategy overlaps with Hall's strategy of structural role definition or taking steps to minimize one's work load, either by getting rid of respon-

[3]A principal components factor analysis followed by a varimax rotation identified three factors in the work domain and four in the home domain with eigenvalues greater than 1. The four "home" factors correspond to those described in the text. In the work domain, no "planning" factor emerged. To develop the final scales, items that loaded .40 or higher on a particular factor were first included, then other similar questions which did not load as highly but that "fit" conceptually were added. At this point, a computer algorithm that iteratively computes scale reliability coefficients was employed to identify the set of items that produced the best alpha coefficient. These are the scales described in Tables 1 and 2.

Table 1. Coping Scales in the Work Domain

Scale	Number of items	Scale reliability	Representative item
Superwoman	3	.73	I tried to work as hard as possible, so that I could do all the work that was expected of me on the job.
Planning ahead	5	.65	I tried to anticipate stressful periods at work and plan ahead for them.
Cognitive reinterpretation	3	.68	I told myself that it wouldn't be the end of the world if I didn't get all my work done on time.
Divesting of responsibilities	4	.53	I was careful not to take on additional professional activities that would have increased the sense of time pressure I felt.

sibilities or by recruiting additional assistance. There is no parallel in Hall's scheme for our strategy of time planning and management. When others have used Hall's scheme as a basis for new categories of coping strategies, time planning and management has rarely emerged as a discrete strategy (Elman & Gilbert, 1984). An exception to this trend was a

Table 2. Coping Scales in the Home Domain

Scale in home domain	Number of items	Scale reliability	Representative item
Superwoman	3	.66	When at home, I tried to be as efficient as possible—for example, I tried not to waste time talking on the phone.
Planning ahead	7	.66	I tried to prioritize things that needed to be done at home by making lists and then figuring out when I'd be able to do each thing.
Cognitive reinterpretation	5	.71	I tried to recognize that I'd have to lower my standards about such things as how clean my house is and how elaborate meals are.
Divesting of responsibilities	4	.54	I talked with my husband or others in the house to eliminate or reduce some of the work for which I am responsible.

study by Lang and Markowitz (1986) who found evidence that a two-item coping index called "planned task management" was empirically distinct from Hall's three traditional coping strategies. Several items designed to tap this strategy were included in the present study because it was frequently mentioned by pilot respondents as a predominant coping strategy.

To determine the relative frequencies with which women used the four coping strategies within each domain, repeated-measures analyses of variance were performed. The result in the work domain was an overall difference between the means of the four strategies ($F[3,402]$ = 39.74, $p < .0001$). Scheffe tests were then used to compare pairs of strategies. The strategy most favored in the professional domain was the "superwoman" response ($M = 3.13$, $SE = .62$). Women rated this strategy as significantly more characteristic of the way they coped at work than any of the other three strategies. Time planning was the second most characteristic strategy used by these women at work ($M = 2.59$, $SE = .66$). It was reported to be significantly more characteristic than divesting ($M = 2.22$, $SE = .62$), but not more characteristic than cognitive reinterpretation ($M = 2.28$, $SE = 1.24$). The mean levels of divesting and cognitive reinterpretation, the least used strategies, were not significantly different from each other.

In the home domain, there was also an overall difference between the means of the four coping strategies ($F[3,402]$ = 24.30, $p < .0001$). Scheffe tests suggested that the relative frequencies with which women used each of the four coping strategies at home was only somewhat different from the way they used them at work. In the home domain, the superwoman strategy was once again the dominant coping response ($M = 2.68$, $SE = .76$). It was found to be significantly more characteristic of the way women said they coped at home than were divesting ($M = 1.89$, $SE = .59$), and planning ($M = 2.27$, $SE = .54$); but was no different than cognitive reinterpretation ($M = 2.35$, $SE = 1.18$). In this domain, then, cognitive reinterpretation was quite frequently used, significantly more so than was divesting. Finally, planning, the third most called-upon coping response, was significantly more characteristic of women than was divesting, the least used response.

Although the efficacy of these coping strategies cannot be evaluated with cross-sectional data, it is somewhat informative to examine the bivariate correlations between each strategy and measures of both the quality of experience in each role and of mental health. In the work domain, three facets of the quality of women's role experience were examined: job stress, job functioning, and job satisfaction. In the home domain, four variables were investigated: marital stress, marital satisfaction, parental stress, and parental satisfaction. Two dimensions of mental health were also investigated: depression and general well-being. The correlations of the coping scales in each domain with all of these "outcome" measures, including those not directly relevant to the role from which the coping responses were taken, were examined. This was done to investigate whether a coping response in one domain can influence outcomes in another.

The correlations between the four coping strategies in the work and home domains and the various measures of role quality and mental health appear in Tables 3 and 4. In both the work and home domains, planning showed consistent significant relationships to the "outcome" measures. Planning at home was particularly important in this regard, as it was significantly related to eight of the nine role quality and mental health measures investigated, including those relevant to the work role. Planning at work did not significantly correlate with any of the home-related outcomes.[4] Also of note is that the superwoman strategy as a coping response at home was significantly related to the two parenting outcomes. The more a woman tried to do everything at home, the more parenting satisfaction and the less parenting stress she experienced.

Comparisons of Wives' and Husbands' Views

The Effect of Each of the Wife's Roles on Her Other Roles. The husbands of the women in this sample agreed with their wives' assessments of how much her career was enhanced by and suffered because of her family life. They also agreed with their wives regarding how much her relationships with them and with their children were enhanced by her career. Husbands disagreed with their wives, however, about how much her relationship with them and with the children suffered because of her career. Specifically, wives thought these relationships suffered significantly more than did their husbands ($t[112] = 3.00, p < .01$ for the wife's relationship with her husband, and $t[112] = 4.40, p < .0001$ for the wife's relationship with the children).

Husbands also agreed with their wives about the relative effect of

---

[4]To get some notion of the direction of influence between the four coping strategies and the various "outcome" measures, a series of standardized path analyses were performed. The use of time planning as a coping strategy at work significantly influenced job satisfaction ($B = .243, SE = .121, p < .05$), and well-being ($B = .32, SE = .118, p \leq .01$). Planning at home also positively influenced well-being ($B = .55, SE = .168, p < .01$). However, the opposite path was significant where the marital and parental stress variables were concerned. Marital stress negatively influenced planning at home ($B = -.402, SE = .187, p < .05$), as did parental stress ($B = -.55, SE = .268, p < .05$).

Table 3. Correlations between Coping Strategies in the Work Domain and Measures of Role Quality and Mental Health

Coping strategies used at work	Job stress	Job functioning	Job satisfaction	Marital stress	Marital satisfaction	Parenting stress	Parenting satisfaction	Depression	Well-being
Superwoman	-.06	.09	.07	-.01	.00	-.14	.12	-.13	.14
Planning	-.18*	.15	.21*	-.07	.01	-.10	.13	-.06	.32**
Cognitive reinterpretation	-.01	.05	.08	.09	.07	-.09	.13	-.11	.17
Divesting	.04	-.03	.10	.03	-.06	.11	-.03	-.12	.05

$*p < .05.$
$**p < .01.$

Table 4. Correlations between Coping Strategies in the Home Domain and Measures of Role Quality and Mental Health

Coping strategies used at home	Job stress	Job functioning	Job satisfaction	Marital stress	Marital satisfaction	Parenting stress	Parenting satisfaction	Depression	Well-being
Superwoman	-.07	.12	.12	-.03	.11	-.18*	.21*	-.09	.14
Planning	-.19*	.21*	.25*	-.21*	.14	-.24**	.23**	-.21*	.38**
Cognitive reinterpretation	.11	.00	.01	.03	.01	-.03	.09	-.06	.08
Divesting	.09	.06	-.01	.06	-.06	.04	-.16	.16	.08

$*p < .05.$
$**p < .01.$

each of their wives' roles on one another. For example, husbands agreed with their wives that the wife's relationship with their children suffered more because of her career than did her marital relationship ($t[112] = 2.48$, $p < .02$). They also agreed with their wives that the marital relationship was enhanced by her career to a significantly greater extent than it was harmed ($t[112] = 6.96$, $p < .0001$).

Career Support Giving in the Marriage. Like their wives, husbands perceived a high level of reciprocity in career support giving in their marriages. When husbands' responses to the questions about the specific ways they supported their wives' careers were compared to their responses regarding the support they received from their wives, there was only one significant difference. Husbands thought they encouraged their wives to take advantage of professional opportunities significantly more often than their wives encouraged the husbands to do so ($t[129] = 4.55$, $p < .0001$). There was also a high level of agreement between husbands and wives regarding the frequency with which the husband supported his wife's career. When wives' responses to the questions about the support they received from their husbands were compared with their husbands' responses about the support they gave their wives, no significant differences were found for any of the four supportive behaviors. The husbands and wives in this sample were also largely in agreement regarding how equitable career support-giving was in their marriages.

Problems at Home as a Result of Wife's Multiple Roles. Husbands were asked how often they encountered seven of the 10 problems asked of their wives, as a result of their wives' trying to balance the demands of a career, a marriage, and a family. For all but two problems, the husbands reported experiencing the problem significantly less often than did their wives. Specifically, husbands thought the house was not as clean as they would like it to be significantly *less often* than did their wives ($t[111] = 10.04$, $p < .0001$). They were also *less likely* than their wives to think that big projects like cleaning the garage were not getting done ($t[111] = 10.52$, $p < .0001$), that little projects and errands were not getting done ($t[111] = 10.68$, $p < .0001$), that the family was not eating well-balanced meals ($t[110] = 10.65$, $p < .0001$), or that their wives were not devoting as much time to family finances as they would like them to be ($t[110] = 5.12$, $p < .0001$). Husbands tended to agree with their wives, however, about how often the wife was too tired to enjoy the time she spent with the family, and how often the husband had to worry about coordinating his schedule with his wife's so that child care responsibilities would be covered.

Role Conflict and Role Overload. Husbands reported experiencing conflict between work and family responsibilities an average of once a week during the past month, whereas their wives reported having such conflicts two or three times per week during the past month ($t[111]=$ $-.6.02, p < .0001$). Although husbands said their wives experienced role conflict significantly more often than they, themselves, did (t [111] = 3.45, $p < .001$), their estimation of their wives' role conflict was still significantly lower than their wives reported for themselves (t [132] = -4.09, $p < .0001$). Husbands' perceptions of the role overload their wives experienced at work during the past month, however, were essentially the same as their wives.' That is, both said the wife felt between "somewhat" to "moderately" overwhelmed at work during the past month because of having too much to do and not enough time to do it in.

Husbands' Preferences Regarding How Their Wives Spent Their Time. In addition to the high standards these women seemed to set for themselves, they also appeared to have unrealistic perceptions of their husbands' expectations of them. Wives were asked how much time they thought their husbands would like them to be spending on a number of activities compared with the amount of time they were currently spending. Husbands were asked how much time they thought their wives should be spending on these activities, compared with the amount of time they were currently spending. For every activity, the wives' perceptions of their husbands' preferences were significantly different from what their husbands said they actually preferred.

In terms of specific activities, husbands said they thought their wives should be spending "about the same amount of time" as they were currently spending on career-related activities in the evening and on weekends, whereas the wives thought their husbands would prefer them spending "a little less time" ($t[118] = -5.33, p < .0001$). Husbands also said they thought their wives should be spending "a little more time" alone relaxing, whereas the wives thought their husbands were satisfied with the amount of time they were currently spending in this manner ($t[119] = -2.86, p < .005$). Conversely, the wives thought their husbands would prefer them to be spending "a little more time" with the children ($t[119] = 1.99, p < .05$) and alone with them ($t[117] = 3.93, p < .0001$), whereas the husbands said they preferred their wives to be spending "about the same amount of time" as they were currently spending. Finally, wives tended to think that their husbands were satisfied with the amount of time they were currently spending on housework, meal preparation, and home maintenance, whereas their husbands actually preferred their wives spend "a little less time" on these activities ($t[119] = 2.16, p < .05$).

DISCUSSION

Although women with young children are joining the paid labor force at an unprecedented rate, these women are, at the same time, continuing to maintain their traditional homemaking and motherhood roles (Bianchi & Spain, 1986). Relatively little systematic research has been done on the problems such women encounter in trying to reconcile their roles of wife and mother with their role of paid worker. Even less is known about how these women integrate, organize, and balance the various problems and activities in their different roles simultaneously. The current study was designed to investigate the problems encountered by women professionals with pre-school-age children and their strategies for balancing the demands of their multiple roles.

The overall picture that emerges from these data is one of reserved optimism. On the one hand, the majority of women in this sample felt that the net effect of their family lives on their careers was either positive or neutral and that the net effect of their careers on their marriages was definitely positive. Most of these women also reported high levels of support from their husbands for their careers, satisfaction with the contributions their husbands were making to housework and child care, and an equitable division of household chores within their marriages. The husbands also seemed concerned that their wives were often too tired to enjoy time with the family, and were aware of the amount of role overload their wives experienced at work.

On the other hand, large percentages of these women viewed their careers as having a negative effect on their relationships with their children, said their husbands' careers generally took precedence over their own, and reported still having to take responsibility for seeing to it that household chores got done. Women also reported doing more child care than their spouses, especially in areas of physical care, getting up during the night, staying home with sick children, and driving children to day care and other activities. Moreover, these women reported experiencing conflicts between work and home an average of two or three times a week, and appeared to be engaged in a continuous tug-of-war between their responsibilities at work and their responsibilities to their families. Whereas husbands agreed that their wives experienced more role conflict than they themselves did, they still did not perceive the severity or degree to which their wives experienced conflicts between their roles.

Some insight into the daily stresses experienced by this group of women comes from examining the problems they encountered as a result of trying to balance multiple demanding roles. For example, the majority of our respondents reported that they experienced such problems as not having time to keep the house sufficiently clean, not being able to tackle big projects around the house, and not being able to keep up with little projects and errands "often" or "all the time." In short, these women seem to regard the home as a setting that defies their efforts to get caught up. As one woman expressed it, "My house provides constant evidence of my shortcomings and inadequacies. No matter how hard I try, things at home are almost never as clean and orderly as I would like them to be."

Perhaps these women would have been more tolerant of this lack of order at home if they perceived themselves as deliberately *choosing* to spend less time on household tasks so they could spend more time with their husbands, their children, or just by themselves. However, this clearly was not the case. The majority of respondents reported, at least sometimes, that they were bothered by not being able to do things with or for the children. Moreover, insufficient time to spend with their husbands, or on themselves, were experienced as pervasive problems. The vast majority of women reported experiencing these problems "often" or "all the time."

In the work domain, women's problems seemed to center primarily around perceived time constraints imposed by their family lives. The majority of respondents reported being bothered at least sometimes by such problems as not being able to spend enough time working and not being able to stay late or work in the evenings as much as they thought they should. Because of this acute time shortage, the hours spent at work counted a great deal and had to be spent wisely. Virtually all of our respondents felt burdened by having to carefully plan their time at work so as to make every minute count.

As in previous research, the women in this study reported experiencing conflicts between work and family responsibilities significantly more often than did the men. Hall (1972) hypothesized that women should experience greater interrole conflict than men because women's multiple roles are likely to be salient simultaneously, whereas men's multiple roles are more likely to operate sequentially. If this is true, then one might expect a woman's work day to be frequently interrupted by family matters. A closer look at the types of conflict situations reported by the women in this sample, however, revealed that such situations occurred most frequently at the beginning and end of the woman's work day. For example, these women reported frequently having to rush to get their children ready in the morning so that they, themselves, would not be late for work and often having to leave work earlier than they would have liked because of their children. However, very few reported being distracted with family matters while they were at work. This suggests that women professionals can successfully integrate work and family responsibilities.

This effort, however, often left the women in this sample feeling overwhelmed at work *and* at home. This is not surprising. What is surprising is how they coped with their situations. The only coping strategy to show consistent significant relationships with measures of role satisfaction and mental health in this sample was time planning, particularly time planning at home. Yet, the dominant coping response among these women, both at home and at work, was to work as hard and efficiently as possible in order to get everything done. Use of this strategy at home did hold some benefits for the parenting role, perhaps because doing many things for one's children alleviates worries that the children are suffering because of one's career. However, no other benefits were associated with this response. In both domains, women also rarely attempted to reduce the demands on them by divesting themselves of some of their responsibilities.

Given the lack of congruence between the strategy that appears to be most effective in dealing with role conflict and the strategy that is most frequently employed, it may be instructive to examine these two strategies in more detail. What we call the "superwoman" strategy involves cutting back on activities like lunch, leisure activities, and sleep in order to have more time available for work, and trying to work as hard and efficiently as possible in order to meet all role demands. This may be considered to be a reactive coping style (cf. Hall, 1972), that is, one that is used in *response* to feelings of role conflict and role overload. What we call time planning involves trying to anticipate stressful periods and plan ahead for them: prioritizing things that need to be done, making lists and allocating certain times for various activities regarded as important (e.g., high priority work, one's children, one's husband, and oneself) and not letting other pressures interfere with those activities. This coping strategy, which to our knowledge has not been carefully investigated in other studies, is *proactive.* By employing such a strategy, women may be able to prevent or avoid feelings of role conflict, role overload, and strain (Lang & Markowitz, 1986). Interestingly, however, women in our sample reported the act of planning itself to be stressful: One of the major problems that women reported experiencing at work was the need to carefully plan all of their time. Moreover, our results provide some evidence that those women who were most stressed were least likely to engage in time planning.

Taken together, these findings suggest that women may get trapped in a vicious cycle where stress, role demands and insufficient time to plan, result in increased stress and role demands in the future. Coping theorists have argued that when coping failure is due to a lack of knowledge or skill, it may be appropriate to develop interventions to fill this gap (cf. Lazarus & Folkman, 1985). Our findings suggest that women professionals with family responsibilities would benefit from training in time planning and time management. Perhaps such training should emphasize the importance of adhering to such techniques at the very times that it may be most difficult to do so—when role demands and perceived stress are at high levels.

The discussion up to this point, however, ignores the fact that the findings in this study reflect women's coping strategies at a single point in time and therefore do not tell us anything about how these strategies came to characterize women's responses to role overload. Rather than merely reacting to the stress of the moment, as the analysis suggests, these women may be responding to environmental factors (perceived or real) that preclude the use of certain coping strategies. For example, an unpredictable work load or an unreliable day care provider would frustrate attempts at time planning. Alternatively, these women may be attempting to demonstrate (perhaps to themselves) the extent of their role commitment. In this regard, a woman may consider the effort she puts into being a good wife, mother, professional as a sign of her commitment to each of those roles. Delegating role responsibilities to others, therefore, would indicate a lack of commitment.

Comparisons of husbands' and wives' views of the wife's life situation revealed a number of intriguing differences and suggested that the women in this sample had higher standards regarding their role performance than their husbands had for them. For example, the wives thought their relationships with their husbands and children were suffering because of their careers more than their husbands did. Also, husbands were far less likely than their wives to report experiencing problems at home resulting from their wives' attempts to balance multiple roles. Although the vast majority of the women in our sample were bothered by the house not being as clean as they would like, and by insufficient progress on both big and small home projects, husbands appeared less sensitive to such problems.

Furthermore, our data provide clear evidence that wives have unrealistic perceptions of their husbands' preferences regarding how they should allocate their time. Whereas wives thought that husbands would prefer them to spend less time on work during the evenings and weekends and more time with the children and with them, this was not actually the case. In fact, husbands in our sample expressed satisfaction with their wives' time use in these categories. Husbands would prefer their wives to relax alone more than they do and to spend less time on housework and meal preparation than they are now spending. Of course, it is possible that the husbands in our sample provided such answers not because this is what they really believed but because they wanted to present themselves in a favorable light. We believe that such an explanation is unlikely because, as noted, husbands also reported not being bothered by a messy house or by uncompleted household projects in a separate series of questions.

CONCLUSION

Although much remains to be done, at a societal level, to relieve working women of the burden of two full-time jobs, a more immediate solution to these women's problems may depend on their relaxing their own standards of role performance[5] and adopting different ways of handling the multitude of demands on their time. The problems the women in this study encountered at home as a result of attempting to balance multiple demanding roles were, in part, the result of failing to delegate. In regard to delegating, it is also interesting to note that despite their financial resources, only 57% of the women in this sample employed paid domestic help beyond their child care arrangements. This pattern of coping may be a response to the cultural stereotype of the wife/homemaker role into which women are socialized. While able to fully participate in the world of work, these women are apparently unable to overcome their deep-rooted value system concerning the woman's proper role in the home. As Bernard (1975) noted over a decade ago, "It is easier for working women to accept the feminist position in the outside world than it is in the world of the family" (p. 188).

A number of issues emerged in our results that may be interesting to explore in more detail. One unanswered question concerns the underlying reason for the inequities that were found in the study regarding taking responsibility for household chores and engaging in various child care activities. Although the husbands in our study made a significant contribution to household chores, it was the women who were responsible for seeing to it that the chores got done. Moreover, women took much more of the responsibility for child care activities than their husbands. Such findings are often interpreted as incriminating the husband for not doing or taking more responsibility for home tasks. An alternate hypothesis is that the "superwoman" coping style of these women professionals may make it difficult for them to relinquish tasks and/or re-

[5]This conclusion may seem at odds with our failure to find an effect of cognitive reinterpretation on the outcomes examined in the chapter. We wish to point out, however, that our measure of cognitive reinterpretation did not focus exclusively on lowering one's personal standards of role performance and therefore does not permit a strict test of the efficacy of this particular coping strategy with respect to the outcomes examined.

sponsibilities to their husbands. Even when such tasks are relinquished, husbands may not be socialized to do them according to their wives' high standards. A challenge for future investigators involves disentangling the processes that lead to inequities in distribution of household tasks, and hence greater role conflict, for women professionals with small children.

Another question raised by the study concerns the long-term career consequences of women's family responsibilities. Virtually all of the women in this sample reported spending less time on work-related tasks than they thought they should be spending. In general, the women also regarded themselves as not having the time to take advantage of professional opportunities that might advance their careers in the long run and not having the time to develop professional relationships with their colleagues. An issue that cannot be addressed from the current design is whether the problems of time allocation experienced by these women will have detrimental effects on career advancement. It would also be interesting to determine whether those women who devote significant portions of their time and energy to their husbands, their children, and themselves will ultimately show less success in their careers than those women who compromise time with their families in order to spend more time at work. Long-term longitudinal studies that follow women in various role combinations from the early career years until midcareer could begin to address such questions. Even longer-term follow-up may be indicated to monitor career trajectory if a more accommodative career style is considered (Bailyn, 1977). Such a style allows for mutual development in family and career roles and implies a slow and consistent career pattern rather than a quick and meteoric one.

Although it is true that time allocation problems may have detrimental effects on career advancement, one will recall that women seldom faced problems from loss of concentration at work due to preoccupation with family. Furthermore the number, age, and temperament of children were unrelated to job stress and job functioning. These findings argue that in the immediate work situation mothers are at no disadvantage in regard to productivity. Problems with role conflict seem to occur, rather, at the beginning and end of workdays, where worry about the negative effect of career on children takes over.

The lives of married women professionals with young children are complicated "juggling acts" in which conflicting role demands and time shortages often detract from overall quality of life. Fortunately, at least partial remedies for this situation may exist at several levels. As a society, our employers and courts should follow the leads of other countries and institute paid maternity leave and child care benefits for working parents to ease financial and other worries over starting and maintaining healthy families. Closer to home, husbands of working mothers can consciously work toward more egalitarian division of responsibility for household tasks, and of care for their children. Although husbands in this sample appeared quite supportive of their wives' professional endeavors, much room remains for recognizing the degree to which their wives experience role conflicts and for communicating that domestic standards can be relaxed with no loss of regard for a woman's performance as a wife and mother. Finally, women themselves might improve their lives through practical actions, such as hiring household help, and through relaxation of the deep-rooted standards concerning the wife/homemaker/mother role by which they judge themselves. As noted, interventions might be developed to help women to alter their styles of coping with life stresses. "Planning ahead" proved the most effective coping strategy in this sample of women, and it is one that other research indicates is quite teachable. Efforts from within and outside the family unit may help working mothers not only withstand the stresses of their busy lives but also gain enjoyment and satisfaction from them.

ACKNOWLEDGMENTS

This research was supported by a grant from the National Institute for Mental Health (MH40255-01) and a grant from the National Science Foundation (BNS-8417745) to Camille Wortman and Carol Emmons. The authors wish to thank the project interviewers and support staff for their committed, quality service. Special appreciation is due to all the respondents who so generously contributed their time and effort for this study.

REFERENCES

Abidin, R. R. (1983). *Parenting stress index* (PSI). Charlottesville, VA: University of Virginia.
Bailyn, L. (1970). Career and family orientations of wives and husbands. *Human Relations, 23*, 97–113.
Bailyn, L. (1977). Involvement and accomodation in technical careers: An inquiry into the relation to work at mid-career. In J. Van Maanen (Ed.), *Organizational careers* (pp. 109–133). London: Wiley.
Behrman, D. L. (1982). *Family and/or career plans of first-time mothers.* Ann Arbor, MI: UMI Research Press.
Bernard, J. (1975). *Women, wives and mothers. Values and options.* Chicago: Aldine.
Bianchi, S. M., & Spain, D. (1986). *American women in Transition.* New York: Russell Sage Foundation.

Bradburn, N. M. (1969). *The Structure of Psychological Well-Being*. Chicago: Aldine Publishing Company.

Bryson, R., Bryson, J. B., & Johnson, M. F. (1978). Family size, satisfaction and productivity in dual-career couples. *Psychology of Women Quarterly, 3,* 167–177.

Chassin, L., Zeiss, A., Cooper, K., & Reaven, J. (1985). Role perceptions, self-role congruence and marital satisfaction in dual-worker couples with preschool children. *Social Psychology Quarterly, 48*(4), 301–311.

Conners, C. K. (1970). Symptom patterns in hyperkinetic, neurotic, and normal children. *Child Development, 41,* 667–682.

D'Arcy, D., & Siddique, C. M. (1984). Social support and mental health among mothers of pre-school and school age children. *Social Psychiatry, 19,* 155–162.

Derogatis, L. R. (1977). SCL-90-R Manual-I. John Hopkins University School of Medicine.

Elman, M. R., & Gilbert, L. A. (1984). Coping strategies for role conflict in married professional women with children. *Family Relations, 33,* 317–327.

Fielding, J., Gerdau, R., Crichton, J. (Producers). Gonzalez, C., & Stafford, V. (Directors). (1985). *After the sexual revolution* (transcript of ABC News report). New York: Journal Graphics, Inc.

Fraker, S. (1984). Why women aren't getting to the top. *Fortune,* April 16, pp. 40–45.

Gilbert, L. A., Holahan, C. K., & Manning, L. (1981). Coping with conflict between professional and maternal roles. *Family Relations, 30,* 71–79.

Gore, S., & Mangione, T. W. (1983). Social roles, sex roles and psychological distress: Additive and interactive models of sex differences. *Journal of Health and Social Behavior, 24,* 300–312.

Gove, W. R. & Geerken, M. R. (1977). The effect of children and employment on the mental health of married men and women. *Social Forces, 56,* 66–77.

Hall, D. T. (1972). A model of coping with role conflict: The role behavior of college educated women. *Administrative Sciences Quarterly, 17,* 471–489.

Hall, D. T., & Gordon, F. E. (1973). Career choices of married women: Effects of conflict, role behavior and satisfaction. *Journal of Applied Psychology, 58,* 42–48.

Harrison, A. O., & Minor, J. H. (1978). Interrole conflict, coping strategies, and satisfaction among black working women. *Journal of Marriage and the Family, 40,* 799–805.

Hayghe, H. (1986). Rise in mothers' labor force activity. *Monthly Labor Review, 109*(2), 43–45.

Herman, J. B. & Gyllstrom, K. K. (1977). Working men and women: Inter- and intra-role conflict. *Psychology of Women Quarterly, 1,* 319–333.

Hofferth, S. L., & Phillips, D. A. (1987). Child care in the United States. *Journal of Marriage and the Family, 49,* 559–571.

Kahn, R. L., Wolfe, D. M., Quinn, R. P. & Snoek, J. D. (1964). *Organizational stress: Studies in role conflict and ambiguity.* New York: Wiley.

Kessler, R. C., & McRae, J. A. (1981). Trends in the relationship between sex and psychological distress: 1957–1976. *American Sociological Review, 46,* 443–452.

Kessler, R. L., Price, R. H., & Wortman, C. B. (1985). Social factors in psychopathology: Stress, social support, and coping processes. *Annual Review of Psychology,* 531–572.

Ladewig, B. H., & McGee, G. W. (1986). Occupational commitment, a supportive family environment, and marital adjustment: Development and estimation of a model. *Journal of Marriage and the Family, 48,* 821–829.

Lang, D., & Markowitz, M. (1986). Coping, individual differences, and strain: A longitudinal study of short-term role overload. *Journal of Occupational Behavior, 7,* 195–206.

Lazarus, K., & Folkman, S. (1985). *Stress, appraisal and coping.* New York: Springer Publishing.

Parry, G. (1986). Paid employment, life events, social support, and mental health in working class mothers. *Journal of Health and Social Behavior, 27,* 193–208.

Pearlin, L. I. (1975). Sex roles and depression. In N. Datan & L. H. Ginsberg (Eds.), *Proceedings of Fourth Lifespan Developmental Psychology Conference: Normative Life Crises* (pp. 191–208). New York: Academic Press.

Pearlin, L. I., & Schooler, C. (1978). The structure of coping. *Journal of Health and Social Behavior, 19,* 2–21.

Pleck, J. H. (1978). The work-family role system. *Social Problems, 24,* 417–427.

Pleck, J. H. (1985). *Working wives, working husbands.* Beverly Hills: Sage Publications.

Radloff, L. S. (1975). Sex differences in depression: The effects of occupation and marital status. *Sex Roles, 1,* 249–265.

Rapaport, R., & Rapaport, R. (1971). *Dual-career families.* Baltimore: Penguin Press.

Sekaran, U. (1983). How husbands and wives in dual-career families perceive their family and work worlds. *Journal of Vocational Behavior, 22,* 288–302.

Sieber, S. D. (1974). Toward a theory of role accumulation. *Americal Sociological Review, 39,* 567–578.

Smith, D. S. (1985). Wife employment and marital adjustment. *Family Relations, 34,* 483–490.

Staines, G. L., & Pleck, J. H. (1986). Work schedule flexibility and family life. *Journal of Occupational Behaviour, 7*(2), 147–153.

Staines, G. L., Pleck, J. H., Shepard, L. J., & O'Connor, P. (1978). Wives' employment status and marital adjustment: Yet another look. *Psychology of Women Quarterly, 3,* 90–120.

Thoits, P. A. (1983). Multiple identities and psychological well-being: A reformulation and test of the social isolation hypothesis. *American Sociological Review, 48,* 147–187.

Weingarten, K. (1978). The employment pattern of professional couples and their distribution of involvement in the family. *Psychology of Women Quarterly, 3,* 43–52.

Weissman, M. M., & Bothwell, S. (1976). Assessment of social adjustment by patient self-report. *Archives of General Psychiatry, 33,* 1111–1115.

Welch, S., & Booth, A. (1977). The effect of employment on the health of married women and children. *Sex Roles, 3,* 385–397.

White, L. K., Booth, A., & Edwards, J. N. (1986). Children and marital happiness—Why the negative correlation? *Journal of Family Issues, 7,* 131–147.

Windle, M., & Lerner, R. M. (1986). Reassessing the dimensions of temperamental individuality across the life span: The revised dimensions of temperament survey (DOTS-R). *Journal of Adolescent Research, 1,* 213–230.

Wright, J. D. (1978). Are working wives really more satisfied? Evidence from several national surveys. *Journal of Marriage and the Family, 40,* 301–313.

Yogev, S. (1981). Do professional women have egalitarian marital relationships? *Journal of Marriage and the Family, 43,* 865–871.

5

The Microstructure
of Daily Role-Related Stress
in Married Couples

NIALL BOLGER, ANITA DeLONGIS, RONALD C. KESSLER, and ELAINE WETHINGTON

As large numbers of couples have adopted life-styles in which both members have jobs outside the home and share the work of parenting, there has been a corresponding increase in research on the effects of multiple role demands on psychological functioning. Nonetheless, even after a decade of research, we do not have a firm grasp of even the most fundamental issues, such as whether the participation of wives and mothers in the labor force promotes good or bad mental health among men and women in dual-earner families.

There are three positions on this issue, each supported by some evidence. The first is the role stress perspective, which argues that the combination of family and employment demands creates role overloads (more demands than one can handle) and role conflicts (the perception that role demands in one area affect the adequacy of one's role performance in another area). This increased exposure to stress is thought to create higher psychological distress among women in dual-earner cou-

NIALL BOLGER • Department of Psychology, University of Denver, Denver, Colorado 80208.   ANITA DeLONGIS • Department of Psychology, University of British Columbia, Vancouver V6T 1Y7, British Columbia, Canada.   RONALD C. KESSLER • Survey Research Center / ISR, University of Michigan, Ann Arbor, Michigan 48109.
ELAINE WETHINGTON • Department of Human Development and Family Studies, Cornell University, Ithaca, New York 14853.

ples than in couples where the wife is a homemaker (Coser & Rokoff, 1971). Less has been written about the emotional effects of multiple roles on men, but the general position seems to be that they are less adversely affected than women (Cleary & Mechanic, 1983; Holahan & Gilbert, 1979).

The second position is the role expansion perspective, which argues that multiple roles in general have positive effects on health and well-being and consequently that the combination of family and work roles should be associated with improved mental health (Marks, 1977; Sieber, 1974; Thoits, 1983; Verbrugge, 1983). Although acknowledging that multiple roles increase exposure to role-related overloads and conflicts, role expansion theorists argue that the alternative resources provided by multiple roles outweigh these stresses and help dampen their emotional effects. Women employed outside the home have greater access to social support than homemakers. They have more control over personal finances. And their experiences in the labor force are thought to promote more positive feelings of self-esteem and personal control than homemakers typically have. All of these resources are known to play a part in helping ameliorate the effects of stress.

The third is the selection perspective, which argues that the association between multiple roles and emotional functioning is due to role incumbency being influenced by prior emotional characteristics or their determinants. This interpretation is not favored by anyone who does research on the influences of roles; rather, it is treated as a nuisance that must be rejected before getting on with the interesting analysis. In our view, most researchers are overly quick to dismiss selection as unimportant on the basis of fairly naive arguments, even though much of the evidence that has been offered in support of the role stress and role expansion perspectives is equally consistent with a selection argument. This position is discussed more fully by Kessler and McRae (1984).

The available evidence does not unequivocally support any one of these interpretations over the others. Almost all of this evidence comes from cross-sectional surveys of the general population. Among women, data of this sort show that employment outside the home is associated with somewhat better mental health than is homemaking, although this association is neither strong nor entirely consistent. The evidence on this point is reviewed by Mirowsky and Ross (1986). The data also show that mental health is somewhat worse among men whose wives are employed compared to the husbands of homemakers. This association is stronger among men with traditional sex role orientations (Kessler & McRae, 1982), though, and there is reason to believe that the association will disappear with time. Ross, Mirowsky, and Huber (1983) review the evidence on this point.

Survey data also show that children, particularly young children, are associated with worse mental health among the adults who raise them compared to married men and women who do not have children (McLanahan & Adams, 1987). This association is more pronounced among women than men, although it becomes stronger among men and weaker among women as the children get older (Gove & Geerken, 1977). The association among women, finally, seems to be more pronounced when they are employed outside the home (Cleary & Mechanic, 1983).

Because of these complex findings, it is naive to think that any single influence—role stress, role expansion, or selection—totally accounts for the relationship between roles and emotional functioning. The fact that women in the labor force are in better mental health than homemakers, for example, does not mean that there is nothing stressful about having a job outside the home. It means either that the good things about having a job outweigh the bad or that the determinants of female labor force participation are associated with good mental health. The critical issue for the debate, obviously, is to determine the relative contributions of role stresses, role resources, and selection processes to the observed relationships between roles and mental health. Unfortunately, there is no way that the typical study of this process—gross comparisons of psychological distress across different role statuses and combinations—can partition these three influences.

As an appreciation of this limitation has developed, researchers have moved beyond a focus on role status *per se* to an analysis of specific characteristics of roles that might be associated with emotional adjustment. Baruch and Barnett (1986), for example, have shown that individuals' assessments of the rewarding and distressing aspects of their various roles relate more strongly to psychological well-being than having the roles themselves. The obvious problem with this approach is that these assessments are subjective perceptions that may be confounded with the psychological outcomes they are intended to explain.

Some efforts have been made to develop more objective survey-based measures of role experiences (Pearlin & Schooler, 1978). Analyses making use of these measures show that chronic role-related stresses are much more important than the roles themselves in explaining the distribution of emotional distress (Pearlin, 1983). Even with more objective measures, though, causal ambiguity still exists. Does chronic marital conflict, for example, cause depression? Or is it chronic depression that brings about marital conflict? Conventional survey data provide no way of distinguishing between these two possibilities nor of estimating their relative contributions to the overall association between marital conflict and depression.

In this chapter, we describe a program of research designed to deal more effectively with these problems of causal interpretation by using daily diaries to focus on the level of analysis where chronic stress is manifest—in day-to-day events and activities. As such, this work can be seen as part of a growing tradition of research using daily diaries to study chronic stress (e.g., DeLongis, Coyne, Dakof, Folkman, & Lazarus, 1982; Eckenrode, 1984; Stone & Neale, 1982). Diaries provide more concrete and reliable information about the actual experience of stress in a role than can be obtained in a conventional survey. Rather than ask the respondent to provide a summary assessment of how often he fights with his wife, for example, we can calculate an actual count of daily arguments over a period of time. Furthermore, because diaries record day-to-day *variations* in stress and mood, they make it possible to study the dynamics of stress in role situations that appear static in more highly aggregated cross-sectional surveys. In this way we can directly address the problem of causal confounding that has proved to be so intractable in the past. Finally, because daily diaries permit one to examine multiple role stresses within individuals over time, findings based on diary data are relatively immune to selection effects (Kessler, 1987). Therefore, in discussing many of the findings we can restrict ourselves to the relative merits of the role stress versus the role expansion perspectives.

Our analysis begins with a discussion of the relationship between multiple roles and the prevalence of various role-related daily stresses, focusing particularly on the effects of the wife's employment status and the presence of children in the home. Next, we evaluate whether these role statuses buffer or exacerbate the effects of daily stresses on mood in ways that are predictable from the theoretical positions outlined here. Having traced these links between roles and daily stresses, we then turn to exclusively daily-level analyses to see whether, within any given role, various combinations of daily stresses at home and at work have effects that conform to theoretical predictions. Finally, we use the diary data to provide direct empirical evidence on what is thought to be a key source of multiple role stress: the spillover of stresses between work and family roles.

THE STUDY DESIGN

Respondents were men and women in 166 married couples, volunteers from a larger sample of 778 white couples in the Detroit metropolitan area who participated in a community survey about marital stress and coping. Respondents in the diary study were asked to complete a short diary on each of 42 consecutive days (6 weeks). Respondents were not paid for their participation, although a $5 gift was sent along with the first diary booklet. Seventy-four percent of those who agreed to participate in the diary phase of the study completed the full set of 42 diary days. Just under 90% completed 28 days.

Table 1 presents descriptive information on the diary sample as well as on the respondents from the larger survey who did not participate in the diary study. Couples in the diary sample had an average of 2.5 children, and their average family income was almost $43,000. Husbands were slightly older than wives (43.3 vs. 40.5 years) and had slightly higher levels of education (13.7 vs. 13.3 years). Nearly 90% of husbands were employed compared to 61% of wives. Approximately half of the sample were Protestant, and another 40% were Catholic.

A comparison of the diary and nondiary subsamples shows that these are similar on most of the characteristics considered here. Exceptions are education and employment status: Husbands in the diary sam-

Table 1. Comparison of Diary Respondents with Other Respondents in the Baseline Survey

	Diary subsample (n = 166)		Other respondents (n = 612)		Mean difference (a − b)	p (two-tailed)
	$\overline{X}$	s.d.	$\overline{X}$	s.d.		
Couple characteristics						
Number of children	2.5	1.8	2.5	1.8	0.0	.85
Family income (dollars)	42,800	19,800	41,600	20,600	1,200	.52
Husband characteristics						
Age (years)	43.3	12.2	43.5	13.0	−0.3	.83
Education (years)	13.7	2.5	13.3	2.7	0.4	.06
Employed (%)	89.8	30.3	84.1	36.6	5.7	.07
Religion						
Protestant (%)	46.4	49.9	44.8	49.7	1.6	.71
Catholic (%)	39.8	48.9	39.5	48.9	0.3	.94
Other (%)	13.8	34.5	15.7	36.4	−1.9	.55
Wife characteristics						
Age (years)	40.5	11.7	40.9	12.3	−0.4	.67
Education (years)	13.4	2.0	13.1	2.1	0.3	.25
Employed (%)	60.8	48.8	55.1	49.7	5.7	.19
Religion						
Protestant (%)	49.4	50.0	48.7	50.0	0.7	.87
Catholic (%)	43.4	49.6	41.2	49.2	2.2	.61
Other (%)	7.2	25.8	10.1	30.1	−2.9	.26

ple had slightly higher levels of education (.4 of a year), and they were more likely to be employed (90% vs. 84%); wives were also more likely to be employed (61% vs. 55%).

The diary contained a wide range of questions, but only two of these are considered in this chapter. The first is a checklist of 24 stresses that occurred over the past 24 hours. We consider seven of these stresses here. Two involve overloads, "a lot of work" at home or on the job. The other five involve interpersonal stresses, "tensions or arguments with" one's spouse, children, supervisor at work, co-workers, or work subordinates. On the basis of preliminary analyses, the three interpersonal work stresses were combined into a single measure.

The second diary measure considered in this chapter is an inventory of daily mood. This inventory includes 18 items based on the Affects Balance Scale (Derogatis, 1975) subscales of anxiety (e.g., nervous, tense, afraid), hostility (e.g., irritable, angry, resentful), and depression (e.g., helpless, worthless, depressed). Respondents were asked to rate "the number that best describes your feelings during the past 24 hours" on a 4-point scale ranging from "Not at All" to "A Lot." Responses to all 18 items were combined to create a scale of distressed mood. The alpha reliability of this scale is .91 among men and .92 among women. Consistent with prior research on gender differences, women report significantly more distress than men.

THE PREVALENCE OF DAILY ROLE STRESS

One point of agreement among virtually all writers on the topic is that multiple roles are associated with increased stress. Even advocates of the role expansion perspective grant this point. This could occur because multiple roles cause overloads and conflicts or because of selection. An example of the former would be the conflicting demands of family and work creating marital conflict between an employed woman and her husband. An example of the latter would be a woman taking a job outside the home as a way of coping with a conflictual marriage.

Several analyses have been carried out to study the relationship between roles and role stress in cross-sectional survey data, and the results are generally consistent with the view that multiple roles are associated with increased role stress. See Thoits (1987) and Emmons, Biernat, Tiedje, Lang, and Wortman (Chapter 4 this volume) for reviews. As noted, though, many of these studies use subjective measures, whereas others rely on retrospective reports about the frequency of particular stressors over a period of time. Our data help resolve these problems by obtaining concrete information about role-related stresses on a daily basis over a period of several weeks. This makes it possible to aggregate daily reports to arrive at more accurate prevalence estimates.

Based on the role stress perspective, at least three predictions can be made about how roles and role-related daily stresses should covary in the diary data. The first is that role stress of all kinds will be more common in couples where the wife is in the labor force rather than a homemaker. As noted earlier, the available evidence suggests that female labor force participation has a more negative emotional effect on husbands than wives, so a related prediction is that stress increases more for men than women when the wife has a job outside the home.

The diary data partially support these predictions. There are eight daily stresses (family and job overloads among men; family overloads among women; spouse, child, and job arguments among men; and spouse and child arguments among women) that can be compared across couples who differ in the wife's labor force participation. Three of these are more prevalent in dual-earner couples: family overloads among men and spouse arguments among both men and women. A fourth, job arguments among men, is significantly less prevalent among the husbands of women in the labor force than the husbands of home-makers. These results are presented in Table 2. (Note that the statistical tests in Table 2 assess the generalizability of our findings to the popula-tion of *person-days* associated with the persons in our sample; they do not assess generalizability to the population of *persons* from which our sam-ple was drawn [see Cohen & Cohen, 1983, Chapter 11].)

It is particularly important that there is no relationship between female labor force participation and overloads at home among women because this stress has been thought to increase considerably when a married woman takes a job outside the home. (See Emmons *et al.*, Chap-ter 4 this volume.) The absence of this relationship could help explain why most surveys find labor force participation to be associated with somewhat better mental health among married women rather than the somewhat worse mental health predicted by the role stress perspective.

It is also important to note that the family overloads reported by husbands in dual-earner couples are greater than those found among the husbands of homemakers. This could help account for the associa-tion of wives' employment with worse mental health among their hus-bands.

It is not clear how to interpret the one significant association in the opposite direction from the prediction, that husbands of women in the labor force report comparatively few job arguments. It might be that multiple roles are health promoting in this case, in that men in dual-

Table 2. Prevalence of Daily Role Overloads and Arguments by Role Status for Husbands and Wives

	Role status				Tests of significance	
	Wife employed		Wife homemaker			
	No children at home	≥1 child at home	No children at home	≥1 child at home	Wife's work status (t)	Parental status (t)
	Percentage of days	Percentage of days	Percentage of days	Percentage of days		
A. Husbands						
Home						
Role overload	22.1	25.9	15.4	22.7	3.30***	3.66***
Argument with spouse	6.0	5.3	2.7	5.0	1.60	0.26
Argument with child	—	5.7	—	5.9	-0.16	—
Work						
Role overload	34.6	35.5	26.7	36.5	0.79	2.51*
Argument with spouse	3.3	2.5	1.3	5.0	-2.85**	0.88
n (days)	1,036	2,282	371	1,505		
B. Wives						
Home						
Role overload	23.0	37.3	26.8	36.4	-0.12	8.39***
Argument with spouse	6.0	6.6	2.9	5.5	2.31*	1.61
Argument with child	—	10.3	—	11.4	-0.92	—
Work						
Role overload	30.9	32.4	—	—	—	0.78
Argument with spouse	4.0	1.3	—	—	—	-5.56***
n (days)	910	2,408	385	1,491		

*p < .05; **p < .01; ***p < .001.

earner couples experience less pressure to compete at work because they are not shouldering the total responsibility for family financial maintenance (Pleck, 1985).

A second prediction about the relationship between roles and the prevalence of daily role stress is that this stress will be more common in couples with children. The available evidence shows that children are more strongly associated with distress among mothers than fathers, so a related prediction is that the prevalence of role stress increases more for women than men when there is a child in the home.

The data are partly consistent with these predictions. Of eight role stress measures that could be compared across couples who differ in the presence of children (family and job overloads and arguments among both men and women), three are significantly more prevalent in couples with a child, and two of these are found among men rather than women: family overloads (both sexes) and job overloads among men. As shown in Table 2, four of the five remaining stresses are unrelated to the presence of children in the home, whereas arguments at work are significantly less common among women if they have children at home.

It is noteworthy that family overload is the stress thought to be most strongly affected by the presence of children. The fact that this stress is significantly related to children among both men and women is consistent with this thinking. Furthermore, family overloads are more prevalent among women than men in comparison to couples without children in the home. This, too, is consistent with the prediction.

It is less clear how to interpret the findings that children are associated with increased job stress (overload) among fathers and decreased job stress (arguments) among mothers. Most theories of role stress would predict that job stress would increase more among women than men (Coser & Rokoff, 1971). It is, of course, possible to offer *post hoc* interpretations (e.g., increased overload among fathers could be due to their trying harder to get ahead than they would if they did not have children; women with children at home might select less challenging jobs or invest themselves less in their jobs, either of which might decrease their exposure to arguments at work).

An important implication of these results is that the stronger association between children and emotional distress that surveys typically find among women than men is probably not due to a greater increase in chronic role stresses among women. Our data show that mothers experience more family overloads than men, but we also find that job overloads are more prevalent among fathers. These differential prevalences add up to roughly equal exposures to excess stress for men and women. Furthermore, women in the labor force experience at least one kind of job stress (arguments) less often than other women, whereas there is no comparable benefit associated with children among men. On the basis of these considerations alone, we would expect the distress of fathers to increase more than that of mothers when a child is added to the family. The fact that the opposite occurs argues that differential exposure to role stress is probably not the fundamental intervening link between children and higher psychological distress among women.

A third prediction consistent with prior literature is that role stress will be particularly high in couples where there are children and the mother works outside the home (Holahan & Gilbert, 1979). On the basis of available survey data, we would also predict that this interactive effect is considerably stronger among women than men.

There is absolutely no support for these predictions in the diary data. We evaluated four stresses (family overloads and spouse arguments reported by both men and women). Regression equations were estimated in which dummy variables for wife labor force participation, the presence of children, and the interaction between these two variables were used to predict prevalence of role stress. In no case was there a significant interaction. It is particularly important that we failed to find interactive effects among women, for role stress theory clearly predicts that they should exist. This offers another basis of support for the conclusion that differential exposure to role stress does not explain the relationship between multiple roles and psychological distress among women.

THE STRESS-BUFFERING EFFECTS OF MULTIPLE ROLES

A central issue in the debate between the role stress and role expansion perspectives involves emotional reactivity to role-related stress. The role stress perspective predicts that role stresses will be more emotionally damaging to people who have multiple roles. Overloads at home, for example, are predicted to be more distressing to women in the labor force than to homemakers because of the conflicts they create between the competing demands of family and job (Coser & Rokoff, 1971; Gove & Tudor, 1973). The role expansion perspective makes exactly the opposite prediction—that the greater social and emotional resources available to women in the labor force allow them to cope more effectively with family overloads than homemakers (Thoits, 1983).

Cross-sectional evidence on this issue is consistent with the role expansion perspective. Marital stress, for example, has been shown to be more strongly related to emotional functioning among homemakers than among women in the labor force (Veroff, Douvan, & Kulka, 1981). Nevertheless, as we noted earlier, this finding lends itself to multiple interpretations. It could be that employment helps buffer the effects of marital difficulties on psychological distress. It is equally plausible, though, that selection explains the association. This could happen if stress reactivity increased the likelihood of women becoming home-makers rather than seeking employment outside the home.

The diary method provides a unique opportunity to see whether the role stress perspective is consistent with more dynamic data linking role stress and emotional functioning. Our approach to this test was to use time series models of the relationship between daily variations in role stress and mood to evaluate whether emotional reactivity to daily stress differs among people who have different roles. The implications of this approach for the control of selection effects is discussed by Kessler (1987).

The analyses we have carried out so far make use of fairly simple time series models of the general form

$$\Delta DM_{it} = b_0 + b_1 JS_{it} + b_2 FS_{it} + b_3 C_t \tag{1}$$

where the outcome ΔDM_{it} refers to the difference between the daily mood of person i on day t and his or her *average* mood across all diary days, and the predictors include job stress (JS) and family stress (FS) on the same day, as well as controls (C) for confounding variables that differ across time (for example, day of the week). The b_1 and b_2 coefficients in these models are interpreted as the effects of role-related stress on daily mood. Using the residual score as an outcome results in a pooled within-person analysis; this effectively controls for the additive effects of any confounding variables that vary across individuals (e.g., age or educa-tion).

These sorts of models were estimated separately in four subsamples of couples in which the wife was either employed 20+ hours a week (referred to subsequently as women in the labor force) versus either a homemaker or employed less than 20 hours a week (both of whom are referred to here as homemakers) and couples in which there was either one or more children living at home or no children at home. The cross-classification of these two dichotomies yields four types of couples. Al-though admittedly coarse, this typology provides a useful way of obtain-ing preliminary information about the structure of stress reactivity in the data.

The results of the subgroup time series analyses rather dramatically disconfirm both sets of predictions among women. All five of the stresses considered (overloads at home and work, arguments with spouse, child, and co-workers) significantly increase distress on the day they occur, yet there is no evidence that these effects vary depending on whether the woman is in the labor force or not, has a child at home or not, or is in any combination of these two roles. In particular, the data fail to document either of the two moderating effects most widely discussed by advocates of the two perspectives. Contrary to the prediction of role stress theory, the impact of job stress on mood is not greater among women with children at home than among those without children. This is consistent with cross-sectional evidence reported by Baruch and Barnett (1986). Contrary to the prediction of the role expansion theory, the impact of family stress is no weaker among women in the labor force than among homemakers.

An important implication of these results is that the better mental health of women in the labor force compared to homemakers typically found in general population surveys is not due to coping resources that help these women reduce the emotional distress otherwise associated with role-related stress. Indeed, if we combine our results on differential exposure to daily stress (which shows women in the labor force to experience more spouse arguments) with the finding that stress reactivity does not vary by labor force status, we would predict that women in the labor force would be in worse mental health than homemakers. The opposite is true, though, in our data.

Neither the role stress or role expansion perspective has as much to say about the relationship between roles and stress reactivity among men. Interestingly, though, our data show that family roles influence reactions to stress among men much more than among women. Consistent with the role stress perspective, the emotional effects of family role stress (both overloads and arguments) are significantly greater among the husbands of women in the labor force than the husbands of homemakers. With respect to the effects of job stress, though, just the opposite is true. The husbands of women in the labor force are significantly less affected by these stresses than the husbands of homemakers.

It is likely that a complex combination of influences is involved in these different interactions. Greater demands on the husband for time and energy around the house could be responsible for the greater distress associated with family overloads among the husbands of women in the labor force. This is unlikely to account, though, for the greater distress created by spouse arguments. A more plausible interpretation is that an argument with one's wife is more upsetting in dual-earner marriages because the wife has more marital power. This possibility has been hypothesized by Burke and Weir (1976), although it has not been tested empirically. We have some ability to make such a test in future analyses by making use of data obtained in our baseline survey about marital power and spouse conflict resolution styles.

The opposite sign interactions involving the effects of job stress might be due to the protective effects of multiple roles. The most likely possibility of this sort is that men have more access to support from their wives if labor force participation among these wives allows them to empathize more deeply with their husbands' problems at work (Simpson & England, 1981). This more effective support could help reduce the emotional effects of job stress. An alternative interpretation is that job problems are less upsetting because dual-earner couples have more financial resources and breadth of earning capacity, which help protect the husband from the anxieties associated with work stress (Pleck, 1985).

These results begin to uncover the kinds of complexities that we had envisioned when we first began this line of investigation—a variety of different positive and negative implications of each role combination that produce an aggregate association with psychological functioning that depends on the relative prevalence and power of counteracting forces. We have not yet taken the next step of rigorously decomposing the relationships between roles and distress in terms of exposure and reactivity to daily stress to see whether these influences can explain the aggregate relationships, but the preliminary results presented here provide some clues about what we might expect to find when we do this. We return to this issue in the discussion section.

THE STRESS-POTENTIATING EFFECTS
OF MULTIPLE DAILY STRESSES

Before dismissing entirely the possibility that particular combinations of family and employment roles are associated with differences in stress reactivity among women, we considered another possibility. This involved multiple stresses that occur on the same day. One role stress perspective, explicitly, role conflict, predicts that the conflicting demands of the two roles create a stress that is greater than the sum of its parts (Coser & Rokoff, 1971). We broadened this prediction somewhat and searched for interactions between any two daily stresses that occurred on the same day in the job and the family domains. We reasoned that arguments at work on a particular day might make it particularly difficult to cope with arguments at home at the end of the day and that other kinds of simultaneous stresses (for example, overloads at work followed by spouse arguments at home) might create a synergistic effect that promotes particularly high distress. (See also the chapters by Pearlin and McCall [Chapter 3] and by Weiss [Chapter 2] in this volume.)

We investigated this possibility by creating time series models to predict daily mood that included as predictors interaction terms between pairs of daily stresses. Our working hypothesis was that these interaction terms would have positive signs and be significantly different from zero—indicating that the overload and conflict created by the occurrence of stress in two role domains has an emotional effect over and above the effects of the component stresses.

This turned out not to be the case. None of the interactions we examined, either among men or women, was both positive and significant. In particular, the interaction predicted by the role stress perspective between overload at home and overload at work was virtually zero among both men and women. This result calls into question the importance placed on role conflict in theories of role stress.

At the same time, a significant negative interaction was found among both men and women involving arguments at work and at home. The distress found among men and women who experienced these two stresses on the same day was less than we would have predicted on the basis of an additive model. This could reflect the possibility that the distress created by arguments at work is to some extent dissipated by taking it out on one's spouse or child later in the day. Or it could be explained by the work argument preparing the person to cope more effectively with the subsequent argument at home.

One attractive feature of the diary data is that we have the capacity to investigate these speculations directly. For example, the dissipation interpretation suggests that some people pick a fight with their spouse or child as a way of coping with the emotions created by work arguments. If this interpretation is correct, we would expect to find that job arguments predict subsequent family arguments in daily time series analyses and that this is more true for persons who use displacement as a coping strategy. We can carry out analyses to see whether these predictions hold up in the data, using within-person time series to study variation in the relationship between work arguments and subsequent home arguments and using data on coping styles obtained in the baseline interview to link this variation to broader coping styles that involve displacement. Analyses of this sort are currently underway.

The argument that arousal increases coping effectiveness can be evaluated in a similar way. We obtained data in the diary about patterns of coping with daily stress, and we can see whether the coping strategies used in spouse arguments differ on days that vary in whether or not there was an argument at work.

Irrespective of the resolution of this interpretive uncertainty, the existence of significant negative interactions is consistent with the role expansion perspective. Indeed, one proponent of this perspective explicitly predicted the existence of a negative interaction of precisely this sort and offered the arousal interpretation in support of the prediction (Marks, 1977). Clearly, we need to examine the mechanisms involved in this interaction more carefully in future analyses. We also need to take it into consideration in subsequent analyses of differential exposure and reactivity to daily role-related stress. The interaction shows that the greater exposure to multiple daily stresses that is found among people with multiple roles is, to some degree, counteracted by reduced stress reactivity.

STRESS SPILLOVER

In the last section, we speculated that arguments at work might trigger subsequent arguments at home. This process is an example of an emotional contagion that has been called stress "spillover" in the literature on multiple roles (Crouter, 1984; Staines, 1980). It is widely believed by advocates of the role stress perspective that this kind of spillover helps explain why people with multiple roles experience more role stress. To date, though, evidence presented in support of the notion that stress spillover occurs across employment and home roles has been largely indirect and qualitative (McDermid & Crouter, 1986; Pearlin & McCall, Chapter 3 this volume; Weiss, Chapter 2 this volume).

The diary data provide an opportunity to obtain more direct evidence. Researchers who have studied job–family linkages (e.g., Billings & Moos, 1982) have presumed that spillover operates at the level of daily stress—a problem at work creating problems at home the same night or problems at home leading to difficulties at work the next day, but they have not tested this presumption. Unlike previous cross-sectional analyses, we can see whether this kind of process occurs by means of time series analysis of daily stress and mood. The analysis we used is a fairly simple one that has many features in common with the kinds of models used earlier to study the effects of stress on mood. In this case, we studied whether stress in one role predicts subsequent stress in another role.

The results consistently document significant spillover effects among both men and women. These effects are bidirectional, with stresses at home spilling over into the employment role and stresses on the job spilling over into the family. Overloads on the job, for example, predict a significant increase in home overloads the same evening. Arguments at work predict an increased probability of arguing with one's spouse at home the same evening. Overloads at home, in turn, are associated with a significant increase in the probability of overload at work the next day, whereas arguments at home predict subsequent arguments at work. Even though there are some small differences in the spillover effects that we find among men and women, the overall consistency in the broad patterns is striking. These results contradict the claims of Pleck (1977) on the differential permeability of the job–family boundary for husbands and wives. He argues that job-to-family spillover is more likely for husbands, whereas family-to-job spillover is more likely for wives. No such differences are evident using our direct measures of spillover.

The results also help us interpret some of the aggregate patterns described earlier. The high prevalence of spouse arguments in couples where the wife is in the labor force, for example, can be explained by the fact that job arguments often spill over to create arguments at home. Similarly, the higher prevalence of job overloads in couples with children at home can be explained by the joint effects of children on home overloads and of home overloads on subsequent job overloads.

There are other aggregate patterns, however, that the time series analysis shows to be unrelated to spillover. One of these is the high prevalence of job overloads among the husbands of homemakers with children at home. We find no evidence that spillover of home stress can account for why these men have so many overloads at work. Some other processes are apparently involved.

Nor can the results involving spillover explain why mothers have significantly fewer job arguments than other women in the labor force. Indeed, we find that arguments between mother and child significantly increase the risk of subsequent arguments at work. This means that, all else equal, we would expect women with children at home to report more, rather than fewer, arguments at work. Apparently, something we have not considered is negating this spillover effect from family to work. Further analysis might show that selection is involved.

Despite these two patterns that cannot be attributed to spillover, the overall evidence for its existence is much more powerful and pervasive than previous arguments have suggested. In many cases, we find that stress in one role more than doubles the risk of a subsequent stress in the other role. Effects as large as this can totally explain role-based variation in the aggregate prevalence of most of the daily stresses we examined.

An important task for future research will be to begin tracing the magnitude and determinants of variation in spillover. In the last section

we speculated about the processes involved in a spillover of job arguments to family arguments, and we discussed some analysis strategies for
investigating which of these processes is actually at work. Theoretical
work of this sort is underway (see Pearlin and McCall, Chapter 3 this
volume, and Weiss, Chapter 2 this volume). This theoretical work will
need to be linked with careful empirical work in larger, more representative populations.

DISCUSSION

At the beginning of this chapter we described some of the relationships between social roles and psychological functioning that others
have documented in general population surveys. Distress is somewhat
higher among homemakers than women in the labor force, but lower
among the husbands of homemakers than the husbands of women in the
labor force. The presence of children in the home is associated with
increased distress, particularly among employed women. We also described two theoretical perspectives that have attempted to make sense
of these associations. The first perspective emphasizes the health-
damaging effects of multiple roles, the other their health-promoting
effects. We began our work on the assumption that both influences are at
work. We also assumed that social selection factors are probably of some
importance and that the aggregate patterns found in previous survey
research reflect a complex balance of these different counteracting
forces.

Any attempt to disentangle these influences with conventional
cross-sectional survey data is likely to be inadequate to the task, even
though considerable progress has been made in recent years in measuring and evaluating the effects of the experience of particular roles. We
consequently turned to a disaggregated analysis of role-related micro-
stressors. The preliminary analyses presented in this chapter support
our belief that scientific understanding of the relationship between multiple roles and psychological functioning can be advanced in this way.
Even though these results represent only the most preliminary work on
an enormously complex data array, they already demonstrate the enormous power of this method to look inside a situation that is usually
considered static and chronic to uncover its dynamic characteristics.

These analyses show that the processes linking roles to psychological
distress are considerably more complex than suggested by the role stress
and role expansion perspectives. Combining employment and family
roles has been shown to have both positive and negative effects for both

men and women. Support for the role stress perspective was found in the observations that combinations of roles are significantly associated with the prevalence of some daily stresses and that stress spillover effects between job and home are pervasive. The greater emotional effects of family stress on the husbands of women in the labor force compared to the husbands of homemakers is also consistent with this perspective. At the same time, we found support for the role expansion perspective in the finding that the husbands of women in the labor force are buffered from the distress otherwise associated with job stress as well as in the finding of a consistent negative interaction between arguments at work and at home on the same day in predicting distress.

We also found some results that contradict central assumptions of the two perspectives. Regarding the role stress perspective, there is no evidence, for example, that women in the labor force experience family overloads more often than homemakers. Nor could we find any evidence to suggest that the occurrence of stress at work and stress at home on the same day leads to more psychological distress than predicted on the basis of an additive model. This calls into question the importance of role conflict, which is a central concept in the role stress perspective. Our disaggregated time series analyses also failed to find any evidence among women that certain combinations of roles are associated with reactivity to stress. This calls into question a basic aspect of the role expansion perspective, which argues that women in the labor force are better able to cope with stress because of the social and emotional resources provided by employment outside the home.

These findings point to the need for more thorough analyses along several lines. For example, the analyses we have carried out up to now have not examined fine-grained aspects of roles—such as whether children are preschoolers or school age, whether or not the mother has outside help with housework and child care, the extent to which the husband has an egalitarian sex role orientation or helps around the house, and a wide range of other differences between couples that may affect exposure to stress and stress reactivity. Nor have we yet examined the full range of daily stresses that are linked to family and employed roles or the processes of coping associated with them when they occur. These extensions will almost certainly help to clarify some of the obscure aspects of the results found so far.

It is difficult to draw any firm conclusions from this complex array of findings, especially as we have not yet attempted to integrate them into a comprehensive model of the relationship between social roles and distress. Nonetheless, two broad conclusions seem to be warranted as a way of directing subsequent research efforts.

The first of these is that the roles occupied by married women are more strongly associated with the psychological functioning of their husbands than of the women themselves. Given that previous research on changing gender roles has concentrated on women to the neglect of men, this result suggests that such an emphasis has been misleading and that serious effort is needed to understand the ways changing female roles affect the lives and attitudes of men. As the chapter by Weiss in this volume makes clear, much of the daily interaction between husbands and wives, even among dual-earner couples, appears to be directed toward minimizing the psychological distress of the husband, often to the neglect of the wife. Thus, husbands in dual-earner families may perceive their wives' employment as a direct threat to their emotional security.

The second conclusion is that daily stress does not seem to play a major part in mediating the aggregate relationship between multiple roles and distress among women. We can see this in the finding that the distress of women in the labor force is lower than that of homemakers despite the fact that women in the labor force are exposed to more daily stress and appear to have no advantage in stress reactivity.

This observation raises the possibility that either selection or stable characteristics of role situations explain the aggregate patterns found among women. We hope that some insights into these different possibilities will be obtained with future analyses making use of information about role experiences obtained in our baseline survey.

As we have been working with these data for only 3 months, we are painfully aware of the fact that we have many more questions than answers. Nonetheless, the results we have been able to obtain in this short time encourage us in thinking that an analysis of day-to-day experiences in roles will eventually increase our understanding of emotional reactions to the enormous changes in family and employment roles that are occurring in contemporary society.

ACKNOWLEDGMENTS

The research described in this chapter was supported by NIMH grants R01 MH41135, K01 MH00507, and T32 MH16806 and by a Research Scientist Development Award to Ronald Kessler (MH00507). We would like to thank John Eckenrode, William Mason, Arthur Stone, and Lois Verbrugge for helpful discussions about the design, implementation, and analysis of the diary study and our colleagues in the Social Environment and Health Program at The Institute for Social Research for their support throughout the course of the investigation.

REFERENCES

Baruch, G. K., & Barnett, R. C. (1986). Role quality, multiple role involvement, and psychological well-being in midlife women. *Journal of Personality and Social Psychology, 51,* 578–585.

Billings, A. G., & Moos, R. H. (1982). Work stress and the stress-buffering roles of work and family resources. *Journal of Occupational Behavior, 3,* 215–232.

Burke, R. J., & Weir, T. (1976). Relationship of wives' employment status to husband, wife and pair satisfaction and performance. *Journal of Marriage and the Family, 38,* 279–287.

Cleary, P. D., & Mechanic, D. (1983). Sex differences in psychological distress among married people. *Journal of Health and Social Behavior, 24,* 111–121.

Cohen, J., & Cohen, P. (1983). *Applied multiple regression/correlation analysis for the behavioral sciences* (2nd ed.). Hillsdale, NJ: Erlbaum.

Coser, R. L., & Rokoff, G. (1971). Women in the occupational world: Social disruption and conflict. *Social Problems, 18,* 535–554.

Crouter, A. C. (1984). Spillover from family to work: The neglected side of the work-family interface. *Human Relations, 37,* 425–444.

DeLongis, A., Coyne, J. C., Dakof, G., Folkman, S., & Lazarus, R. S. (1982). Relationship of daily hassles, uplifts, and major life events to health status. *Health Psychology, 1,* 119–136.

Derogatis, L. R. (1975). *Affects Balance Scale.* Baltimore, MD: Clinical Psychometrics Research Unit.

Eckenrode, J. (1984). The impact of chronic and acute stressors on daily reports of mood. *Journal of Personality and Social Psychology, 46,* 907–918.

Gove, W. R., & Geerken, M. R. (1977). The effect of children and employment on the mental health of married men and women. *Social Forces, 56,* 66–76.

Gove, W. R., & Tudor, J. F. (1973). Adult sex-roles and mental illness. *American Journal of Sociology, 78,* 812–835.

Holahan, C. K., & Gilbert, L. A. (1979). Interrole conflict for working women: Careers versus jobs. *Journal of Applied Psychology, 64,* 86–90.

Kessler, R. C. (1987). The interplay of research design strategies and data analysis procedures in evaluating the effects of stress on health. In S. V. Kasl & C. L. Cooper (Eds.), *Stress and health: Issues in research methodology* (pp. 113–140). New York: Wiley.

Kessler, R. C., & McRae, J. A., Jr. (1982). The effect of wives' employment on the mental health of married men and women. *American Sociological Review, 47,* 216–227.

Kessler, R. C., & McRae, J. A., Jr. (1984). A note on the relationships of sex and marital status to psychological distress. In J. A. Greenley (Ed.), *Research in community and mental health, Vol. 4,* (pp. 109–130). New York: JAI Press.

MacDermid, S., & Crouter, A. C. (1986, November). *An examination of crossover: Relationships among aspects of work and the marital satisfaction of workers' spouses.* Paper presented at the meeting of the National Council on Family Relations, Dearborn, MI.

Marks, S. R. (1977). Multiple roles and role strain: Some notes on human energy, time, and commitment. *American Sociological Review, 42,* 921–936.

McLanahan, S., & Adams, J. (1987). Parenthood and psychological well-being. *Annual Review of Sociology, 13,* 237–257.

Mirowsky, J., & Ross, C. E. (1986). Social patterns of distress. *Annual Review of Sociology, 12,* 23–45.

Pearlin, L. I. (1983). Role strains and personal stress. In H. Kaplan (Ed.), *Psychosocial Stress* (pp. 3–32). New York: Academic Press.

Pearlin, L. I., & Schooler, C. (1978). The structure of coping. *Journal of Health and Social Behavior, 19,* 2–21.

Pleck, J. H. (1977). The work-family role system. *Social Problems, 24,* 417–427.

Pleck, J. H. (1985). *Working wives/working husbands.* Beverly Hills, CA: Sage.

Ross, C. E., Mirowsky, J., & Huber, J. (1983). Dividing work, sharing work, and in-between: Marriage patterns and depression. *American Sociological Review, 48,* 809–823.

Sieber, S. D. (1974). Toward a theory of role accumulation. *American Sociological Review, 39,* 567–578.

Simpson, I. H., & England, P. (1981). Conjugal work roles and marital solidarity. *Journal of Family Issues, 2,* 180–204.

Staines, G. L. (1980). Spillover versus compensation: A review of the literature on the relationship between work and nonwork. *Human Relations, 33,* 111–129.

Stone, A. A., & Neale, J. M. (1982). Development of a methodology for assessing daily experiences. In A. Baum & J. Singer (Eds.), *Advances in environmental psychology: Environmental health* (pp. 49–83). Hillsdale, NJ: Erlbaum.

Thoits, P. A. (1983). Multiple identities and psychological well-being: A reformulation and test of the social isolation hypothesis. *American Sociological Review, 48,* 174–187.

Thoits, P. A. (1987). Negotiating roles. In F. J. Crosby (Ed.), *Spouse, parent, worker: Gender and multiple roles* (pp. 11–12). New Haven, CT: Yale University Press.

Verbrugge, L. M. (1983). Multiple roles and physical health for women and men. *Journal of Health and Social Behavior, 24,* 16–30.

Veroff, J., Douvan, E., & Kulka, R. A. (1981). *The Inner American.* New York: Basic Books.

6

Single Parenthood and Employment
Double Jeopardy?

PATRICIA COHEN, JIM JOHNSON, SELMA A. LEWIS, and JUDITH S. BROOK

INTRODUCTION

Many investigations of the effects of maternal employment on mothers and children have focused on married women. However, it is plausible that these effects may be different when women are sole heads of households than they are in two-parent homes. In this work an empirical examination of the circumstances and consequences of maternal employment in one- and two-parent homes is presented, taking into account potentially correlated variables that may impact on the well-being of mothers and children.

THEORETICAL BASES FOR EFFECTS OF EMPLOYMENT ON MATERNAL PSYCHOPATHOLOGY

Several studies have found that working women are likely to have fewer symptoms of depression and demoralization than are nonworking women (Kessler & McRae, 1981; Radloff, 1975). These positive effects of

PATRICIA COHEN • School of Public Health, Columbia University, New York, New York 10032.   JIM JOHNSON • New York State Psychiatric Institute, 722 West 168th Street, New York, New York 10032.   SELMA A. LEWIS • Committee of Special Education, District 10, 5500 Broadway, Bronx, New York 10463.   JUDITH S. BROOK • Mount Sinai School of Medicine, New York, New York 10029.

paid employment also hold for married women; however, they appear to be primarily attributable to those without dependent children.

It has often been argued that mothers who are employed are likely to experience stress as a result of a conflict between their work responsibilities and the demands of homemaking and parenthood—the *role overload* hypothesis. Nevertheless, most comparisons of employed with nonworking mothers find no significant differences in depression or other indexes of emotional distress. It is at least possible that mental health differences between working and nonworking mothers are obscured by the presence of important subgroups in different proportions in these groups. When the popular press discusses working mothers, the implicit reference is typically to well-educated women for whom employment is not an absolute financial necessity. However, in the United States the work force of mothers is predominantly made up of women for whom the financial position of the family would be precarious without their income, including many who are the sole, or nearly sole, source of support of their family. Among these women the positive benefits of employment may be entirely attributable to the income produced by the employment (Downey & Moen, 1987).

Alternatively, divorced mothers, not having the role of marital partner, may experience psychological benefits from the additional role, identity, and social contacts available in the workplace (Sieber, 1974; Thoits, 1983). This hypothesis we will call the *role expansion* hypothesis.

POTENTIAL SOURCES OF CONFOUNDING OF EFFECTS OF MATERNAL EMPLOYMENT

Several variables complicate the examination of the effects of employment among divorced mothers. First, single mothers may be demoralized because of recent or current marital conflict (Hess & Camara, 1979), rather than because of overload in ongoing responsibilities or loss of social support. Second, divorced mothers are likely to have lower family incomes than those in two-parent families, and low income is related to stress and demoralization. And when divorced mothers are not working, they may have to depend on public assistance for support, which has itself been implicated in child and maternal demoralization. Third, large family size has tended to be predictive of both mothers' and children's problems (Rutter, Yule, Quinton, Rowlands, Yule, & Berger, 1975), a relationship that is generally interpreted as attributed to overload on mothers. However large families are less common in divorced families, as is maternal employment. Therefore, in order to demonstrate effects of employment on divorced mothers, it is critical to take into account the effects of these potential confounders.

STUDIES OF MATERNAL EMPLOYMENT EFFECTS ON CHILDREN

A large number of studies have investigated the potential effects of maternal employment on the achievement and adjustment of children. One of the earliest studies (Glueck & Glueck, 1957) failed to find maternal employment differences between delinquent and nondelinquent boys or between symptomatic and nonsymptomatic boys, but another early study found that boys with employed mothers were more delinquent if the home was also unstable (McCord, McCord, & Thurber, 1963). Research in the two decades since these early studies has examined children from infancy to adolescence with samples varying demographically from inner-city ghetto minorities (e.g., Woods, 1972) to the offspring of professionals (e.g., Lerner & Galambos, 1985).

The vast majority of these studies have looked at maternal employment in intact homes (e.g., Gold & Andres, 1980), and attempts to determine whether effects on children may have been due to differences in family structure or family income are extremely rare. Findings have varied considerably from study to study, but on the whole they have led three reviewers to dismiss maternal employment as a significant risk factor (Hoffman, 1979; Rutter, 1979; Siegel, 1984). In the words of one reviewer, "on average, children of working mothers develop just as well as those whose mothers remain at home, and there are no differences between these two groups in rates of psychologic disorders" (Rutter, 1979, p. 148). By adolescence, the overall picture is one of very few negative effects and frequent positive ones, especially on girls (Hoffman, 1979). As Siegel (1984) has noted, however, although maternal employment *per se* is apparently not a very powerful influence on the way children develop, it is important to separate it from divorce, poverty, and other associated factors.

One of the very few studies to examine a carefully drawn sample in which sociodemographic status and other factors could be controlled (Faret, 1980) found significant negative relationships between maternal employment and both achievement and adjustment of kindergarten children. However, these effects were generally not significant when maternal education, family income, and race were controlled. A specific examination of single parenthood was not presented; however, the author states that no significant family composition effects were observed.

This may have been because of a confounding of these effects with other variables.

THEORETICAL EXPLANATIONS OF NEGATIVE EFFECTS OF MATERNAL EMPLOYMENT ON CHILDREN: MEDIATORS

Children with a working single parent may show adjustment problems for any of several reasons. First, there is considerable evidence that distress and demoralization in the mother tends to be reflected in elevated rates of distress in the children (Kashani, Burke, & Read, 1985; Weissman *et al.*, 1984). Several studies have shown that children may be adversely affected by maternal employment when mothers' attitudes toward their role is negative (Benn, 1986; Lerner & Galambos, 1985; Trimberger & Maclean, 1982). On the evidence, negative maternal attitudes toward their roles typically indicate general depression or demoralization (Warr & Parry, 1982). We will call this the *stress contagion* hypothesis of children's reactions to single maternal employment.

Second, although early concerns about the effects of nonmaternal care on young children have been largely laid to rest (Etaugh, 1980), a number of studies suggest that adolescent children of employed mothers may have less supervision (Hoffman, 1974; Woods, 1972) that may result in more delinquent behavior (conduct disorder). On the other hand, some research has suggested that low income working mothers are more likely to have structured rules and to enforce them (Hoffman, 1974). The "latchkey" child has been the object of much recent concern (Fosarelli, 1984), and it appears that an increased vulnerability to peer pressure for antisocial activity may be present in these youth (Steinberg, 1986). This evidence is consistent with reported earlier sexual activity in daughters of employed mothers (Hansson, O'Connor, Jones, & Blocker, 1981). This mechanism for potential negative effects of single-mother employment we will call the *supervision* hypothesis.

A third potential problem associated with the employment of single mothers is in the area of parent–child relationship. Although the evidence is not strong (e.g., Colangelo, Rosenthal, & Dettmann, 1984), some work has suggested that both adolescent sons (Montemayor, 1984) and adolescent daughters (Burke & Weir, 1978) may experience some negative effects of maternal employment on parent–child relationships. Clear differences in sex role and sex steryotyping of occupations have been demonstrated depending on the employment and occupations of mothers (e.g., Gilroy, Talierco, & Steinbacher, 1981; King, Abernathy, & Chapman, 1976; Selkow, 1984). These attitudes may have negative repercussions on the relationship between parent and children. This mechanism for an employed single mother effect will be referred to as the *relationship* hypothesis.

POTENTIAL SYNERGISTIC EFFECTS

It is also plausible that the combination of employment and single parenthood would produce an effect on mental health of children and mothers that is more than additive. In many areas of effort an inverted "U"-shaped relationship between the difficulty of fulfilling task demands and performance is noted, with optimal performance with moderate, where demands are present but within achievable levels and poorer performance and more stress at both higher and lower levels. For many contemporary mothers of school-age children, employment may present more nearly optimal environmental demand than does no employment, providing that household and child-rearing tasks can be shared with a partner. However, when home responsibilities are not shared, the level of demand may pass the point where adequate demand fulfillment can be maintained, and stress may rise.

THE SAMPLE AND DATA SET

The current study is based on data from a longitudinal study of a random sample of children in families living in two upstate New York counties. Families were originally sampled in 1975, when the children were ages 1 to 10 (Kogan, Smith, & Jenkins, 1977) and were recontacted for interview in 1983 when they were ages 9 to 18. Eighty-four percent of the families were located, and 74% were interviewed at the time of the follow-up. Because attrition was greatest in the urban, poor, young families, an additional sample of 54 families was added at the time of the follow-up. As shown in Table 1, the resulting sample covers the full range of income and is quite representative of families with children of these ages in the northeastern United States, with the exception of a higher rate of Catholic religious background and fewer minority families, both due to the characteristics of the sampled counties.

At the time of the follow-up, both mothers and youth were interviewed separately but simultaneously in their homes by pairs of interviewers. Interviews covered family characteristics and relationships, extrafamilial environment, and assessment of characteristics of mothers and youth, including a full diagnostic interview of youth and of mothers

**Table 1. Demographic Characteristics of the
Follow-Up Sample (*N* = 711)**

1983 median family income	$23,000
Percentage white	92
Percentage Catholic	55
Percentage families intact	68
Maternal mean years of education	13

regarding the youth. Interviews typically took about 2 hours each. The current study examines the 711 mother–child pairs living together, excluding families with father custody or other living arrangements.

The Measures

The measure of maternal distress or demoralization was taken from the Anxiety and Depression scales of the SCL-90 (Derogatis, Lipman, Rickels, Uhlenhuth, & Covi, 1974). Cronbach's alpha on the current sample was 0.86.

Measures of child psychopathology used in the current analyses are scaled versions of diagnostic syndromes, taken from the pooled maternal and child interviews. Data on the reliability and validity of these instruments are provided in Cohen, O'Connor, Lewis, and Malachowski (1987). Measures of three of the most common syndromes were used, namely conduct disorder, anxiety, and depression. Although derived from an interview designed to produce diagnoses rather than unidimensional scales, the scaled versions are quite reliable, with internal consistencies over 0.70 for each syndrome and each source of information.

At the time of the follow-up interviews, 40% of the sample mothers were working full-time, 20% were working part-time, and 40% were not employed. Because the families with part-time employed mothers occupied an intermediate position on most other risk factors, as well as on the dependent variables, this risk factor was measured as a three-level scale in the following analyses. Twenty-two percent of the sample children were living in mother-only families; three mothers had never been married, and the remainder were divorced or separated. Divorces or separations had taken place on the average about 5 years previously.

The potential mediators, parental conflict, parenting, and parent–child relationship used in the current study, were measured as follows. Parental conflict was reported by the mother on an adaptation of the Locke–Wallace Marital Conflict scales (r_{xx} = .55). Three scales of parenting were as reported by the youth. Maternal time spent with child was an original measure with $r_{xx} = .64$, whereas mother–child communication came from Schaefer (1965) as did the measure of youth's autonomy from the mother ($r_{xx} = .70$).

Analytic Strategy

The basic models were tested in multiple regression analyses along the lines described in Cohen and Cohen (1983, Chapter 9). Variables that may be common causes of divorce and maternal employment as well as maternal and child symptoms were examined first, to determine whether the hypothesized effects were independent of these variables. These potential confounders of the psychopathology–single employed mother relationship included family income, welfare status, maternal education, and family size. Although parental conflict might well have preceded the divorce, we have chosen to interpret our measure of current parental conflict as representing an essentially postdivorce variable and therefore have included it among the mediators, rather than with the confounders.

Having established that certain examined effects are independent of the confounders, the next series of analyses examine potential mediating variables representing each of the theories regarding the origins of the effects. To the extent that a theory is correct, we would expect that including more proximal representatives of the theory in the analysis will reduce the magnitude of the effects of maternal employment. The mediators exployed in the current analyses of child syndromes included maternal demoralization (the contagion hypothesis), maternal time spent with child and autonomy from mother (the supervision hypothesis), and mother–child communication (the relationship hypothesis).

Finally, we examine the possibility that the employed single-mother risk of psychopathology was conditional on family size, recency of divorce, or prior employment. Potential moderators of effects on children's psychopathology included the age or sex of the child and the recency of the divorce.

FINDINGS

Relationships of Maternal Employment and Marital Status with Other Risk Factors, Including Confounders, Mediators, and Moderators

On the whole, working-mother families in our sample did not differ in average income from families in which mothers did not work. This was because these groups are further subdividable into those living in

Table 2. Income, Maternal Employment, and Marital Status

	Adjusted mean income[a]
Single mother, not working ($n = 46$)	$11,300
Single mother, employed full-time ($n = 90$)	$17,495
Two parents, mother not working ($n = 239$)	$28,300
Two parents, mother full-time worker ($n = 193$)	$30,600

[a]Adjusted for age of the child. Each mean is significantly different from all others, $p < .01$. The 143 women working part-time had family incomes at intermediate values.

two-parent homes and single parents as shown in Table 2. When the groups were disaggregated, differences due both to family structure and to maternal employment were evident.

Parental conflict was higher in divorced families, as anticipated, and was also slightly higher in families where wives were working. However, the difference in parental conflict between married couples and divorced couples did not vary as a function of maternal employment status.

Mothers were, as expected, more likely to work if they were single and were also more likely to work when they had had more education. However, the tendency for more educated mothers to work did not differ between single and married mothers.

Maternal employment was not related to the age of the study child. Although many studies have found mothers more likely to work when children enter school, given the age range of these children, 9 to 18, and the variable ages of their siblings, the lack of such a relationship in these data is not surprising. However, mothers with small families were more likely to be employed. There was no difference between single mothers and two-parent families in the relationship between the number of children and the tendency for the mother to work. Nor was the relationship between divorced status and maternal employment conditional on the age or sex of the child.

Maternal Employment and Parenting

The amount and quality of maternal–child supervision and interaction did not differ between families with working mothers and nonworking mothers or between single-mother and two-parent homes. Although there was a trend ($p < .10$) for single mothers to spend *more* time with their children (as reported by the youth), this relationship was redundent with the fact that single-mother families tend to be smaller, and children in smaller families tend to spend more time with their mothers. Neither autonomy from mother, as reported by the child, nor quality of mother–child communication was related to either maternal employment or single-parent status.

Maternal Employment, Family Structure, and Maternal Psychopathology

Maternal psychopathology was related to divorced status (see Table 3). At the zero-order level there was no relationship to maternal employment; however we continued to examine this relationship as it might have been distorted by confounding covariates. The relationship between single parenthood and maternal psychopathology was not conditional on the employment status of the mother. Therefore the basic hypothesis of a role-overload effect was not supported, nor was there evidence of beneficial effects of role expansion.

Table 4 demonstrates the partial relationships of marital status and maternal employment status with maternal demoralization when controls for potential confounding and mediating variables were introduced. When income was included as a covariate, the relationship between marital status and maternal psychopathology was no longer significant. When parental conflict was also controlled, the relationship between maternal psychopathology and single motherhood was (not significantly) negative.

Controlling for marital status, there was a slight tendency for working mothers to have higher levels of psychopathology. However, when the remaining confounders, family size, income, welfare status, and maternal employment, were introduced into the maternal employment–demoralization relationship, all trace of a relationship disappeared.

Table 3. Psychological Symptom Means of Mothers as a Function of Marital and Employment Status

Mother	Single mothers	Two-parent families
Not working	.24[a]	−.13
Part-time	.31	−.09
Full-time	.38	−.05

[a]Mean on standardized variable.
Marital status: $t = 2.45$, $p < .05$; maternal employment: $t = .88$, n.s.; and marital status $\times$ maternal employment: $t = .27$, n.s.

Table 4. Partial Regressions of Marital Status and Maternal Employment on Maternal Psychopathology Controlling Potential Confounders and Mediators

	Marital status B (SE)	Maternal employment B (SE)
Simultaneous entry	.40 (.09)*	.05 (.04)
+ Confounders:		
Family size, income, mother education, welfare	.17 (.11)	−.02 (.05)
+ Mediator:		
Family conflict	−.11 (.11)	.04 (.04)

*$p < .01$.

Several potential moderators of the relationship between maternal demoralization and marital status or maternal employment status were examined. No interactive effects of either variable with family size, age or sex of the child, or with whether the mother also worked at at time of the original interview (8 years previously) were significant in predicting maternal psychopathology.

Maternal Employment, Family Structure, and Child Psychopathology

Conduct disorders in the children were related to both maternal employment and single mothers, and both relationships were conditional on the age of the child (see Table 5). Although boys exhibit more symptoms of conduct disorder, none of the relationships shown here varied as a function of the sex of the child, and means are therefore

Table 5. Mean Estimated Conduct Disorder Scores in 9- to 18-Year-Old Children by Marital Status, Maternal Employment, and Child Age

	Single mother	Two-parent family
Younger child (age 10)		
Mother not employed	.78	.13
Employed full-time	.88	.23
Older child (age 16)		
Mother not employed	.35	.22
Employed full-time	1.06	.91

Note. Marital status: $t = 3.38$; $p < .01$. Maternal employment: $t = 2.20$; $p < .05$. Age × marital status: $t = 2.70$; $p < .01$. Age × maternal employment: $t = 2.67$; $p < .01$.

shown for the combined sex groups. As shown in the table, the tendency for offspring of working mothers to exhibit more symptoms of conduct disorder was greater in the older children than in the younger children (shown here illustratively for 10- and 16-year-olds). On the other hand, the tendency for children in single-parent homes to have more symptoms of conduct disorder than those in two-parent homes was much larger in the younger children.

Both single-mother status and maternal employment were significantly related to both child anxiety and child depression, although the relationship between these variables and single motherhood was not quite significant at conventional levels when these variables were considered simultaneously. There was a trend ($p = .06$) for the hypothesized interactive effect of marital status and maternal employment on child anxiety (see Table 6), showing the negative effect of maternal employment to be greater for children with single mothers. The difference in the effect of maternal employment on child depression for single mothers compared to two-parent homes was not significant. None of these relationships was conditional on the age or sex of the child.

Removal of Potential Confounders and Mediators

Controlling for confounders and mediators left the relationships of marital status and maternal employment with offspring conduct disorder, including the age differences in these relationships, essentially as given in Table 5.

Anxiety and depression in the children were not related to maternal marital status independently of income and welfare status. However, the effect of maternal employment persisted even when controls for income, welfare status, family size, and maternal education were introduced (see Table 7).

Table 6. Mean Child Anxiety Scores by Marital Status and Maternal Employment[a]

	Single mothers	Two-parent families
Mother		
Not employed	.189	.245
Employed	.629	.349

[a]Controlling for age and sex of the child.
Note. Marital status: $t = 1.601$; $p = .11$. Employment status: $t = 2.111$; $p < .05$. Interaction: $t = 1.863$; $p = .06$.

Table 7. Partial Effects of Marital Status and Maternal Employment
on Child Depression and Anxiety

	Dependent variable	
	Depression B (SE)	Anxiety B (SE)
Marital status, controlling		
Age and sex of child and maternal employment	.166 (.091)*	.146 (.096)
+ Confounders		
Income, welfare, family size, maternal education	−.150 (.100)	.050 (.125)
+ Mediators		
Family conflict, time with mother, autonomy, com- munication, maternal psychopathology	−.077 (.117)	−.010 (.108)
Maternal employment, controlling		
Age and sex of child and marital status	.088 (.042)**	.089 (.042)**
+ Confounders		
Income, welfare, family size, maternal education	.102 (.040)***	.075 (.041)*
+ Mediators		
Family conflict, time with mother, autonomy, com- munication, maternal psychopathology	.106 (.039)***	.079 (.041)*

*$p < .10$.
**$p < .05$.
***$p < .01$.

The effects of maternal employment on child anxiety and depression were not (entirely) mediated by family conflict, maternal psychopathology, maternal time with child, mother communication with the child, or autonomy from mother. However, the relationship of maternal employment with child anxiety was marginal throughout these analyses, whereas the relationship with child depression was quite robust.

Finally, we examined the possibility that the increase in income associated with maternal employment might be as beneficial as a "full-time mother." We found, however, that psychopathology differences associated with maternal employment were much larger than the offset effect of the expected family income increase, particularly for conduct disorder in older children.

SUMMARY AND DISCUSSION

There was consistent evidence of risk to mothers and to children for all three kinds of child psychopathologies associated with maternal employment, regardless of family size or structure. Risks for children were, on the whole, not mediated by deficiencies in the time the mother spent with the child, in the communication between mother and child, or in the level of autonomy granted the child by the mother, as measured in this study. Although other aspects of maternal–child relationship not included in these analyses might have accounted for the maternal employment effects, in fact, an examination of these measures in our data failed to reveal significant associations with maternal employment.

Several other possibilities for factors mediating the maternal employment–child psychopathology relationships include the child's involvement with peers, child care and supervision provided by maternal proxies, and the child's relationship and identification with a father or father substitute. As noted, several studies suggest that adolescent children of working mothers may be more involved with peers, and it is empirically true that a peer-centered adolescent is more liable to delinquent acts. Adolescents for whom peers take on even more importance because of maternal employment may also be more subject to anxiety and depression when not well accepted by peers. Also, a large body of research has led to strong evidence that children experiencing adequate substitutes for maternal care are indistinguishable from children cared for by their mothers. Therefore the children with psychopathology in families where mothers are employed may be those without such adequate substitutes.

Another potential mechanism not examined in the current study is identification with a father or father substitute. The literature suggests that adolescents, and especially boys, may have difficulties in this area when mothers are employed, and probably especially if the fathers are not employed or are not very successful.

What accounts for the finding of significant negative effects of maternal employment in this study, when the literature so strongly suggests that effects are nil at worst, and positive at best? One reason may lie in the large size and broad representative nature of our sample, characteristics of almost no other study of he issue. Another may lie in the simultaneous consideration of potential confounders, again a very unusual characteristic of published reports on this topic. A third may lie in the nature and measurement of the child outcome variables. Much of the literature concentrates on potential consequences for children's achievement and competence. It may be that these effects are quite different than those on psychopathology. In reviewing this area, Piotrkowski and Repetti (1984) note that in view of changing public attitudes and expectations regarding mother's employment, findings from earlier decades may well not generalize to current samples. Furthermore, those studies that have examined adjustment have done so with global instruments, without the specificity of measurement of the current study.

Both maternal and child problems of psychopathology were elevated in single-mother families. However, these effects were very predominantly accounted for by the low income levels of these families, and where income was adequate no excess risk was apparent. This is, of course, not to deny the excess risk in these families but only to suggest that if preventive efforts were targeting children in particular kinds of families it would make more sense to select for low income rather than for family structure.

Finally, on the basis of these data there is little evidence of an *excess* risk to mothers or offspring when a single parent (mother) is employed, and definitely no evidence of a role-overload effect.

ACKNOWLEDGMENTS

This study was supported by NIMH Grant # MH36971, NIDA Grant # DA03188, by a grant from the William T. Grant Foundation, and by the New York State Office of Mental Health.

REFERENCES

Benn, R. K. (1986). Factors promoting secure attachment relationships between employed mothers and their sons. *Child Development, 57,* 1224–1231.

Burke, R. J., & Weir, T. (1978). Maternal employment status, social support, and adolescents' well-being. *Psychological Reports, 42,* 1159–1170.

Cohen, J., & Cohen, P. (1983). *Multiple regression/correlation for the behavioral sciences.* Hillsdale, NJ: Erlbaum.

Cohen, P., O'Connor, P., Lewis, S. A., & Malachowski, B. (1987). A comparison of the agreement between DISC and K-SADS-P interviews of an epidemiological sample of children. *Journal of the American Academy of Child Psychiatry, 26,* 662–667.

Colangelo, N., Rosenthal, D. M., & Dettmann, D. F. (1984). Maternal employment and job satisfaction and their relationship to children's perceptions and behaviors. *Sex Roles, 10,* 693–702.

Derogatis, L. R., Lipman, R. S., Rickels, K., Uhlenhuth, E. H., & Covi, L. (1974). The Hopkins Symptom Checklist (HSCL). *Behavioral Science, 19,* 1–15.

Downey, G., & Moen, P. (1987). Personal efficacy, income, and family transitions: A longitudinal study of women heading households. *Journal of Health and Social Behavior, 28,* 320–333.

Etaugh, C. (1980). Effects of nonmaternal care on children: Research evidence and popular views. *American Psychologist, 35,* 309–319.

Faret, A. M. (1980). Effects of preferred maternal roles, maternal employment, and sociodemoghraphic status on school adjustment and competence. *Child Development, 51,* 1179–1186.

Fosarelli, P. D. (1984). Latchkey children. *Developmental and Behavioral Pediatrics, 5,* 173–177.

Gilroy, F. D., Talierco, T. M., & Steinbacher, R. (1981). Impact of maternal employment on daughters' sex-role orientation and fear of success. *Psychological Reports, 49,* 963–968.

Glueck, S., & Glueck, E. (1957). Working mothers and delinquency. *Mental Hygiene, 41,* 327–352.

Gold, D., & Andres, D. (1980). Maternal employment and development of ten-year-old Canadian francophone children. *Canadian Journal of Behavioral Science, 12,* 233–240.

Hansson, R. O., O'Connor, M. E., Jones, W. H., & Blocker, T. J. (1981). Maternal employment and adolescent sexual behavior. *Journal of Youth and Adolescence, 10,* 55–60.

Hess, R. D., & Camara, K. A. (1979). Post-divorce family relationships as mediating factors in the consequences of divorce for children. *Journal of Social Issues, 35,* 79–86.

Hoffman, L. W. (1974). Effects of maternal employment on the child—A review of the research. *Developmental Psychology, 100,* 204–228.

Hoffman, L. W. (1979). Maternal employment: 1979. *American Psychologist, 34,* 859–865.

Kashani, J. H., Burk, J. P., & Reid, J. C. (1985). Depressed children of depressed parents. *Canadian Journal of Psychiatry, 30,* 265–269.

Kessler, R. C., & McRae, J. A. (1981) Trends in the relationship between sex and psychological distress: 1957–1976. *American Sociological Review, 46,* 443–452.

King, K., Abernathy, T. J., & Chapman, A. H. (1976). Black adolescents' view of maternal employment as a threat to the marital relationship: 1963–1973. *Journal of Marriage and the Family, 38,* 733–737.

Kogan, L., Smith, J., & Jenkins, S. (1977). Ecological validity of indicator data as predictors of survey findings. *Journal of Social Service Research, 1,* 117–132.

Lerner, J. V., & Galambos, N. L. (1985). Maternal role satisfaction, mother-child interaction, and child temperament: A process model. *Developmental Psychology, 21,* 1157–1164.

McCord, J., McCord, W., & Thurber, E. (1963). Effects of maternal employment on lower-class boys. *Journal of Abnormal and Social Psychology, 67,* 177–182.

Montemayor, R. (1984). Maternal employment and adolescents' relations with parents, siblings, and peers. *Journal of Youth and Adolescence, 13,* 543–557.

Piotrkowski, C. S., & Repetti, R. L. (1984). Dual-earner families. *Marriage and Family Review, 7,* 99–124.

Radloff, L. (1975). Sex differences in depression: The effects of occupation and marital status. *Sex roles, 1,* 249–265.

Rutter, M. (1979). Separation experiences: A new look at an old topic. *Pediatrics, 95,* 147–154.

Rutter, M., Yule, B., Quinton, D., Rowlands, O., Yule, W., & Berger, M. (1975). Attainment and adjustment in two geographical areas. III. Some factors accounting for area differences. *British Journal of Psychiatry, 126,* 520–533.

Schaefer, E. S. (1965). Children's report of parental behavior: An inventory. *Child Development, 36,* 413–424.

Selkow, P. (1984). Effects of maternal employment on kindergarten and first-grade children's vocational aspirations. *Sex Roles, 11,* 677–689.

Sieber, S. D. (1974). Toward a theory of role accumulation. *American Sociological Review, 39,* 567–578.

Siegel, A. E. (1984). Working mothers and their children. *Journal of the American Academy of Child Psychiatry, 23,* 486–488.

Steinberg, L. (1986). Latchkey children and susceptibility to peer pressure: An ecological analysis. *Developmental Psychology, 22,* 443–439.

Thoits, P. A. (1983). Multiple identities and psychological well-being: A reformulation and test of the social isolation hypothesis. *American Sociological Review, 48,* 147–187.

Trimberger, R., & MacLean, M. (1982). Maternal employment: The child's perspective. *Journal of Marriage and the Family, 44,* 469–475.

Warr, P., & Parry, G. (1982). Paid employment and women's psychological well-being. *Psychological Bulletin, 91,* 498–516.

Weissman, M. M., Prusoff, B. A., Gammon, G. D., Merikangas, K. R., Leckman, J. F., & Kidd, K. K. (1984). Psychopathology in the children (ages 6–18) of depressed and normal parents. *Journal of the American Academy of Child Psychiatry, 23,* 78–84.

Woods, M. B. (1972). The unsupervised child of the working mother. *Developmental Psychology, 6,* 14–25.

7

Spillover between Work and Family
A Study of Blue-Collar Working Wives

EVELYN J. BROMET, MARY AMANDA DEW,
and DAVID K. PARKINSON

The goal of this chapter is to explore the overlap and potential health consequences of work and family stress among women employed in blue-collar jobs. Women currently comprise more than 40% of the labor force in the United States. In 1980, 6 million women, or 14% of the total female labor force, were employed in blue-collar occupations. In spite of the size of this segment of the work force, little information exists on the nature and magnitude of work stress such women experience, the spillover between work and domestic stress, and the health and mental health consequences of these stressors. These issues are particularly crucial in female employees, as Nieva (1985) noted, because "problems of integrating work and family lives still fall more heavily on women than men" (p. 175). They may be even more important among blue-collar women, whose jobs are often neither desirable, flexible, or lucrative, and who typically have total responsibility for home and child care.

In examining the overlap between work and family stress, we use

EVELYN J. BROMET • Department of Psychiatry and Behavioral Science, SUNY at Stony Brook, Stony Brook, New York 11794-8790.   MARY AMANDA DEW • Department of Psychiatry, University of Pittsburgh, Pittsburgh, Pennsylvania 15213.   DAVID K. PARKINSON • Department of Preventive Medicine, SUNY at Stony Brook, Stony Brook, New York 11794-8790.

the term *spillover* to refer to stress spreading from work to family, from family to work, or in both directions simultaneously. Before discussing existing evidence for spillover in blue-collar women, it is important to identify the types of stresses often encountered in the workplace and at home that may produce overlapping effects across domains. In this section, we first discuss the types of occupational and domestic stressors that blue-collar workers report as well as the health effects shown to be associated with such stressors. We then turn to a consideration of the concept of spillover and its potential contribution to the health of female workers.

OCCUPATIONAL STRESS

What stressors are engendered by blue-collar jobs? The vast majority of descriptive information comes from assessments of male workers. Stresses emanating from their jobs include understimulation, monotony, boredom, and social isolation (e.g., Cox, 1980; Kasl, 1978; Poulton, 1978). Assembly-line work has been shown to be particularly stressful. Caplan *et al.* (1975) found that among male blue-collar workers, machine-paced (assembly-line) workers reported more stress associated with their jobs than workers in any other manual occupation studied. Similarly, Frankenhaeuser (1977) showed that catecholamine excretion during work was significantly greater in high-risk sawmill workers functioning in constricted and repetitious jobs compared to other workers in the same mill.

Although less information is available on the nature of occupational stress in blue-collar women, some knowledge has accumulated on this issue. One source of information comes from reports by the National Institute of Occupational Safety and Health (NIOSH) concerning presumed "hysterical epidemics" in the workplace. During these "epidemics," workers typically complained of a variety of psychological and somatic symptoms that they attributed to environmental stresses, such as chemical exposures. However, it is striking that the women also reported an array of occupational stresses, including concerns about repetitive and rigidly paced jobs, pressure to increase production, and a work environment characterized by poor labor/management relations (Colligan & Murphy, 1979).

Our research group conducted a detailed study of occupational stress and solvent exposure in a sample of 168 female employees of a small appliance plant in central Pennsylvania (Dew, Bromet, Parkinson, Dunn, & Ryan, 1989). These workers were engaged in assembly-line work in which small appliances, such as toasters and coffee pots, were put together. The plant had not been modernized over the years. More-over, the company had decided that they would eventually close the plant, and the workforce was gradually being laid off. The workers expressed a great deal of dissatisfaction with their jobs, with most stating that the job did not measure up to their initial expectations and that they would not advise good friends to undertake such a job. Not surprisingly, we also found a high level of occupational stress among these workers. The types of job stress most frequently described were often being required to work very fast, have a great deal to be done, and not being able to use skills and knowledge learned in school or in previous jobs or training experiences.

What are the effects of such job stress on the health and mental health of blue-collar workers? The several studies conducted have primarily focused on male workers. These studies have almost all been cross-sectional, and thus inferences about causal direction cannot be made. The findings indicate a significant relationship, with greater work stress associated with more psychological as well as somatic symptoms (Cooper & Marshall, 1976; House *et al.*, 1979; Kasl, 1978). There is some evidence from our longitudinal study of male power plant workers that occupational stress may also make a modest *predictive* contribution over a 1-year period to the development and/or exacerbation of psychological symptoms, clinical affective disorder, and alcohol-related problems (Bromet *et al.*, 1988). Although there are fewer studies of female blue-collar workers, recent evidence suggests that the findings observed in male workers are generalizable to women in comparable jobs. For example, in our study of female assembly-line workers, perceptions of greater work load led to significantly more reports of somatic, respiratory, and nervous system symptoms after controlling for an array of other known risk factors for these health variables, namely age, education, marital status, number of children under 6 living at home, smoking, and support from supervisor, co-workers, and friends. Other findings also suggest that one-quarter to one-third of blue-collar women experience significant "nervous strain at work" (Cherry, 1984) and that higher levels of work stress are associated with poorer health in women working in non-blue-collar jobs as well (Verbrugge, 1982). More research on the nature and magnitude of this relationship is clearly needed (Haw, 1982; Sales & Frieze, 1984).

DOMESTIC STRESS

By contrast to occupational stress, domestic stress—especially that emanating from the marital relationship—has been examined in a number of clinical and general population studies with large female samples (e.g., Hinchliffe, Hooper, & Roberts, 1978; Pearlin & Schooler, 1978; Spanier, 1976). Furthermore, although women employed in blue-collar occupations have not been studied *per se,* marital stress in working class women has been examined, particularly in samples of mothers of young children. The degree of reported marital difficulties is as variable as the methods by which this construct has been operationalized. At one extreme is the finding of Brown and Harris (1978) that 60% of working class women with children under age 6 lacked a confiding relationship with their spouse. By contrast, in Richman's (1977) sample of similar women from a blue-collar area in London, 29% reported poor marital relationships, for example, frequent arguments, decisions not being made together with one's husband, and low satisfaction with the marriage. Similarly, Roy (1978) found that 31% of a sample of married working class women had poor marriages. Earlier we noted that blue-collar working women often have major responsibility for housework and child care in addition to their full-time jobs. In our sample of assembly-line workers, a variety of marital stresses were mentioned, such as husbands' being unwilling to listen to personal problems or to problems related to their working conditions. However, the most frequently cited difficulty was their husband's failure to help with the housework.

The physical and mental health effects of domestic stress have been examined extensively in women although often without stratifying by employment status (e.g., Blumenthal & Dielman, 1975; Bullock, Siegal, Weissman, & Paykel, 1972; Ilfeld, 1982). A positive relationship between perceived adequacy of marital intimacy and the onset of affective disorders has been particularly consistent (Waring, 1985). In a largely blue-collar sample of mothers of young children, we showed that marital conflict (frequently thinking about marital problems; seeking advice about the marriage; discussing divorce or separation; seeking professional intervention about the marriage; leaving the house because of a fight with one's husband) bore a striking relationship to both clinical depression and subclinical depressive symptomatology (Bromet & Cornely, 1984).

SPILLOVER

To what extent does occupational stress have a negative impact upon the marriage, and vice versa, in employed blue-collar women? Prior to the last decade, little data of any type were available regarding this question in part because, as Piotrkowski (1979) noted,

The assumption that the connections between work and family life are minimally important for working-class . . . groups . . . derives from a limited conception of these connections and from workers' self-reports that work does not interfere with their lives. (p. 276)

Piotrkowski's qualitative study of working-class families clearly demonstrated the importance of viewing work and family from an integrated perspective in order to understand fully the dynamics of family life in this segment of the population. Pleck, Staines, and Lang (1980) analyzed responses to the Quality of Employment Survey regarding the question: "How much does your job and your family life interfere with each other?" Among employed women, 35% reported moderate or severe conflict, with "excessive work-time, schedule conflicts, and fatigue and irritability" cited as the major causes. Crouter (1984) conducted one of the few descriptive studies focusing on blue-collar workers, concentrating on spillover effects from family to work. Overall, two-thirds of her sample of 38 male and 17 female workers reported that their family life affected their work in either a positive or negative way. However, the ratio of negative to positive spillover was far greater in women than in men, and greatest in younger women with small children. The latter finding is consistent with the higher absenteeism and tardiness in younger compared to older female employees attributable to child care demands, as well as with findings from mixed social class samples showing that women (and men) with young children experience greater work–family strain than older people (e.g., Keith & Schafer, 1980).

The occurrence of spillover in our sample of female assembly-line workers was apparent from the comments made during the interview about the ways in which their jobs interfered with their family lives. For example, several women said that they often became upset at work and took these feelings home with them. Many described their jobs as making them exhausted and irritable and hence unable to get the housework and cooking done, or done well. Still other women said that their work was more affected by problems at home than vice versa. Thus, although the prevalence of spillover has not been studied *per se*, its existence has been well documented.

From a public health perspective, the significance of spillover of work and marital stress derives from its potential as a risk factor for poor physical and/or mental health. As reviewed, the health effects attributable to each type of stressor have been examined and found to be significant. Moreover, in one study of employed married women, both types of stresses were considered simultaneously, and the correlations of family environment measures with depressive and psychosomatic symptoms were similar in magnitude to the correlations of work environment measures with these symptom dimensions (Holahan & Moos, 1981). However, a critical question that remains to be addressed is whether women who report spillover between work and home are at special risk for poor health. Indirect evidence based on Radloff's (1975) study of co-occurring job and marital stress suggests that this might indeed be the case. That is, Radloff reported that among married female workers, those rating both marriage and job as unhappy had the highest (most symptomatic) scores on a depression symptom inventory compared to women unhappy in only a single sphere or in none at all.

The present chapter considers three questions. First, do blue-collar women who report spillover differ from those who do not with respect to demographic characteristics, absolute levels of occupational and marital stress and/or support, and physical and mental health problems? Second, are there systematic differences between women reporting spillover of work and family stress as a function of the direction of the spillover? Third, to what extent does spillover contribute to physical and mental health problems after taking into account other known demographic, psychosocial and clinical risk factors for these problems, including degree of work and marital stress?

METHOD

Subjects

We collected data from a sample of female blue-collar workers that included 389 married women. These workers were all employed in a large electronics plant in eastern Pennsylvania and had been interviewed as part of a larger investigation of the effects of the work environment on female blue-collar work forces in Pennsylvania. Most of the women were engaged in semiskilled (38.3%) or skilled (35.5%) manual jobs, such as wire bonders, etchers, machine operators, testers, parts aligners, and assemblers. A smaller percentage had unskilled manual jobs (3.1%), clerical jobs (11.6%), or had supervisory responsibility (11.6%), although these women often performed skilled manual work as well.

Eligibility criteria for the study included current employment at the electronics plant for at least 6 months, and being female, 18 to 65 years of age, a native English speaker and Caucasian. The latter four criteria reflected the dominant characteristics of the work force in the plant. All eligible subjects were randomly selected from lists provided by Local 1898 of the International Brotherhood of Electrical Workers (IBEW). Introductory letters about the work environment study were mailed to 831 married and unmarried eligible workers at the eastern Pennsylvania plant, among whom 230 (28%) refused to be interviewed, and 34 (4%)

could not be scheduled before the field work ended, most often because of health problems.

Measures

A structured, face-to-face 90-minute interview was conducted by trained interviewers in offices provided by the IBEW. The major variables for the present analysis include (1) job strain; (2) marital strain; (3) spillover of work and family stress; (4) social support from each domain; and (5) health and well-being.

Job Strain. Job strain was assessed by two scales derived from the work of Caplan *et al.* (1975). The first measured workload and consisted of four items concerning whether the women often had to work very fast, work very hard, had little time to get things done, and had a great deal to get done (alpha coefficient of internal consistency = .74). The second scale measured intrinsic rewards and consisted of three items focused on how often the women had an opportunity to use skills learned at school, the job gave them the chance to do the things they did best, and they used skills from their previous experience and training (alpha = .67). A measure to assess total degree of job strain in these areas was created by averaging the two scale scores.

Marital Strain. Marital strain was assessed by averaging the responses to four items reflecting level of strain in the marriage. These items were also derived from Caplan *et al.* (1975) and concerned whether their husband was easy to talk with, was willing to listen to personal problems, helped around the house, and the degree of happiness in their marital relationship (alpha = .78).

Spillover. After asking extensive questions about work and marital stress, including those noted, workers were asked: "In general, do you think that work problems spill over into the family, that family problems spill over into work, or does it happen about equally or not at all?" Their responses were recorded verbatim and coded in terms of spillover direction.

Social Support. Social support from co-workers, supervisor, and friends/relatives was assessed using items adapted from the Caplan *et al.* (1975) social support scales. The three indexes were created by averaging five items reflecting support in each sphere. The alpha coefficients were .74 for the co-worker support scale, .83 for the supervisor support scale, and .72 for the friends/relatives support scale. Examples of items used in these scales include: "How much does your immediate supervisor go out of his/her way to make your work life easier?" "How much can your department co-workers be relied on when things get tough at work?" "How easy is it to talk with friends and relatives?"

Health. Current as well as past health was assessed. With respect to prior well-being, women were classified as having depression or anxiety in the past year if they had sought help from a professional for such feelings or if they were so depressed or anxious (upset) that they felt they needed professional help, even though they did not actually see someone. Women who reported drinking too much at some point in their lives or that friends or relatives told them they had a drinking problem were considered to have a history of alcohol problems. With respect to current well-being, six variables were included in the analyses: (1) perception of general health (1 = excellent, 4 = poor); (2–4) the somatic complaints, depressive symptoms, and anxiety symptoms subscales of the Hopkins Symptom Checklist (for each symptom, 1 = not at all, 4 = extremely) (HSCL; Derogatis, Lipman, Rickels, Uhlenhuth, & Covi, 1974); (5) an alcohol index adapted from Cahalan and Cisin (1980) based on quantity/frequency information that produced five groups—abstainers and infrequent, light, moderate, and heavy drinkers; and (6) a smoking index indicating whether and how much the women smoked, ranging from not smoking to smoking more than one pack per day.

Analyses

The analyses focus on differences between women who (1) did and did not report spillover of stress, and (2) reported spillover from work to family only, from family to work only, in both directions, or not at all. After examining group differences using univariate procedures, a set of linear multiple regression analyses was then performed to determine whether the experience of spillover in either or both directions (1) contributed uniquely to each of the six health indexes after taking into account other known risk factors, such as demographic characteristics, prior health status, and work and family stress and support, and (2) exacerbated the health effects of stress from each domain.

RESULTS

Among our sample of 389 married women, 220 (56%) reported spillover of stress from either or both work and family domains. Of these, slightly more than half ($n = 123$; 56%) reported that spillover occurred in both directions, whereas fewer reported spillover to occur exclusively from work to family ($n = 60$) or from family to work ($n = 37$) (see Table 1).

Differences between Women Depending on Type of Spillover

The first two columns of Table 1 display the demographic, domain-related strain and support, and health characteristics of women according to whether or not they experienced any spillover. As shown in the sixth column of the table, comparisons between these two groups indicate that women who reported spillover were more likely to be younger, somewhat more educated, and experienced more job strain, less co-worker support, and somewhat more marital strain. With respect to health, these women also reported substantially more depression and anxiety-related problems in the year prior to interview and reported poorer health and health habits—as indicated by their psychological symptoms, drinking and smoking levels—at the time of our assessment.

We also include in Table 1 descriptive data for our sample according to the three patterns of spillover women could have reported. We were particularly interested in whether women with certain patterns of spillover could be distinguished from each other and from those who did not report spillover. Such comparisons show that the groups of women did differ in several respects (see seventh column in Table 1). However, examination of the descriptive data shows that the major differences between women in the areas we assessed concern whether or not women experienced *any* spillover, rather than the specific pattern in which spillover occurred. Thus in most cases where statistically significant between-group differences occurred, the three spillover groups appear similar to each other but are distinct from the group with no spillover.

Three understandable exceptions to this pattern occur: Women who report spillover exclusively from work to family experience the highest levels of job strain, whereas women who report spillover exclusively in the direction of family to work experience the most marital strain; women who report spillover in both directions were most likely to report depression or anxiety in the year prior to interview. *Post hoc* contrasts designed to assess the statistical reliability of these latter three observations were significant for the relationship of marital strain to direction of spillover (F [1,387] = 33.89; $p < .001$, effect size eta = .28) and depression/anxiety to spillover direction ([1, $n = 389$] = 13.64; $p < .01$, effect size phi = .19). The relationship of job strain to specific

Table 1. Relationship of Demographic, Strain, Support, and Health Characteristics to Spillover

Characteristic	Spillover		Direction of spillover			Analysis[a]	
	Yes (n = 220)	No (n = 169)	Work to family (n = 60)	Family to work (n = 37)	Both directions (n = 123)	Spillover vs. no spillover comparison[b]	Four-group comparison[c]
Demographic							
Age (years)	41.8	46.0	40.0	41.4	42.8	4.09***	6.64***
Education (% > high school)	20.8	13.1	16.7	16.2	23.0	3.29†	4.88
Income (% > $35,000)	74.5	72.8	70.0	75.7	76.4	0.15	1.04
Domain-related stress and support							
Work: Job strain (1 = less, 5 = more)	3.04	2.89	3.12	2.95	3.01	2.40*	2.76*
Co-worker support (1 = less, 4 = more)	3.04	3.21	2.90	3.13	3.09	2.27*	2.24
Supervisor support (1 = less, 4 = more)	3.13	3.18	2.95	3.04	3.24	0.59	0.68
Home: Marital strain (1 = less, 5 = more)	2.57	2.44	2.45	3.00	2.50	1.80†	7.34***
Friend/relative support (1 = less, 4 = more)	3.19	3.28	3.19	3.14	3.20	1.34***	6.92***
Health							
Past							
Depression or anxiety in past year (% yes)	22.7	7.0	20.0	16.0	26.0	17.43***	19.92***
History of alcohol problems (% yes)	11.0	7.7	13.3	8.1	10.7	1.18	1.93
Current							
Perception of general health (1 = excellent, 4 = poor)	2.03	1.94	2.07	2.11	1.98	1.24	1.04
Depressive symptoms[d]	1.49	1.34	1.44	1.53	1.50	3.97***	5.75***
Anxiety symptoms[d]	1.46	1.33	1.47	1.45	1.46	3.22**	3.68*
Somatic complaints[d]	1.60	1.51	1.66	1.52	1.60	2.44*	2.56*
Alcohol index (1 = abstainer, 5 = heavy drinker)	3.07	2.75	3.07	2.94	3.11	2.36*	2.00
Smoking index (1 = do not smoke, 5 = smoke > 1 pack per day)	2.12	1.82	2.25	2.08	2.06	2.05*	1.64

[a]Each test statistic was calculated excluding cases without data on a given variable. At most, two cases were omitted for any variable.
[b]χ^2 for dichotomous variables, t for all other variables.
[c]Comparing no spillover, work to family, family to work, both directions groups; χ^2 for dichotomous, F for all other variables.
[d]Log transformed prior to analysis to reduce skewness. Group means are presented in original, untransformed units (1–4 scale).
†$p < .07$; *$p < .05$; **$p < .01$; ***$p < .001$.

spillover direction was of marginal statistical importance (F [1,388] = 4.73; $p < .10$; eta = .11). (*P* levels for all three *post hoc* contrasts were corrected with the Bonferroni procedure.)

Given these observations of differences in the degree of marital and job strain experienced by women with various patterns of spillover, we reexamined the individual items on which our two composite measures of strain were based in order to identify the types of stresses most commonly encountered by the women in our sample. Of the four marital strain items used to form our composite index, women who reported spillover exclusively from family to work were particularly likely to state that their husband rarely or never helped around the house (56%), as compared to women in the remaining three study groups (24 to 27%). The family to work spillover group was also substantially more likely to report that their relationship with their husband was unhappy (22% as compared to 7% in each of the remaining groups).

Concerning perceptions of job strain, reexamination of the individual items we used to create our composite measure revealed that women who reported spillover exclusively from work to family were most likely to report that they rarely used skills learned in school (62% of this group as compared to 46 to 53% in the remaining three groups) and rarely used experiences from other jobs (48% compared to 30 to 41% for the remaining three groups).

Unique Effects of Spillover on Health

In light of the evidence we presented earlier that the women's current health was related to spillover (regardless of the specific direction in which spillover occurred), our final research question concerned whether this relationship would remain intact once we took effects of other known risk factors for ill health into account. We used linear multiple regression analysis to address this question and performed a separate analysis for each physical and mental health measure. Specifically, we estimated a hierarchical series of three regression models for each health measure, in which we added three groups, or blocks, of predictor variables to the analysis in consecutive steps. First, we included all variables assessing women's background characteristics—the demographic and health history risk factors—in order to determine their effects on current health. In the second step, we included effects for the indexes of stress and support from work and family domains, as well as for the presence of absence of spillover. Thus at this second step each of these effects was estimated controlling for the background characteristics entered previously. Third, to determine whether the presence of spillover in either direction exacerbated any health effects of job or marital strain, multiplicative interaction terms representing strain and spillover (i.e., job strain by spillover; marital strain by spillover) were included in the final step of the analysis.

Table 2 presents results of these analyses for each health measure. Two types of coefficients are presented to depict each predictor's relationship to a given health measure: the zero-order correlation (r) prior to controlling for the influence of any other variable on current health and the regression coefficient (b), which reflects the importance of a given predictor in affecting a particular area of current health controlling for other variables included in the analysis at a given stage. Considering first those predictors entered in the first block, we note that, as would be expected, a positive mental health history was associated with a greater likelihood for current mental health symptoms. Similarly, a history of alcohol problems was associated with heavier current drinking, as well as with smoking more heavily. Finally, younger women in our blue-collar sample were likely to drink and smoke more heavily.

After addition of the second block of variables, we note that higher levels of both job strain and marital strain remain at least modestly associated with poorer health after other background variables were controlled. The exception to this pattern concerned the small and non-significant effects of the strain variables on current drinking behavior. Our present findings mirror the pattern of strain–health relationships we observed previously in male power plant workers (Parkinson & Bromet, 1983) and in a sample of blue-collar women employed in a light manufacturing plant (Dew, Bromet, Parkinson, Dunn, & Ryan, 1989).

In the present sample, perceptions of social support in either work or home domains, while correlated with many of our health measures, tended not to affect health after other variables' effects were taken into account (hence precluding our examining social support as a variable potentially buffering the effects of spillover). Regarding a central issue in our analysis, we note that the experience of spillover continued to be associated with several areas of current health, even after the array of background and clinical characteristics as well as the strain and support measures were included in the analyses. Specifically, women who reported any type of spillover also reported more current depressive and anxiety-related symptoms and tended to drink more than women who did not experience spillover. Thus, over and above the individual impact of health history, strain from each domain, and any ameliorative effects of domain-specific support, spillover continued to exert a negative impact on several health areas for these blue-collar women.

Finally, our data provide some evidence that, at least for mental

Table 2. Correlations and Standardized Regression Coefficients from Hierarchical Regressions for Current Health Measures[a]

	General health		Depressive symptoms		Anxiety symptoms		Somatic complaints		Alcohol index		Smoking index	
	r	b	r	b	r	b	r	b	r	b	r	b
Block I: Background characteristics												
Age	.04	.05	.01	.01	.02	.04	−.01	.01	−.16***	−.13**	−.17***	−.17***
Education	−.01	−.02	.05	.05	.05	.05	.05	.04	.10*	.07	.00	−.03
Income	.04	.05	−.05	−.04	.02	.04	.04	.04	.04	.02	−.03	−.05
Depression/anxiety in past year	.19***	.19***	.31***	.30***	.27***	.28***	.22***	.22***	.01	.00	.06	−.01
History of alcohol problems	.00	.00	.02	.01	−.02	−.03	.05	.04	.14**	.12**	.14**	.13**
Multiple correlation (R)	.20*		.31***		.28***		.23***		.21**		.22***	
Block II: Stress												
Work: Job strain	.12**	.10	.21***	.11**	.18***	.12**	.25***	.20***	.05	.04	.15**	.11*
Co-worker support	−.04	.04	−.20***	−.11*	−.16**	−.06	−.10*	−.01	.08	.09	.03	.09
Supervisor support	−.06	−.06	−.14**	−.08	−.15**	−.12*	−.14**	−.12*	.00	.01	−.09	−.07
Home: Marital strain	.21***	.18**	.29***	.23***	.18***	.11	.16**	.10*	.02	.04	.10*	.07
Friend/relative support	−.09	.00	−.11*	.06	−.10*	.01	−.06	.04	−.01	−.04	−.05	−.03
Spillover (0 = no, 1 = yes)	.06	.01	.19***	.10*	.16**	.09†	.13**	.06	.12*	.10†	.10*	.07
Increment in R	.10**		.15***		.11***		.13***		.04		.07*	
Block III: Strain by spillover interactions												
Job strain × spillover	.20		.39*		.34		.07		.12		.05	
Marital strain × spillover	.32		.36		.45*		.12		.11		.02	
Increment in R	.01		.002		.01		.01		.002		.002	

[a]See text for scoring criteria for each variable. Analyses included all women with complete data on all variables (N = 377).
†p < .07; *p < .05; **p < .01; ***p < .001.

health outcomes, spillover exacerbated the effects of stress emanating from both work and family domains. In particular, with respect to symptoms of depression, the interaction of job strain with spillover plus the direction of main effects for these variables indicates that at high levels of job strain, women reporting spillover were significantly more likely also to report depressive symptoms, whereas at lower levels of job strain the effect of spillover was much less pronounced. The interaction effect of marital strain with spillover was similar in direction but was of marginal statistical significance. For symptoms of anxiety, the interaction terms plus relevant main effects indicate that the presence of spillover significantly exacerbated the effects of marital strain on symptomatology, whereas the interaction of job strain and spillover was of marginal significance.

DISCUSSION

The pattern of results obtained shows that, as predicted, blue-collar women who experience spillover differ systematically on an array of demographic and psychosocial variables. Compared to women who reported no spillover, blue-collar working wives who acknowledged the occurrence of spillover are younger and are generally more "distressed," for example, they report more job and marital strain, perceive less co-worker support, are three times more likely to have been depressed or anxious in the year preceding the interview, have higher current levels of depressive, anxiety, and somatic symptoms, consume more alcohol, and are more likely to be heavier smokers. The present findings are also among the first to provide quantitative evidence supporting the significance of spillover as a risk factor for poor mental health, even after a variety of known demographic and psychosocial risk factors were taken into account.

Labor force participation is becoming increasingly common in women, including those with young children. In our sample, women's age and the presence of young children in the household were confounded (e.g., younger women were more likely to have children under 6 years of age at home) and could not be examined separately. However, it is reasonable to infer that younger women were more likely to report spillover because of the inevitable conflicts between parenthood and employment (Crouter, 1984). As one women stated: "I'm tired when I come home and then everyone demands things that need to be done." Many women feel pulled in both directions, as indicated by the following response: "I sometimes feel I should be home with the children, but I also want to work." Finally, some women expressed the conflict directly: "I get angry and disgusted at work, then go home and take it out on my family," or "I'm constantly preoccupied with my daughter's mental health problems and get distracted and irritable at work."

The significance of these work–family conflicts for working women's health and well-being has until now been obscured. One reason is the belief that spillover is relatively uncommon in blue-collar samples (e.g., Piotrkowski, 1979). It is noteworthy that in our study, the *majority* of women reported experiencing spillover even though their mean age was greater than 40 and their children were no longer preschoolers. By contrast, a smaller percentage of employed wives with a child under 18 in the Quality of Employment Survey responded positively to a similar question, namely, "How much do your job and your family life interfere with each other—a lot, somewhat, not too much, or not at all?" (10.5% a lot; 26.5% somewhat; Pleck, Staines, & Lang, 1980). One explanation for the higher prevalence in our sample is that our question followed a section of the interview in which women provided detailed information about work and marital stress and perceived support. They therefore had the opportunity to think about whatever difficulties they were experiencing, and their responses to the spillover question may have been influenced by their verbalizing the specific problems at work and at home. Thus we would argue that the prevalence found in the present sample represents an informed reflection by these women of the degree of spillover they experienced. Had we asked the question prior to inquiring about specific problems, we might have seriously underestimated the extent to which spillover was occurring.

By inquiring about the presence of spillover after focusing on marital and work-related stresses, did we overestimate the prevalence of spillover in the sample? It is our belief that the inherent consistency of our data (e.g., women experiencing spillover from work to home reported the most work stress; women experiencing spillover from home to work reported the greatest marital stress), as well as the unique predictive value of spillover in relation to mental health mitigate against this interpretation of the findings. Moreover, our finding that women reporting spillover of any type were more likely to experience a variety of stresses in their lives suggests that among blue-collar working women, the acknowledgment of spillover may signify generalized psychosocial difficulties and is consistent with the conceptualization that spillover may be a sensitive indicator of emotional distress.

A more complete understanding of the dynamics of spillover will require carefully designed studies capable of disentangling the extent to which its expression reflects a generalized personality or coping style versus a specific effect of role overload or interrole conflict due to simultaneous, conflicting demands of multiple roles. We do not wish to imply that engaging in multiple roles necessarily has negative consequences (Spreitzer, Snyder, & Larson, 1979). By its very wording, our interview schedule was concerned with uncovering the adverse aspects of spillover rather than the benefits accruing from our sample's dual role as worker and homemaker. Because of the cross-sectional nature of our study, we are unable to choose between alternative interpretations of our findings on the relationship between spillover and health, namely that women who experience spillover become highly distressed or that stress either at work or at home leads to poor health that in turn causes women to experience such conflicts between work and home. Although our findings on the prevalence and unique health effects of spillover may raise more questions than answers, they further erode the myth that blue-collar employees' work and family lives are minimally connected (Greenhaus & Beutell, 1985). Rather they underscore the importance of carefully assessing this variable in all occupational groups.

It is important that future studies examine the effects of spillover on physical and mental health in additional occupational groups of female employees, including white-collar workers, as well as in male employees. As men come to assume more domestic responsibility, spillover may become a more salient issue. Herman and Gyllstrom (1977) showed that interrole conflict—which is presumably highly correlated with and may be a precursor of spillover—was a function of the number of social roles held for both men and women. Because men tend to express distress differently from women, the specific health effects may be associated with gender. Of more theoretical importance is whether the mechanisms underlying these effects are linked to gender in samples of employed men and women of comparable age, education, and occupational attainment.

With respect to examining such issues in white-collar workers, we are currently conducting an epidemiologic study of male and female managers and professionals focused on the prevalence of depression and alcohol abuse and the extent to which occupational and marital stress contribute to their occurrence. Cooperation from the corporation was obtained in part because of the corporate medical director's belief that stress-related mental health problems contributed both directly and indirectly to a significant proportion of the company's insurance payments. If we can identify and isolate the contribution of specific stressors, including spillover, to health and productivity, the company will consider developing targeted intervention strategies to reduce the level of psychiatric morbidity in their population. If the present findings on the effects of spillover are confirmed in our white-collar study and in research on workers in other occupations and organizations, their practical implications for the design of workplace interventions in general should then be considered.

It is also imperative that future studies of spillover be conducted prospectively in order to understand its origins, dynamics, and subsequent effects. Women first entering the labor force or entering after a prolonged absence provide an ideal cohort from which to observe the onset of feelings of spillover, its natural history (the extent to which it fluctuates or is stable over time and the factors associated with such course), its potential as a unique risk factor for poor health, and effective coping strategies that may reduce its impact.

In conclusion, the present study represents an initial effort to assess the magnitude and health effects of spillover in married women employed in blue-collar jobs. Our empirical results confirm recent suggestions from qualitative sociological studies that a significant proportion of blue-collar women experience spillover between home and work. In addition, our findings suggest that spillover is uniquely associated with a variety of health problems.

ACKNOWLEDGMENTS

This research was supported by NIMH Grant MH 39972. We would like to thank Leslie Dunn for coordinating all aspects of the field work for the study, Sandra Mitstifer for facilitating the interviewing process, the International Brotherhood of Electrical Workers Local 1898 for their help in implementing the study, and Ben Locke of the National Institute of Mental Health for his continuing support of our occupational mental health endeavors.

REFERENCES

Blumenthal, M., & Dielman, T. (1975). Depressive symptomatology and role function in a general population. *Archives of General Psychiatry, 32*, 215–232.

Bromet, E., & Cornely, P. (1984). Correlates of depression in mothers of young children. *Journal of the American Academy of Child Psychiatry, 23*, 335–342.

Bromet, E., Dew, M. A., Parkinson, D., & Schulberg, H. (1988). Predictive effects of occupational and marital stress on the mental health of a male workforce. *Journal of Organizational Behavior, 9*, 1–13.

Brown, G., & Harris, T. (1978). *Social origins of depression*. New York: The Free Press.

Bullock, F., Siegal, R., Weissman, M., & Paykel, E. (1972). Marital relations of depressed women. *Journal of Marriage and the Family, 34*, 488–495.

Cahalan, D., & Cisin, I. (1980). American drinking practices: Summary of findings from a national probability sample. In D. A. Ward (Ed.), *Alcoholism: Introduction to theory and treatment* (pp. 101–118). Dubuque, IA: Kendall/Hunt Publishing Company.

Caplan, R., Cobb, S., French, J., Harrison, R., & Pinneau, S. (1975). *Job demands and worker health.* Washington, DC: DHEW (NIOSH) Publication No. 75-160.

Cherry, N. (1984). Women and work stress: Evidence from the 1946 birth cohort. *Ergonomics, 27,* 519–526.

Colligan, M., & Murphy, L. (1979). Mass psychogenic illness in organizations. *Journal of Occupational Psychology, 52,* 77–90.

Cooper, C., & Marshall, J. (1976). Occupational sources of stress: A review of the literature relating coronary heart disease and mental ill health. *Journal of Occupational Psychology, 49,* 11–28.

Cox, T. (1980). Repetitive work. In C. Cooper & R. Payne (Eds.), *Current concerns in occupational stress* (pp. 23–41). New York: Wiley.

Crouter, A. (1984). Spillover from family to work: The neglected side of the work–family interface. *Human Relations, 37,* 425–442.

Derogatis, L., Lipman, R., Rickels, K., Uhlenhuth, E., & Covi, L. (1974). The Hopkins Symptom Checklist (HSCL): A self-report symptom inventory. *Behavioral Science, 19,* 1–15.

Dew, M. A., Bromet, E. J., Parkinson, D. K., Dunn, L. O., & Ryan, C. (1989). Effects of solvent exposure and occupational stress on the health of blue collar women. In K. Ratcliffe, M. Ferree, M. Freston, G. Mellow, G. Price, B. Wright, & K. Yanoshik (Eds.), *Women, health and technology.* Ann Arbor: University of Michigan Press.

Frankenhaeuser, M. (1977). Job demands, health and well-being. *Journal of Psychosomatic Research, 21,* 313–321.

Greenhaus, J., & Beutell, N. (1985). Sources of conflict between work and family roles. *Academy of Management Review, 10,* 76–88.

Haw, M. A. (1982). Women, work and stress: A review and agenda for the future. *Journal of Health and Social Behavior, 23,* 132–144.

Herman, J., & Gyllstrom, K. (1977). Working men and women: Inter- and intra-role conflict. *Psychology of Women Quarterly, 1,* 319–333.

Hinchliffe, M., Hooper, D., & Roberts, R. (1978). *The melancholy marriage.* New York: Wiley.

Holahan, C., & Moos, R. (1981). Social support and psychological distress: A longitudinal analysis. *Journal of Abnormal Psychology, 90,* 365–370.

House, J., McMichael, A., Wells, J., Kaplan, B., & Landerman, L. (1979). Occupational stress and health among factory workers. *Journal of Health and Social Behavior, 20,* 139–160.

Ilfeld, F. (1982). Marital stressors, coping styles, and symptoms of depression. In L. Goldberger & Breznitz, S. (Eds.), *Handbook of stress* (pp. 482–495). New York: The Free Press.

Kasl, S. (1978). Epidemiological contributions to the study of work stress. In C. Cooper & R. Payne (Eds.), *Stress at Work.* (pp. 3–48). New York: Wiley.

Keith, P., & Schafer, R. (1980). Role strain and depression in two-job families. *Family Relations, 29,* 483–488.

Nieva, V. (1975). Work and family linkages. In L. Larwood, A. Stromberg, & B. Gutek (Eds.), *Women and work: An annual review, Vol. 1* (pp. 162–190). Beverly Hills: Sage Publications.

Parkinson, D., & Bromet, E. (1983). Correlates of mental health in nuclear and coal-fired power plant workers. *Scandinavian Journal of Work, Environment and Health, 9,* 341–345.

Pearlin, L., & Schooler, C. (1978). The structure of coping. *Journal of Health and Social Behavior, 19,* 2–21.

Piotrkowski, C. (1979). *Work and the family system.* New York: The Free Press.

Pleck, J., Staines, G., & Lang, L. (1980). Conflicts between work and family life. *Monthly Labor Review,* pp. 29–32.

Poulton, E. (1978). Blue collar stressors. In C. Cooper & R. Payne (Eds.), *Stress at work* (pp. 51–79): New York: Wiley.

Radloff, L. (1975). The CES-D Scale: A self-report depression scale for research in the general population. *Applied Psychological Measurement, 1,* 385–401.

Richman, N. (1977). Behaviour problems in pre-school children: Family and social factors. *British Journal of Psychiatry, 131,* 523–527.

Roy, A. (1978). Vulnerability factors and depression in women. *British Journal of Psychiatry, 133,* 106–110.

Sales, E., & Frieze, I. (1984). Women and work: Implications for mental health. In L. Walker (Ed.), *Women and mental health policy* (pp. 229–246). Beverly Hills: Sage Publications.

Spanier, G. (1976). Measuring dyadic adjustment: New scales for assessing the quality of marriage and similar dyads. *Journal of Marriage and the Family, 38,* 15–30.

Spreitzer, E., Snyder, E., & Larson, D. (1979). Multiple roles and psychological well-being. *Sociological Focus, 12,* 141–148.

Verbrugge, L. (1982). Work satisfaction and health. *Journal of Community Health, 7,* 262–283.

Waring, E. (1985). Measurement of intimacy: Conceptual and methodological issues in studying close relationships. *Psychological Medicine, 15,* 9–14.

8

Where Work and Family Meet
Stress across Social Roles

BLAIR WHEATON

INTRODUCTION

When someone gets a divorce, we think of it as a family problem. When someone loses a job, we look to the work situation or the economy for an explanation. Stress occurs within roles, forming natural boundaries for our explanations. But roles are related, although not always in obvious fashion, suggesting in general that the occurrence of stress in one role will have implications for the meaning of stress in other roles. At the same time, stressors may accumulate within a role. Divorce may follow from a history of increasing marital conflict or from positive counter-forces outside the domestic role (Levinger, 1976). Job loss can follow from the individual's incapacity to perform or from larger economic mandates. How such events affect individuals must surely depend on the role history leading to the event. The primary purpose of this chapter is to examine the contextual role contingencies that affect the impact of two major events in work and family roles: divorce and unemployment.

A central reason for concern with stressful events is their implications for changes in mental health. What we know about stress in work and family roles derives from a number of separate, and only sometimes overlapping, research traditions. The recent history of life event research is toward greater differentiation: Where the standard approach

BLAIR WHEATON • Department of Sociology, University of Toronto, Toronto M5S 1A1, Ontario, Canada.

was to count exposure to aggregate numbers of stressful events, increasingly the tendency is to emphasize the content and circumstantial differences among events (Brown, 1981; Dohrenwend *et al.*, 1987; Turner, Avison, & Noh, 1986). Thus issues such as divorce and unemployment have been treated both as if they are functionally equivalent demands for change and as individual events that should be treated as unique. The work on individual events suggests that the full understanding of specific events requires a case-by-case approach to stressors. But at the same time each event becomes the focal point of its own empirical tradition, leaving the possible dependency among events unclear. A middle-ground approach is to study related sets of events.

Divorce and unemployment represent the two most prominent examples of stressful events in work and family roles. Each defines a research tradition with its own concerns. In the case of divorce, for example, a common concern is the possibility that divorce has differential emotional impacts on men and women. Gerstel *et al.* (1985) note that divorce poses typically different problems for women and men but that these problems may add up to the same amount of impact. In fact, this and another study find no differences in the level of impact by sex (Gerstel, Reissman, & Rosenfield, 1985; Menaghan & Lieberman, 1986). There are many sources of variation in impact to consider, including level of postdivorce social support, age, having children, and economic resources (Bloom, Asher, & White, 1978; Gerstel *et al.*, 1985; Leslie & Grady, 1985; Menaghan & Lieberman, 1986). With the significant exception of a few studies (Menaghan & Lieberman, 1986; Pearlin & Johnson, 1977), there has been little explicit attention in the empirical literature to the preexisting marital situation itself or to attendant stressors in other roles.

The same could be said of research on the mental health effects of unemployment. Some have concentrated on the fact and size of health effects of unemployment (Dew, Bromet, & Schulberg, 1987; Kessler, House, & Turner, 1987); some have concentrated on the effects of macroeconomic stress on the effect of unemployment (Brenner, 1973; Catalano, Dooley, & Jackson, 1985; Dooley & Catalano, 1984); and some on the importance of social support in ameliorating effects of unemployment (Gore, 1978; House, 1981; La Rocco, House, & French, 1980). In the area of job stressors, there is a clearer tradition of considering continuing forms of work stress (House, Strecher, Metzner, & Robbins, 1986), but often not in conjunction with discrete events such as unemployment, loss of income, or demotion. The exceptions are again important: Pearlin *et al.* (1981) give context to the problem of job disruptions by also including the simultaneous influence of ongoing economic strains, and Menaghan and Merves (1984) study the conditions under which ongoing occupational stresses affect distress, including some variables that measure family situation.

The exceptions noted to the tendency to study within-role conditions and then to focus more on event stressors or ongoing stressors but not both are all the more noteworthy because they are based on analyses of the same data. Obviously, for the issue of cross-role contingencies or contextual within-role contingencies to be answered, the question must be asked. The question here is how prior circumstances in the same role, and concurrent circumstances in other social roles, affect the experience of major events such as divorce and unemployment.

Context and Contingency in the Effects of Events

Each life event takes place in the context of a set of circumstances that will have a substantial impact on the way the individual perceives the event. For example, divorce will surely mean something quite different when it is imposed than when it occurs by volition. The source of initiation of the divorce process is part of the meaning context of the divorce experience. In general, the circumstances of a divorce must be specified explicitly if we are to understand the possibility of its differential emotional impact.

Specifying contextual factors in life events as a set of attendant role circumstances is just one approach to the specification of "context." There are others. For instance, Dohrenwend et al. (1987) consider five dimensions beyond the simple fact of the event: whether it is independent of the individual's psychological condition, the desirability of the change, the amount of change, the extent to which the individual's behavior precipitated the event, and threat to life. Brown and Harris (1978) and Brown (1981) uses a rather more involved procedure to define the "contextual threat" of an event. Whatever the approach used, the describing contextual factors for an event should be specified as separately operating factors, other independent variables, in an explanatory model of stress responses, rather than as part of the measurement decision in how to score the event. The latter procedure denies the possibility of a "main effect" role for the contextual factor and of course does not allow the estimation of an exact parameter for the contingency introduced by context.

A central claim of this chapter is that a crucial part of this contextual environment is the preexisting history of ongoing, more chronic forms of stress in the same and other roles. Drawing on the discussion in Wheaton (1986), I refer to continuing conditions in life roles that present problematic levels of demand as *ongoing stressors,* to distinguish them from *event stressors.* Because ongoing stressors are necessarily defined in continuous terms, so must the term *problematic.* Ongoing stressors have also been referred to as role strains (Pearlin, 1983) and as chronic stressors (Wheaton, 1983). I use the term to make clear that ongoing and open-ended role problems conform to the notion of social stress in the sense of environmental demand on responses capacities, while avoiding the sometimes presumptuous connotations of the term *chronic* (how long does a condition have to persist to be called chronic?). Ongoing stressors in the family role could refer to long-term marital conflict, individual responsibility for communal issues (e.g., children), or affectional or communication withdrawal, and in the work role to excessive monitoring by a supervisor, continuous repetition, isolation from others, unpredictable or uncontrollable task demands or task rates, or physically dangerous work.

The reason that ongoing stressors form a large part of the context of the consequential meaning of life events can be made more obvious by example. If a divorce follows after an apparently serene marital situation, it is likely the individual will be affected more strongly. If, on the other hand, divorce follows after a long-term escalation of marital conflict, it is likely that the individual will be affected less. The same sort of reasoning could be applied to unemployment as an event: If the job lost was highly stressful and/or generally despised, the fact of unemployment may not seem as comprehensively negative in its connotations. In both cases, the event has multiple meanings, including not only loss and change but also release and freedom. Thus, ongoing stressors help to define the given conditions that determine whether or not events will have any, or for that matter, a negative emotional impact.

Ongoing stressors may also *increase* the impact of life events when they occur; in fact, this is the more usual prediction. When ongoing stressors have this effect it is likely they do so because they stand for independent, unresolved sources of stress that are unaffected by the occurrence of the event. These sources of ongoing stress are also more likely to emanate from social roles other than the one in which the event takes place. Thus a divorce in the context of a difficult job situation will be all the more difficult, in part because coping resources must be allocated to separately existing problems.

The contingencies defined by considering both event and ongoing stressors suggests an intensifying or ameliorative multiplicative impact, depending on whether or not the source of the ongoing stress is within or outside the role in which the event takes place. We can imagine that ongoing problems in a role will make the event that follows have a resolutional impact; the question is whether this will simply reduce the effect of the event or in fact reverse its effect, suggesting distinctly positive emotional impacts for events usually thought as negative in their consequences. There is some precedent in the literature on marital status for predicting an actual reversal of the effect of divorce on distress if the previous marriage was rated as highly problematic. Kitson and Sussman (1982) studied the effect of 14 dimensions of marital stress on five indicators of mental health in a divorced sample. Although they predict "relief" when dimensions producing frustration or irritation are high, only 11% of the predicted associations are significant. Because the sample is divorced, no interaction for the effect of divorce contingent upon previous marital problems could be tested. This interaction was tested by Menaghan and Lieberman (1986), however, but was also found to be nonsignificant.

Within-Role versus Across-Role Stressors

What is needed in the understanding of major family and work event stressors is a general framework that distinguishes between within-role and across-role stress impacts. If these two sources of stress have contrasting effects, note that aggregate measures of both life events and ongoing stressors will mask the interdependency of their effects. The reason is that some combinations may lead to the intensification of the effects of stress, whereas others may lead to buffering the effects of stress.

The contrast in function between cross-role and within-role stressors can be made more explicit by pursuing our previous example a little further. It may seem self-evident that chronic marital problems would precede a divorce, but we also expect significant variability. In fact, most divorces involve a person who initiates and wants the divorce and another who, initially at least, does not want the divorce and is forced to accept it. Although generally recognized, this fact has not found expression in the empirical literature on divorce, in part because longitudinal data on couples is rare. One likely concomitant of the "harm doer" versus "victim" problem is the preexisting perception of marital problems before the separation process begins. When someone reports marital problems and eventually becomes divorced, it is more likely that he or she initiated the process than if no marital problems are reported. It is the person who is surprised who is in emotional trouble, both because he or she is more unprepared and because it is not his or her choice. When ongoing marital stressors are reported, it is automatically the case that anticipation of further marital stress is greater and coping defenses are activated.

If it was the case that reporting of marital stress tends to be associated just with anticipation of future problems, we would predict that the existence of prior ongoing marital stress would simply reduce, in the sense of buffer, the effect of divorce. Specifically, we would expect the effect of divorce on measures of distress to be less positive. But if prior reporting of stress tends to be associated with not just anticipation but also choice among the eventually divorced, we might expect a stronger effect than just stress buffering. The individual who perceives a great many marital problems, in effect, is in a situation of considerable ongoing and possibly chronic stress. Divorce may then function as a resolution of that stress, a case when more stress is actually stress relief. This is a *catharsis* effect hypothesis, suggesting not only a reduction in the positive impact of divorce on distress but also the possibility of an actual negative effect. The reason for this catharsis effect has wholly to do with the fact that the prior stress is in the same role. The general prediction is this: The greater the prior ongoing stress in a role, the more likely that a role loss or role transition event will have a cathartic effect that will actually improve mental health, or at least, the event will have significantly less impact.

But what if the individual heading for divorce is experiencing ongoing problems in the work role? If we imagine a person who must work long hours at a repetitive, uninteresting job that is also physically demanding, we can also imagine that any complexities in the family role may have more immediate and virulent effects. The problem for the individual is that the problems in one role do not help with problems in the other; in fact, the seeming independence of their resolution may make the accumulation of stress in different roles have a stress-intensifying effect.

What has been predicted in the case of divorce is not at all specific to this event or the family role. The catharsis effect should apply to the case of job loss as well, or any role transition event. Thus, the more severe prior ongoing job problems the individual experiences, the more that unemployment may seem like release from a problem than entry into another. It would take perhaps a more severe job situation to produce an actually negative effect of job loss on distress, but the beneficial mental health effects are clearly still possible.

To make the argument fully symmetrical, we would expect marital problems to exacerbate the effect of a job loss (and vice versa of course). Certainly, the problems of unemployment are likely to be intensified by an already tense family situation, if only because more time will be spent in the home environment.

Predictions

Let us state more generally what has been predicted by these arguments. First, I argued that ongoing state stressors, possibly representing chronic role problems, form an important part of the context within which life changes occur. Thus the mental health consequences of these life changes should be contingent upon these ongoing circumstances. This contingency can be modeled by specifying interactions between, in this case, role loss events and ongoing preexisting stressors. Second, the way in which the impact of life changes will be affected will depend on whether the ongoing stressor is a within-role or out-of-role problem. Within-role ongoing stress will mean that role loss events will have resolutional benefits; this could be manifest as a moderated effect of the role loss or an opposite effect of the role loss, indicating relief from the ongoing stress was more important than the problems of adjustment to the life change. Cross-role ongoing stress will, on the other hand, intensify the effects of role loss. Thus, for within-role stressors, we would predict a negative interaction term, indicating reduction of impact, but for cross-role stressors, we would predict a positive interaction term, indicating intensification of impact.

DATA AND METHODS

Study Design and Sample

The data are from a national panel survey in Canada conducted over the years 1977 to 1981. The target population included all adults in Canada aged 18 or more not in institutions, on native reservations, or living in very remote regions. A multistage, stratified cluster design was used, involving both representative cross-section samples in 1977, 1979, and 1981, and a follow through of the original 1977 sample as a panel with reinterviews in 1979 and 1981. The weighted N in the panel is 1665; this reflects over a 70% completion rate in each of the two follow-up interviews. This sample is based on a larger population than the one at issue in this chapter. We are interested in people who qualify for work and marriage events and thus analysis is restricted to the 781 respondents who were married in 1977, or became married by 1979, and who reported having a job in 1977 and/or 1979.

Description of Measures

Outcome Variable. The outcome considered here is an index of 12 depression and anxiety symptoms measured in 1977 and in 1981. These symptoms include items from known mental health scales, notably the General Health Questionnaire (GHQ) and the Center for Epidemiological Studies Depression Scale (CES-D), as well as a few items measuring general well-being. The items are broadly representative, including reported unhappiness, feeling in low spirits, self-reported perceived state of health, widely thought to be strongly affected by current mental health, frequent headaches, pains in muscles and joints, sleeping problems, nervousness, feeling fearful, feeling depressed, feeling tense, worrying a lot, and feeling hopeless about the future.

Each item was coded for symptomatic status by designating anyone in the upper 25% of responses about frequency of occurrence as a 1 and everyone else as 0. Symptoms were then summed to create a symptom total. This is meant to create a straightforwardly interpretable unit of measurement—symptoms—for the interpretation of results. Actually, all effects to be reported were replicated with a distress index in which frequency variation for each item was fully represented. All items were checked for psychometric status in an item analysis. The indexes were quite reliable, producing an alpha reliability of .77 in 1977 and .83 in 1981.

Stressors. The analytical questions outlined before demand that we have two types of stressors measured in each of the two major life roles, family and work. In the family role, divorce is the event stressor. Forty-six respondents in this subsample reported a divorce after the 1977 interview and before the 1981 interview. The ongoing stressor in this role is a combined measure of marital problems, made up of nine items: absence of love shown by spouse, spouse uninterested in respondent's work, spouse does not help at home, not enough time spent together, spouse not a good parent, low marital satisfaction overall, marriage does not satisfy need for friendship, marriage limits freedom, and marriage does not satisfy sexual needs. These problems were not considered individually due to a lack of power to detect effects and the prohibitive number of individual variables in an already complex model. In fact, the items are related closely, producing an alpha in excess of .80. To provide a metric for interpretation, because each item was measured on an ordinal basis and different items had different numbers of response categories, items were standardized to mean = 0 and standard deviation = 1, and then the index was created as the mean of all items, preserving this interpretation. Marital problems were measured at the last point in time before a reported divorce, which was dated by year, or at the latest in 1979.

In the work role, the major event stressor was nonvoluntary job loss, excluding retirement, over the 5-year period ($N = 54$). Major loss of income was also considered as a control to ensure that any effects of job loss were not due primarily to the resulting loss of income. The ongoing stressor was a measure of reported work problems that focused on issues likely to be a continuing source of work stress: varying and unpredictable hours, excessive overtime hours, having a physically and mentally tiring job, a high frequency of supervision of work, a job that was described as "not at all interesting," and having a dead-end job with no chance of promotion. Because these issues are not necessarily interrelated but likely to be cumulative in impact, a work problems index was constructed by summing the six items after each one was coded for presence versus absence of a problem. The final work problems score assigned was from 1979 if the respondent had a job and was still married that year, and from 1977 if either a divorce or job loss had taken place by 1979.

Control Variables. There are a number of potential confounding variables in assessing the effects of divorce and/or job loss. These variables could play two roles of importance: first, as additive controls that may render part of the effects of ongoing problems or events spurious, and second as factors that may also intervene as contingencies in the effects of divorce or job loss and thus act as alternative interactions that need to be taken into account. Examples here include divorce by age, divorce by number of children, divorce by years married, job loss by dual-career structure, and job loss by income. After screening out some factors that proved to be irrelevant in all models, the remaining control variables were sex, coded to designate females, dual-earner marriage, number of children at home, age of respondent in years, completed education in years, respondent's income, reporting having a confidant outside of one's spouse, years married, and major income loss.

Analytical Strategy

We are interested in the independent influence of contingencies arising in the effects of divorce and job loss due to the presence of ongoing stressors before or at the time of these events. To estimate this influence, we test interaction terms for event-by-ongoing stress combinations in multiple regression models with distress symptoms in 1981 as the dependent variable. Three kinds of effects need to be controlled to establish the plausibility of the contingencies embodied by these interactions. First, the effect of initial distress in 1977 needs to be controlled. Inclusion of this variable ensures that the effects of other independent variables are on changes in symptoms from 1977 to 1981 and that any effects of distress itself on the experience of or the tendency to perceive stress is taken into account. This means that the effects of the stressors measured are independent of previous distress and of any measurement confounding due to the possibility that having distress causes one to perceive more problems—a kind of cognitive rationalization effect. This is a common and serious objection to the use of self-report measures for ongoing stress, but the panel structure allows for partialling out both measurement and causal confounding.

A second type of control incorporated in these models is the additive linear effect of associated causes of distress. These controls are also considered as a third type of effect to be controlled for: plausible interactions between role loss events and social categories or social status that specify the applicability of the effect of these events in other ways, as well as interactions involving only control variables.

RESULTS

Initial Estimates

We begin by considering some initial estimates of the within-role and cross-role effects of ongoing stress on the role loss events, to see first if the predicted effects have any plausibility. The results in Table 1 report mean differences in distress symptoms in 1981 due to a specified event, controlling for symptoms in 1977 as well as the following control variables: sex, dual-earner family, number of children, age, education, respondent's income, and years married. To each basic model, various two-way interactions were added representing in turn within-role and cross-role contingencies in the effects of events.

Both of the within-role effects correspond to predictions. The interaction between divorce and marital problems was significant, and negative, indicating that as marital problems increase, the effect of divorce decreases. The mean difference due to divorce was evaluated at two levels of marital problems: 1 standard deviation below the mean and 1 standard deviation above the mean. To describe interactions throughout, I have chosen values of continuous variables that represent people

Table 1. Initial Estimates of Within-Role and Cross-Role Effects on Major Role Loss Events

	Adjusted mean difference in 1981 symptoms due to event[a]	Probability of interaction term
Within role		
1. Effect of divorce when		.002
Marital problems = −1	1.75	
Marital problems = +1	.60	
2. Effect of job loss when		.005
Work problems = 0	.66	
Work problems = 2	.06	
Across role[b]		
1. Effect of divorce when		.285
Work problems = 0	.69	
Work problems = 2	.94	
2. Effect of job loss when		.437
Marital problems = −1	.31	
Marital problems = +1	.22	

[a]All mean differences reported are derived from regression models in which controls for sex, dual-career status, number of children, age, education, income, years married, and symptoms in 1977 were incorporated.
[b]Two combinations are not tested due to their rarity: divorce plus job loss occurred to only 7 people, and divorce plus major income loss occurred to only 11 people.

roughly 15 to 20% above the lowest point in the distribution and below the highest point in the distribution. At 1 *SD* below the mean in marital problems, we see that those experiencing a divorce report 1.75 more symptoms on the average than those who stay married. At 1 *SD* above the mean, however, this difference is reduced to .60 symptoms. It is quite likely that marital problems reported by these respondents reflect only their own viewpoint and that in many cases information from the other spouse might reveal unrealized disagreement. Thus those reporting few problems are disproportionately likely not to be the initiators of the divorce process; they are the potential victims and are thus also more likely not to have the coping advantage of anticipation. Those who do report problems may see divorce coming and/or may be actively seeking to leave the marriage. If we could isolate those who actively want out, we might find a further basis for interaction that is averaged into the mean difference of .60 for those high in marital problems.

The effect of work problems on job loss is quite similar. When a respondent reports no work problems, the mean difference due to job loss is .66, but when a respondent reports two (out of six) problems, the effect of job loss is essentially zero. This suggests to me that there is some relief resulting from escape from a difficult job environment, somewhat counterbalanced by the stress of unemployment itself, combining to create no overall effect.

The interaction between income loss and work problems was also estimated and found to be nonsignificant. As in all results to follow, the effects of income loss are noncontingent, probably because it has comprehensive impacts on a number of role situations. It is important, at the same time, to control for income loss in further models so that the effect of purely financial issues is taken into account in assessing the effects of job loss.

None of the cross-role interactions added to a basic linear model proved to be significant, and thus the prediction concerning the intensification of role loss impact does not appear at this point to be supported. But there may be an additional second contingency to consider. The literatures on family and work roles both make clear that gender is a basic dividing line and that social processes in each role will almost always be distinguishable by whether the person at issue is male or female.

A line of reasoning that may be important here involves gender differences in the use of contextual information and the extent of perceptual awareness of contextual cues. One type of gender difference identified in the literature on relationships suggests that women are both more sensitive to quality differences and more aware of alternatives due to social comparison (Hill, Rubin, & Peplau, 1976; Rubin, Peplau, & Hill, 1981). In addition, it is clear that women bring more divorces (Jacobson, 1982) and expect more at the beginning of relationships (Hill et al., 1976). Thus the meaning of divorce may depend on the state of the previous marriage more clearly for women than for men.

Women may also be suffering more stress aggregated across roles. Even though women have been entering the labor force in large numbers, it is still common to find that they perform the major portion of housework and child care tasks (Meissner, Humphreys, Meis, & Scheu, 1975; Ross, Mirowsky, & Huber, 1983). Given that coping resources are finite, women will have less room for further stress accumulation in these circumstances. If this is the case, we would expect more cross-role effects for women.

A third possibility, related to the first two, is suggested by Thoits (1987), who hypothesizes that the impact of an event will depend on its identity salience. If family roles are higher in the identity hierarchy of women—as suggested by Thoits due to the fact that social status will determine access to identities and thus importance in a salience hierarchy—then family problems will have more identity-threatening impact for women.

All of the within-role and cross-role contingencies tested in Table 1 were retested as three-way interactions including sex. The probabilities of these interactions under the null hypothesis of no effect are shown in Table 2. Here we see that the dependence of divorce on marital problems is indeed distinguishable by sex but that the dependence of job loss on work problems is not. This finding is of course consistent with any of these explanations. There is also evidence here of one significant cross-role effect, involving the dependence of the effect of job loss on marital problems more for one sex than the other. Note it is marital problems as an ongoing stressor that is implicated in both significant interactions involving sex. But the nature of the sex differences are not yet clear.

Specification and Refinement of Role Loss Effects

The next step in the analysis was to estimate a more complete model incorporating all of the significant interactions, and their nested subcomponents, simultaneously. The regression results for the first model of this sort are shown in Table 3, Column A. This model shows estimates of all of the contingent effects found in separate models in the previous tables. Thus, two three-way interactions were estimated simultaneously, and both were still significant. The first is a within-role effect of marital problems on divorce that depends on sex, and the second is a cross-role effect of marital problems on job loss dependent on sex. The two-way within-role effect of work problems on job loss is also included and is still significant.

To understand these interactions, we note first that the $-.87$ coefficient for the first term indicates that the impact of marital problems on the effect of divorce is more negative among women. This means that

Table 2. Testing for the Specificity of Within-Role/ Cross-Role Interactions by Sex

Term tested	Probability
1. Divorce × Marital Problems × Sex	.027
2. Job Loss × Work Problems × Sex	.292
3. Divorce × Work Problems × Sex	.095
4. Job Loss × Marital Problems × Sex	.001

the stress-resolving function of divorce will be stronger among women. The +1.62 coefficient for the second term indicates that the stress-intensifying impact of marital problems on job loss will be stronger among women.

There is a need to control for further possibilities before Model A in Table 3 is accepted as the best possible rendering. The model as it stands does not include a number of possible interactions that are often cited as important contingencies in the literature, it does not include the possibility that each event is doubly dependent on ongoing stress in both

Table 3. Regression Results for "Best Models" Incorporating Significant Interactions among Event and Ongoing Stressors

	A. Model with additive controls	B. Model with interactions for controls
Intercept	.43	.13
Female	.10	.74**
Dual earners	.03	.02
Number of kids	.10**	.09**
Age	−.002	−.001
Education	−.01	−.01
R's income	−.01	−.005
Confidant	.08	.35*
Symptoms—1977	.72***	.71***
Income loss	.64***	.60***
Job loss	.46	.50*
Divorce	1.12**	.62
Marital problems	.20**	.21**
Work problems	.20**	.19**
Divorce × Number of Kids	—	.31*
Confidant × Female	—	−.77**
Divorce × Marital Problems	.06	.10
Divorce × Female	.25	.05
Marital Problems × Female	−.22*	−.22*
Job Loss × Work Problems	−.21*	−.21*
Job Loss × Female	−.91*	−.84*
Job Loss × Marital Problems	−.65*	−.61*
Divorce × Marital Problems × Female	−.87*	−.83*
Marital Problems × Job Loss × Female	1.62**	1.49**

* = $p < .05$.
** = $p < .01$.
*** = $p < .001$.

roles simultaneously (a three-way interaction for each event involving work and marital problems at the same time), and it does not include the possibility that job loss effects depend on income loss and ongoing stressors simultaneously.

All of the three-way interactions specifying double contingencies of divorce or job loss depending on both kinds of ongoing stress or income loss and ongoing stress were nonsignificant. Further, adding sex as an additional factor and estimating four-way interactions also produced no significant effects. A number of interactions involving the control variables were also estimated. These included divorce by having a confidant by sex, divorce by years married by sex, divorce by education by sex, divorce by age by sex, divorce by dual-earner marriage by sex, divorce by number of children by sex, divorce by income by sex, job loss by income by sex, job loss by age by sex, job loss by dual-earner marriage by sex, marital problems by number of children by sex, and work problems by dual-earner marriage by sex. Most of these three-way interactions and their two-way components were nonsignificant, but two interactions did surface that were retained in later models. These were a two-way interaction between divorce and the number of children that applied equally to men and women and a two-way interaction between having a confidant and gender. The confidant by gender interaction indicated that women gained more from an outside confidant than men, but this interaction did not affect the operation of the effects of either divorce or job loss. Children, as one would expect, increase the impact of divorce.

The additional interactions were included in a "final model" along with the previous interactions of Model A, Table 3. The results are shown as Model B in Table 3. One fact that is clear is that the pattern of interactions involving divorce and job loss is the same (see last two rows of Table 3, for example). The effect of job loss in this model carries with it the same contingencies as before, but this is not the case for divorce. The effects of divorce must be evaluated not only depending on marital problems and sex but also the number of children as well.

The exact mean differences due to divorce and job loss that can be derived from this model are shown in Table 4. The effect of divorce is shown separately by level of marital problems, gender, and number of children. Besides calculating the effect of divorce at 1 SD above and below the mean of marital problems, differences with number of children = 0, 2, and 4 were also incorporated. The average number of children is close to 2, and more than 20% of the sample has no children and at least four children.

Looking at differences in impact due to marital problems first, we see that the impact of divorce among men essentially does not depend

Table 4. Adjusted Mean Difference in 1981 Symptoms Due to Role Loss Events

	Men		Women	
	Marital problems = −1	Marital problems = +1	Marital problems = −1	Marital problems = +1
1. Effect of divorce				
When number of kids = 0	.52	.72	1.40*	−.06
When number of kids = 2	1.14*	1.34**	2.02***	.56†
When number of kids = 4	1.76**	1.96***	2.64***	1.18**
2. Effect of job loss				
When work problems = 0	1.11**	−.11	−1.22†	.54
When work problems = 2	.69	−.53	−1.64**	.12

† = $p < .10$.
* = $p < .05$.
** = $p < .01$.
*** = $p < .001$.

on the level of prior marital problems. When the number of children = 2, men show a mean difference in symptoms of 1.14 when they report few marital problems and a mean difference of 1.34 symptoms when they report many marital problems. Both differences are significant beyond the .05 level. For women, the mean differences show something quite different. When few marital problems are reported (and again setting number of children to 2), eventual divorce has a substantial impact, increasing distress by 2.02 symptoms on the average. But when marital problems have been reported, divorce only leads to a .56 increase in symptoms. This amounts to a reduction in the mean difference of 1.46 due to a two standard deviation increase in marital problems. Thus, it is clear that the contextual importance of prior marital stress applies only to women. And it is only among women that the predicted within-role effect of ongoing stress on divorce occurs.

The results also show that children increase the impact of divorce for both sexes. Each additional two children increases the effect of divorce by .62 symptoms on the average. This effect, combined with the importance of marital problems, leads to a very wide range of divorce experience among women. This range varies from no impact (mean difference = −.06, not significant) for women with no children and many marital problems to an impact of 2.64 symptoms for women with four children who thought they had a good marriage. The increase of 2.64 symptoms reflects a substantial impact, equal to almost 25% of the possible range of 12 symptoms and a 1.5 SD increase in symptoms.

The effects of job loss in Table 4 are distinguished by gender, level of marital problems, and level of work problems. This is done because the effects of job loss depend on marital problems differentially by sex but also depend on work problems equally for both sexes. The effects of job loss are calculated for 0 and 2 reported ongoing work problems, corresponding roughly to values 1 *SD* above and below the mean of 1, and when marital problems are 1 *SD* above average and 1 *SD* below average, as before.

The effect of increasing marital problems among men is to *reduce* the effect of job loss, by .61 symptoms per *SD* increase in level of marital problems. But job loss has a significant impact on men in only one circumstance: when no work problems are reported, indicating possibly a valued job, and when few marital problems were reported. The apparent negative impacts of job loss on distress when there are marital problems are nonsignificant. Still, the relative change in impact requires explanation because it is not at all what was predicted earlier. Among women, the effect is in the opposite direction, as predicted, but this finding requires further consideration as well. Although the relative impact of increasing marital problems is to increase the impact of job loss, the results show that such problems are primarily changing the job loss effect from a beneficial one when there are few marital problems to no impact when there are a number of marital problems. We do not see a case among women where job loss leads to a significant increase in symptoms. What is surprising here is the fact that women in good marriages actually improve in mental health as a result of job loss.

The impact of work problems is straightforward. For both men and women, increasing work problems have the predicted effect of reducing the effect of job loss; it is especially crucial for men in reported good marriages, who suffer distress problems as a result of losing a good job, but not when the job carries with it a number of ongoing problems.

The finding that marital problems reduce the impact of job loss among men forces speculation. It may be that the job loss is actually allowing the marital situation to improve subsequently, by precipitating a situation in which the problems must be addressed. Or, the fact of unemployment could simply cause a common focus of concern—assuming that the male income is often integral to the financial integrity of the household—which may distract attention away from the wearing effects of ongoing marital problems. On the other hand, men still take the breadwinner responsibility seriously, and their identity may be particularly threatened when they feel close to their wife and feel "they have let her down." This would help account for the detrimental effect of unemployment particularly when the marriage is perceived in positive terms.

The other unusual finding concerns the beneficial effect of job loss when women also report good marriages. As noted earlier, some of these women may be pleased by having refuge from a demand overload problem that accumulates across roles. When the marital situation is seen as desirable, this makes all the more sense. In fact, this finding is not an isolated one. Thoits (1986) reports that the employed worker identity appears to distress women more than men when combined with marriage, thus suggesting that leaving a job may actually lead to relief for some women. This is not consistent with the finding of Kessler and McRae (1982) that employment generally benefits women's health, but note that it is specifically in the case of a stressful job that women receive benefits from a job loss (mean difference = -1.64). This is the one case in which the cathartic effect of the event in the face of within-role ongoing stress leads to an actual reversal in the effect of the event.

DISCUSSION

The premise of this chapter has been that the effect of stressful life events is contextually bound. Ongoing stressors within and in other roles constitute an important element in this context, in that they provide part of the "meaning" of the life event to the individual. The general model proposed here is that within-role ongoing stressors reduce, in effect short-circuit, the effects of events in that role, in particular, events that stand for exit from that role, whereas cross-role ongoing stressors exacerbate the effect of the same event. What was predicted, then, were interactive contingencies with effects in the opposite direction.

There was some support for these predictions, but it was bounded as well. First, the predicted pattern occurred only among women, although having a problematic job did reduce the effect of job loss among men as well. Because the emphasis in the predictions was contextual dependence and role interconnectedness, the natural inference is that men tend to be more context independent, but this is not entirely the case, because other forms of context dependence at odds with what was predicted surfaced among men—specifically, the fact that marital problems reduced their distress responses to job loss.

The fact that prior marital stress has direct implications for the impact of divorce only among women is consistent both with the idea that the marital role may be higher in identity salience among women and that women are more willing to interpret a difficult marital situation as such, at the same time that they are less willing to tolerate it. Hill *et al.*

(1976) note the continuing influence of the interpretation that women are the "socioemotional specialists" in relationship situations. Indeed, in these data one clue in this regard is the fact that divorced women have a mean level of reported marital problems before the divorce of 1.31, whereas divorced men have a mean of .50. There is a great deal of overlap in the two distributions, and when marital problems are held constant, there are clearly sex differences in the impact of divorce, but the mean difference in perceived marital problems does suggest that women in problem marriages are more critically evaluative than men.

Second, it is true that the model would have received more straight-forward support if the results were more symmetrical with regards to role. Although it is the case among women that marital problems decrease the effect of divorce and increase the effect of job loss and that work problems generally reduce the effect of job loss, it is not the case that work problems increase the effect of divorce. There is some evidence for three of the four combinations.

A third restriction on the evidence is that the exacerbating effect of marital problems in the face of a job loss for women really only describes the removal of a beneficial effect in one case (when there are work problems).

The results do point to the importance of considering ongoing stress as part of the context of the meaning of life events. In the case of divorce, the interesting point about the mean differences in Table 4 is that the differences among women are greater, but the average of the effects is about the same for men and women. In other words, if we did not consider ongoing stress as part of the event context, we would find very similar overall impacts of divorce among men and women. But these interactions show why this would be quite misleading. Women both receive the greatest impact under certain conditions (many children, few reported marital problems) and the smallest impact (no children, many reported marital problems). Again, this is consistent with the view that women experience a wider range of quality in interpersonal roles.

The approach in this chapter to the specification of contextual factors in the experience of life events has a number of implications for the existing stress literature. The results in Table 4 should make clear the fact that understanding a life event requires careful specification of the accompanying circumstances. This is a fact that may seem obvious when written down, and yet such specification is rarely incorporated into the study of life events.

The results show that in certain situations presumably major life changes such as divorce and job loss will have little or no detrimental effects. In these situations, it is difficult to refer to the event as a "stressor." The view that such events as divorce and unemployment are universally threatening seems questionable in light of the present results. There are circumstances when a divorce or removal from a job situation may be appropriate as a way of coping with ongoing stress.

If there is a general alert to be derived from this chapter, it is the fact that ongoing stressors cannot be ignored, even if they are difficult to measure, if we are to understand the effects of life events properly. The design of this study helped with the measurement problem for ongoing stress, allowing control of confounding with earlier distress. Panel studies may be particularly important in the proper specification of the effects of major life events. Before we hypothesize that differences in social support or coping are essential, it is well to remember that the contextual role circumstances surrounding the occurrence of a life event may provide a clear distinction between situations in which life events require coping intervention and situations in which coping is irrelevant.

ACKNOWLEDGMENTS

This chapter arose from an ongoing series of meetings with my colleagues in the Consortium for Research Involving Stress Processes, supported by the W. T. Grant Foundation. My thanks to John Eckenrode, Susan Gore, and Bruce Link for their comments on a preliminary version.

REFERENCES

Bloom, B., Asher, S. J., & White, S. W. (1978). Marital disruption as a stressor: a review and analysis. *Psychological Bulletin, 85*,(4) 867–894.

Brenner, M. H. (1973). *Mental illness and the economy.* Cambridge, MA: Harvard University Press.

Brown, G. W. (1981). Contextual measures of life events. In Barbara S. Dohrenwend & Bruce P. Dohrenwend (Eds.), *Stressful life events and their contexts* (pp. 187–201). New Brunswick, NJ: Rutgers University Press.

Brown, G. W., & Harris, T. (1978). *Social origins of depression: A study of psychiatric disorder in women.* New York: The Free Press.

Catalano, R. A., Dooley, D., & Jackson, R. L. (1985). Economic antecedents of help-seeking: Reformulation of time series tests. *Journal of Health and Social Behavior, 26*,(2), 141–152.

Dew, M. A., Bromet, E. J., & Schulberg, H. C. (1987). A comparative analysis of two community stressors' long-term mental health effects. *American Journal of Community Psychology, 15*(2), 167–184.

Dohrenwend, B. P., Link, B. G., Kern, R., Shrout, P. E., & Markowitz, J. (1987). Measuring life events: The problem of variability within event categories. In B. Cooper (Ed.), *Psychiatric epidemiology: Progress and prospects.* London: Croom Helm.

Dooley, D., & Catalano, R. (1984). Why the economy predicts help-seeking: A test of competing explanations. *Journal of Health and Social Behavior, 25*(2), 160–175.

Gerstel, N., Reissman, C. K., & Rosenfield, S. (1985). Explaining the symptomatology of separated and divorced women and men: The role of material conditions and social networks. *Social Forces, 64*(1), 84–101.

Gore, S. (1978). The effect of social support in moderating the health consequences of unemployment. *Journal of Health and Social Behavior, 19,* 157–165.

Hill, C. T., Rubin, Z., & Peplau, L. A. (1976). Breakups before marriage: The end of 103 affairs. *Journal of Social Issues, 32,* 147–168.

House, J. S. (1981). *Work stress and social support.* Reading, MA: Addison-Wesley.

House, J. S., Strecher, V., Metzner, H. L., & Robbins, C. A. (1986). Occupational stress and health among men and women in the Tecumseh Community Health Study. *Journal of Health and Social Behavior, 27*(1), 62–77.

Jacobson, G. F. (1982). *The multiple crises of marital separation and divorce.* New York: Grune & Stratton.

Kessler, R. C., & McRae, Jr., J. A. (1982). The effect of wive's employment on the mental health of married men and women. *American Sociological Review, 47*(2), 216–227.

Kessler, R. C., House, J. S., & Turner, J. B. (1987). Unemployment and health in a community sample. *Journal of Health and Social Behavior, 28*(1), 51–59.

Kitson, G. C., & Sussman, M. B. (1982). Marital complaints, demographic characteristics, and symptoms of mental distress in divorce. *Journal of Marriage and the Family, 44*(1), 87–101.

LaRocco, J. M., House, J. S., & French, J. R. P. (1980). Social support, occupational stress, and health. *Journal of Health and Social Behavior, 21*(3), 202–218.

Leslie, L. A., & Grady, K. (1985). Changes in mothers' social networks and social support following divorce. *Journal of Marriage and the Family, 47*(3), 663–673.

Levinger, G. (1976). A social psychological perspective on marital dissolution. *Journal of Social Issues, 32*(1), 21–47.

Meissner, M., Humphreys, E. W., Meis, S. M., & Scheu, W. J. (1975). No exit for wives: Sexual division of labor and the cumulation of household demands. *Canadian Review of Sociology and Anthropology, 12*(4), Part I, 424–439.

Menaghan, E. G., & Lieberman, M. A. (1986). Changes in depression following divorce: A panel study. *Journal of Marriage and the Family, 48*(2), 319–328.

Menaghan, E. G., & Merves, E. S. (1984).Coping with occupational problems: The limits of individual efforts. *Journal of Health and Social Behavior, 25*(4), 406–423.

Pearlin, L. I. (1983). Role strains and personal stress. In H. B. Kaplan (Ed.), *Psychosocial stress: Trends in theory and research* (pp. 3–32). New York: Academic Press.

Pearlin, L. I., & Johnson, J. S. (1977). Marital status, life strains, and depression. *American Sociological Review, 42,* 704–715.

Pearlin, L. I., Lieberman, M. A., Menaghan, E. G., & Mullan, J. T. (1981). The stress process. *Journal of Health and Social Behavior, 22*(4), 337–356.

Ross, C. E., Mirowsky, J., & Huber, J. (1983). Dividing work, sharing work, and in-between: Marriage patterns and depression. *American Sociological Review, 48*(6), 809–824.

Rubin, Z., Peplau, L. A., & Hill, C. T. (1981). Loving and leaving: Sex differences in romantic attachments. *Sex Roles, 7,* 821–835.

Thoits, P. A. (1986). Multiple identities: Examining gender and marital status differences in distress. *American Sociological Review, 51*(2), 259–272.

Thoits, P. A. (1987). *On merging identity theory and stress research.* Presented at the Eastern Sociological Society meetings in Boston, May 1987.

Turner, R. J., Avison, W. R., & Noh, S. (1986). *Sources of attenuation in the stress-distress relationship: An evaluation of modest innovations in the application of event checklists.* Presented at the Second National Stress Conference, University of New Hampshire, June 2–3, 1986.

Wallerstein, J. S., & Kelly, J. B. (1980). *Surviving the break-up: How children and parents cope with divorce.* New York: Basic Books.

Wheaton, B. (1983). Stress, personal coping resources, and psychiatric symptoms: An investigation of interactive models. *Journal of Health and Social Behavior, 24*(3), 208–229.

Wheaton, B. (1986). *On the definition and detection of chronic stress.* Paper presented at the Second National Stress Conference, University of New Hampshire, June 2–3, 1986.

9

Understanding the Individual and Family Effects of Unemployment

JOAN HUSER LIEM and G. RAMSAY LIEM

In spite of Rosabeth Kanter's (1977) persuasive call to treat work and family as interacting rather than independent spheres of influence in studies of socioenvironmental determinants of individual well-being, relatively little research has been done in the last 10 years that explicitly examines the interplay between work and family conditions and individual functioning. Notable exceptions are Piotrkowski's (1979) book, *Work and the Family System,* in which she describes in some detail how jobs both inside and outside the family make demands on workers that influence the quality of family life and the physical and psychological well-being of family members, and Elder's classic study, *Children of the Great Depression* (1974), and related work (Elder & Caspi, 1988) in which he details the relationship between economic stress, family adaptations, and the personality development of children.

Several other researchers, (Larson, 1984; Piotrkowski, Stark, & Burbank, 1983; Schlozman & Verba, 1979; Voydanoff & Donnelly, 1985) have linked economic distress, usually in the form of job loss or stressful occupational conditions, to the quality of family life, for example, family stability, marital adjustment, and supportive versus conflict-laden family

JOAN HUSER LIEM • Department of Psychology, University of Massachusetts–Boston, Boston, Massachusetts 02115.   **G. RAMSAY LIEM** • Department of Psychology, Boston College, Chestnut Hill, Massachusetts 02167.

relationships. Most of the research on the effects of work-related stress, however, has focused on the relationship between occupational stressors and individual or family well-being without taking into account the nature of the family context in which the stress is occurring (Cooper & Marshall, 1976; Cooper & Smith, 1985). A few studies do look at the family as an important source of support for individuals coping with job-related stress, but the precise role played by the family in the coping process is typically left unexamined (Gore, 1978) as are the effects of stress on the family's ability to play a supportive role (Atkinson, Liem, & Liem, 1986).

A much closer examination of the relationship between family processes and individual well-being is characteristic of the family systems literature where the concept of interdependent lives is central (Minuchin, 1974; Minuchin, Rosman, & Baker, 1978). However, little can be found in that literature about the role of stressors external to the family in shaping the family–individual relationship. For example, detailed analyses have been made of communication patterns in families that link disordered parental communication with schizophrenia (Wynne, 1984) and related forms of disturbed behavior in adolescent and young adult offspring (Goldstein, 1984, 1985). Few studies, however, have looked outside the family at events or conditions that may have contributed to the family's deviant patterns of communication (Liem, 1980).

The chapters in this volume share Kanter's (1977) interest in better understanding the relationship between work and family life as determinants of individual well-being. In particular, they examine the ways in which work-related stresses and family conditions interact and are associated with physical and psychological distress among individuals. Our particular contribution, a study of the effects of involuntary unemployment on family and individual functioning, examines the combined effects of a critical occupational stressor, dislocation from the work force, and a number of important family characteristics on individual and family well-being. The model that we will be examining is illustrated in Figure 1.

The model reflects a number of working hypotheses that have guided our research: (1) Unemployment has negative psychological consequences for job losers and through its effects on the unemployed person, for spouses and families as well. For example, a husband's heightened anxiety about being out of work may make him emotionally available to his wife or less effective in carrying out his family responsibilities. His behavior may in turn provoke increased anxiety or depression in his wife and create a less cohesive, more conflicted family environment. (2) Unemployment may affect family functioning directly. It

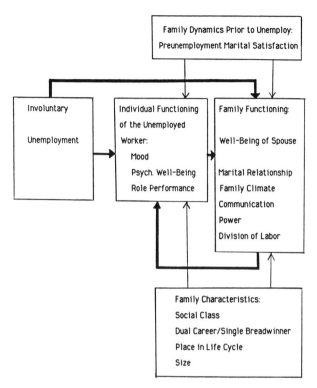

Figure 1. Analytic model of the effects of unemployment on individual and family functioning.

may, for example, require adaptations in the family's standard of living, make it necessary for the family to reorganize its daily routine or create a sense of insecurity that alters the emotional climate within the home. (3) Unemployment may also have negative effects on the unemployed worker through its effects on the family system as a whole. A husband's job loss, to give an illustration, may result in his wife's decision to take a job leaving him with the care of young children, a change in the family's usual routine that may bring with it some financial relief but also new emotional challenges for the unemployed husband. (4) These changes in individual and family functioning occur within a family context involving a variety of dynamic properties that preceded the husband's job loss and structural conditions such as the family's social class background, place in the life cycle, size, and single-breadwinner versus dual-career status. These contextual factors all have a bearing on how an event like unemployment is experienced. They influence the way unemployment is defined and the availability of material and emotional resources with which it can be addressed. They are family conditions, therefore, that are likely to modify the effects of unemployment on individual and family functioning.

Our interest in the mediation of the stress of forced unemployment is related to earlier research findings suggesting strong relationships between broad conditions of unemployment in the economy and institutional indicators of mental illness (Brenner, 1973; Dooley & Catalano, 1980). However, by focusing on a system-level relationship between economic change and mental health, this line of research could not provide insight into the ways in which particular individuals and their families respond in the face of economic pressures. Fortunately, a sizable, more varied body of research on the psychological effects of unemployment now exists. Reviews of this work (Fryer, 1985; Fryer & Payne, 1986; Horwitz, 1984; Warr, 1985) indicate that there is considerable variation in these effects as observed in small sample, cross-sectional and longitudinal studies and large community surveys. Some unemployed workers appear to experience clinical levels of impairment in the form of severe anxiety, depression, or self-harm. Others appear to be positively affirmed and strengthened by the challenges presented by their unemployment. For most, however, the literature strongly suggests that unemployment brings with it discouragement, lowered self-esteem and confidence, and heightened anxiety and depression.

Specifying the conditions under which the more negative outcomes of unemployment are likely to occur remains a major research objective. It is our contention that the family context of unemployment is one important source of the variation in unemployment effects pertaining to emotional health.

Our investigation of the psychological consequences of unemployment, like much of the other research presented in this volume, has been heavily influenced by a social stress conceptualization of human dysfunction. The social stress framework adopts the view that an individual's coping resources can be exhausted by continuous exposure to stressful external events and conditions that impose demands for readjustment in one's life. Under conditions of sufficient external stress, resistance capacities are taxed, increasing the person's vulnerability to physiological and psychological dysfunction (Pearlin, Menaghan, Lieberman, & Mullan, 1981). Having access to a variety of social and economic "resistance resources" has been shown to enhance one's ability to deal effectively with stressful events (Antonovsky, 1974; Dean & Lin, 1977; Lin, Simeone, Ensel, & Kuo, 1979). Each of the demographic and structural characteristics of the family that we have included in this research has an obvious, albeit complex, bearing on the family's access to social and material resources.

Social class standing, for example, suggests more limited economic resources for coping with unemployment among blue-collar workers but greater absolute financial losses as a result of unemployment among white-collar workers. Blue-collar families, on the other hand, often have larger and more closely knit social networks than white-collar families that may make them less dependent on work-related relationships for social support and a sense of rootedness. If it is chronic financial strain that is primarily responsible for the psychological distress caused by unemployment, an hypothesis that is consistent with recent findings reported by Kessler, Turner, and House (1988), we would expect blue-collar families to have a more difficult experience with job loss. To the extent that the loss of status and prestige and separation from important workplace friendships are also critical, the picture becomes more complex.

Competing hypotheses can also be advanced about the differential effects of unemployment for dual-career versus single-breadwinner families. On the one hand, job loss may be more stressful for husbands and wives in single-breadwinner families because it represents the loss of the family's only source of income, whereas dual-career families continue to have one spouse's income to fall back on. The greater financial stress experienced by single breadwinner families might be expected to bring with it greater psychological distress and increased tension within the home. On the other hand, the dual-career family has been described as a chronically stressed family system (Rapoport & Rapoport, 1977, 1978). With both spouses juggling work and family responsibilities, the social and psychological resources of the family are often taxed to the limit, and even relatively unimportant events can overload the system with deleterious consequences. Given the persistence of stress in dual-career families, the added burden of unemployment may have more negative consequences than it does in single-breadwinner families who, in spite of their marginal economic status, may have more social and emotional resources available for coping with the job loss.

Life cycle adaptation such as the birth of a first child or the addition of a second child to the family represent other stressful experiences with which families must cope. When these developmental demands brought about by the family's place in the life cycle coincide with a stressful event like unemployment, one would expect to see increased psychological distress on the part of family members as well as heightened emotional costs for the family as a whole. We expected that younger families coping with the recent addition of children would experience unemployment as more stressful than older families whose composition was likely to be more stable. Similarly, we expected to observe greater distress as a result of unemployment in larger families, especially those with young children, than in smaller families because more children are likely to tax existing resources more heavily. The research reported in this chapter examines these possibilities.

In a more limited way, we have also been able to focus on the role played by family dynamics prior to unemployment in conditioning the psychological effects of unemployment on family members. The interest in preunemployment family dynamics has been influenced by the now extensive clinical research literature linking family processes and individual well-being (Liem, 1980). Within that literature, the quality of the marital relationship, the openness of communication, and the power relationship between spouses, for example, have all been shown to be associated with individual psychological well-being. Furthermore, Komarovsky (1940), in her classic study of unemployment during the Great Depression, has drawn attention to preunemployment structural and relational factors such as patriarchal versus matriarchal patterns of authority and primary versus instrumental marital relations that influence the psychological effects of unemployment.

We were able to look at the relationship between family dynamics and individual well-being in two ways. First, we examined the relationship between spouses' reports of satisfaction with their marriage 6 months prior to the husband's job loss and their psychological responses to unemployment at two later points during the unemployment experience. We also looked at the relationship between various aspects of family functioning that we measured shortly after unemployment occurred and the psychological well-being of husbands and wives 4 months into the unemployment experience.

Although the limited size of our research sample prevents us from testing the model presented in Figure 1 in all its complexity, we are able to report findings relevant to the following aspects of the model:

1. The effects of unemployment on the psychological well-being of the unemployed worker.
2. The effects of unemployment on the psychological well-being of spouses of unemployed workers and on other aspects of family functioning.
3. The role played by preunemployment marital satisfaction and structural family conditions in modifying the effects of unemployment on individual and family functioning.
4. The interrelationships between individual and family effects of unemployment.

THE SAMPLE

Our research sample consists of 82 families in which husbands recently lost their jobs involuntarily. Equal numbers of unemployed blue- and white-collar workers were interviewed together with their wives approximately 2, 4, 7, and 12 months following their job loss. Workers were recruited in the Greater Boston area through screening interviews at local offices of the Massachusetts Division of Employment Security during one of the periods of highest unemployment in Massachusetts in recent years. These workers had experienced stable employment of at least 1-year's duration prior to their job loss; most had been employed for many years before they lost their jobs. Approximately one-third of the wives in the sample were employed full time outside the home. Another third were employed part time, whereas the remainder worked inside the home. All families had at least one child under the age of 18 living at home. Family size varied from 1 to 10 children with the average being 2.4. The age of the workers in the sample is evenly distributed between 21 and 55 years. As might be expected, the ages of the wives and children in these families are similarly varied.

By and large, workers were employed in small- to moderate-sized companies and were laid off during modest but persistent cutbacks rather than as the result of plant closings. The median length of unemployment among this group of workers during the 1-year study period was approximately 4 months; unemployment ranged from 1 month to more than a year with 10% of the workers remaining unemployed at the time of the last interview.

A matched group of 82 continuously employed men and their families were identified through a combination of telephone surveys based on town census data and random screenings at grocery stores in each area from which the unemployed were sampled. Employed families were successfully matched, pairwise, with unemployed families on family size, husband's age and occupation, age of the youngest child, and wife's work status.

THE INTERVIEW

Two-hour conjoint interviews with husbands and wives were conducted by trained interviewers in each family's home four times during the course of a year. Interviews contained both structured and semi-structured questions as well as interviewer initiated and self-administered procedures. For example, spouses recalled recent family problems together but completed paper-and-pencil inventories of psychological symptoms independently. The main topics covered in each of the four interviews were the recent work histories of each spouse, family finances, various areas of family functioning (e.g., household maintenance, child rearing, the marital relationship), relationships with friends, relatives, and neighbors, the job hunt, and physical and psychological well-being.

MEASURES

Individual Functioning of Husbands and Wives

The aspects of individual functioning that are the focus of this chapter were measured in three ways: (1) husbands' and wives' affective states were assessed using the 10-item Bradburn Affect Balance Scale (1969). This measure produces separate, modestly correlated estimates of positive and negative mood; (2) husbands' and wives' psychological well-being was assessed with the Johns Hopkins Derogatis Brief Symptom Inventory (1977). Seven symptom subscales and a total symptom score were used; (3) role performance was assessed with two 7-item measures developed for this research. Spouses were asked to assess their own and each other's performance in various areas of family functioning, that is, as a parent, as a breadwinner, as a sexual partner.

Family Functioning

Five areas of family functioning were also studied. Findings regarding both the effects of unemployment on these aspects of family well-being and the role played by these family factors in conditioning the effects of unemployment on individual functioning are reported next. The areas include (1) the Quality of the Marital Relationship that was assessed using several single-item questions regarding each spouse's satisfaction with the marriage, perceptions of the supportiveness of their relationship, assessments of the quality of their marriage compared to others they know, and estimates of the frequency of arguments between them. An independent measure of the quality of the marital relationship was also obtained from interviewers who were asked to rate the marital relationship in terms of the degree of conflict and tension versus supportiveness they observed during each interview. (2) The Family Climate that was assessed using the family cohesion, family conflict, and family organization subscales of the Moos Family Environment Scale (1974).

The Family Environment Scale is a 27-item true/false scale containing statements describing the emotional climate and degree of organization in the family during the past month.

Other measures of family functioning included (3) the Openness of Communication between husbands and wives that was based on spouses' ratings of three items with which they could strongly agree, agree, disagree, or strongly disagree; for example, "My spouse is someone with whom I can talk about almost anything." (4) The Power relationship in the family that was measured using a decision-making questionnaire completed independently by husbands and wives and a rating by interviewers of who dominated the discussion during the interview. The family decision-making questionnaire is a 10-item scale developed for this research. Through it, husbands and wives indicated who had the final say when there was a disagreement about what to do in various areas of family functioning. (5) The Division of Labor within the family that was based on who performed different family activities, for example, feeding, bathing, or dressing the children, shopping for groceries, doing minor repairs. Subscales were created for child rearing, financial management, household chores, and the coordination of family activities. Spouses indicated on a 5-point scale whether each activity was done more often by the husband, wife, or both spouses equally. The first three measures of family functioning address the quality of interaction within the family, whereas the measures of decision making and division of labor characterize the way in which family roles are defined.

Preunemployment Marital Satisfaction

A single-item measure of the degree of satisfaction with the marriage 6 months prior to the husband's unemployment was completed independently by husbands and wives at the time of the first interview. Because this was a retrospective measure and, therefore, vulnerable to the effects of unemployment, we looked to see if husbands and wives in unemployed families recalled greater dissatisfaction with their marriages than employed husbands and wives. We found no significant differences between the two groups. In approximately 85% of both employed and unemployed families, husbands and wives recalled feeling considerable satisfaction with their marriages six months prior to the interview; 15%, on the other hand, recalled feelings of dissatisfaction. We found substantial agreement between husbands and wives regarding the preunemployment quality of their marriages. Their ratings were significantly correlated ($r = .46$; $p = .0001$), and a case-by-case examination of them revealed that 93 out of 167 pairs were in complete agreement; spouses' ratings differed by more than 1 point in only 14 cases. Our measure of preunemployment marital satisfaction, although imperfect, is therefore a reasonable estimate of the quality of the marital relationship prior to the husband's job loss.

Family Conditions

A determination of the social class standing of each family was made on the basis of the husband's occupation. Husbands in blue-collar families were engaged in occupations requiring skilled or semiskilled manual labor, whereas those in white-collar families worked in professional or managerial positions. Dual-career versus single-breadwinner status was based on the number of hours per week wives worked outside the home. Dual-career families are those in which wives worked 30 or more hours per week outside the home. Single-breadwinner families are those in which wives worked within the home and engaged in fewer than 10 hours per week of paid labor. About one third of the families fell into each of these categories. In another third of the families, wives worked part-time (from 10 to 30 hours per week). The effects of wives' part-time employment outside the home are considered separately in the analyses examining the conditioning effects of dual-career versus single-breadwinner status on the psychological consequences of unemployment. Family size is based on the total number of children in the family, whereas the husband's age serves as our approximation of the family's location in the life cycle. (Husbands' and wives' ages in this sample are very similar.)

RESULTS

The Effects of Unemployment on the Unemployed Worker

We have already reported elsewhere (Liem, Atkinson, & Liem, 1982; Liem & Rayman, 1982; Liem & Liem, 1988) findings of substantial increases in psychological distress among workers as a direct consequence of unemployment. We will, therefore, provide only a brief summary of those findings here.

The psychological effects of unemployment on dislocated workers that we have observed are similar to those reported by Warr, Jackson, and Banks (1988). In comparison to individuals who had not lost their jobs, unemployed workers experienced significantly higher levels of psychological symptoms shortly following their job loss. The differences between the employed and unemployed workers in terms of symptom totals were largely the product of increases in anxiety and depression among the unemployed. Unemployed workers also reported more psychosomatic complaints and greater hostility and paranoia than their employed counterparts though the differences between the two groups on these measures were less dramatic. As one might expect, unemployed men also reported significantly less positive and more negative moods states than did their employed counterparts. They and their wives also agreed that their performance of marital, parental, and household responsibilities diminished as a result of their unemployment.

By the second interview, approximately 4 months following job loss, unemployed workers reported further increases in psychological symptomatology, again primarily in the areas of depression and anxiety. These emotional reactions leveled off at midyear but were followed by a further increase in psychological symptoms at the fourth interview, 1 year after the initial job loss. However, the findings at the end of the year are based on very few cases and must be treated with caution. In fact, for the most part, the findings reported in this chapter pertain only to the first two waves of interviews at which time a substantial number of workers are unemployed.

The response of reemployed workers to securing a job between the first and second interviews was one of considerable emotional relief. There was a dramatic decline in psychological symptoms among this group following their return to work; a pattern that suggests that it is the job loss and not some unmeasured factor that caused the increase in psychological distress among the unemployed men in our sample. The positive effects of reemployment like the stressful effects of continuing unemployment, level off at midyear.[1] However, workers who became reemployed prior to the fourth interview again exhibited a significant decline in symptoms.

---

[1]Although differences in psychological well-being between unemployed workers and their controls continue to be significant at the time of the third interview after approximately 7 months of unemployment, the absolute differences between the two groups did not increase, and in some cases actually decreased. The midyear interviews also revealed less psychological gain as a result of reemployment. That is, workers who became reemployed between the second and third interviews did not show the same immediate reduction in psychological symptomatology demonstrated by workers who became reemployed between the first and second interviews.

The Effects of Unemployment on Spouses
and on Family Functioning

Effects on Spouses. Our data indicate that unemployment has an effect not only on unemployed workers but on spouses and the family system as well. Wives of unemployed workers, like their husbands, experienced increased psychological distress as a result of their husbands' unemployment. Their responses differed from those of their spouses in two ways, however: Significant increases in psychological symptoms (comparing wives of unemployed and employed men) did not occur until the second interview, approximately 4 months after their husband's job loss, and the absolute level of these effects among wives was not as great as among their husbands. There was only a marginal increase in symptoms of depression among wives of unemployed workers when compared to wives of employed workers at the time of the first interview. At the second interview, after 4 months of the husband's unemployment, however, these wives reported significant increases in somatic complaints, interpersonal sensitivity, hostility, depression, and anxiety.

By the time of the third interview, only the wives of unemployed blue-collar workers continued to report increases in symptoms. Wives of unemployed white-collar workers on the other hand reported a significant decrease in anxiety. Furthermore, there was no decline in the emotional distress of spouses of either blue- or white-collar workers who were reemployed by the time of the third interview.

This pattern at midyear is similar to the pattern observed for husbands (see Note 1). We have suggested elsewhere (Liem & Liem, 1988) that it may reflect a certain degree of accommodation to unemployment on the part of continuously unemployed families and a disruption in that accommodation for those who return to work at this point in time. This observation is consistent with findings reported by Warr *et al.* (1988) who describe a stabilization of "affective well-being" following 6 months of continuing unemployment that they attribute to either "constructive" or "resigned" adaptation. Dooley, Catalano, and Rook (1988) have also reported findings that suggest that a return to work following a period of adaptation to unemployment can create new sources of strain.

As might be expected, wives of unemployed workers also reported less positive and more negative mood states than wives whose husbands were employed. These differences in mood were apparent at both the first and second interviews.

The effects of husbands' unemployment on their wives' ability to carry out marital, parental, and household responsibilities followed a pattern similar to the one just reported for psychological symptoms. Although the role performance of husbands was diminished at the time of the first interview, a similar decline was not observed for wives until the second interview. The fact that wives responded to their husband's unemployment with significant increases in psychological symptomatology and diminished role performance only after their husband's unemployment had persisted for at least 4 months suggests that wives' responses may have been mediated at least in part by their husbands' psychological states as a result of job loss. Dew, Bromet, and Schulberg (1987) report precisely this pattern of mediation. We examine the mediating role played by the husband's psychological state later in this chapter.

Effects on Family Functioning: The Quality of Family Interaction. The psychological costs of unemployment are apparent not only in terms of the personal distress experienced by husbands and wives but in terms of changes that occurred in the quality of the interaction between spouses. We have already reported in some detail about deterioration in marital support and the quality of the marital relationship associated with unemployment (Atkinson, Liem, & Liem, 1986). Unemployed workers described their marriages as considerably less supportive than employed respondents. The difference was most pronounced at the time of the second interview after 4 months of unemployment. They also reported arguing with their spouses more frequently than employed men. A significant decline in the marital relationship occurred between the first and the second interviews for men who remained unemployed. For reemployed men, on the other hand, there was an increase in marital supportiveness following reemployment. Wives' assessments of the quality of the marital relationship closely paralleled those of their husbands,[2] though they tended to be aware of the negative effects of unemployment on the relationship somewhat earlier than their husbands were.

The strongest confirmation of these negative effects of unemployment, however, is provided by interviewers' assessments of the marital relationship made immediately after each interview.[3] Interviewers ob-

---

[2]Agreement between spouses regarding the quality of the marital relationship, family cohesion, and the openness of communication was estimated with both correlation coefficients and the percentage of cases in perfect or near-perfect agreement. The Pearson Correlations for these variables are $r = .48$ (marital relationship, $r = .48$ (family cohesion), and $r = .51$ (openness of communication). Percentage agreement or near agreement is 94%, 90%, and 95%, respectively.

[3]Trained interviewers were assigned to families on a rotating basis. For the most part, families were seen and evaluated by different interviewers at each interview. Interviewers

served significantly greater conflict and less support in unemployed as compared to employed families at the first as well as the second interview. They also observed the negative effects on the marital relationship of continued unemployment and the positive effects of reemployment for those families in which the husband returned to work between the first and second interviews. Mean ratings at the first interview based on a scale from 1 to 5 where five equals "tense and conflicted" were 2.65 for unemployed families and 2.18 for employed families; $F = 8.44, p = .004$. At the second interview, the mean rating for unemployed families was 2.92. It was 2.15 for reemployed families and 2.25 for employed families; $F = 7.68, p = .001$.

Reported changes in the overall family climate were similar to changes in the quality of the marital relationship. As indicated by the Moos Family Environment Scale (1974), husbands and wives coping with unemployment reported significantly less cohesion and more conflict in their families than did spouses in control families. These changes were apparent shortly after unemployment occurred (i.e., at the time of the first interview) but were most prominent after 4 months of joblessness, a time when both spouses also described their family role performance as having deteriorated.

One especially important characteristics of families that are able to deal effectively with stressful events appears to be the quality of communication between husbands and wives. Family therapists in particular have observed a close relationship between open and full communication between spouses and the successful resolution of problems in therapy. Pearlin and McCall (Chapter 3 this volume) describe marital support that is effective in reducing occupational stress as a process of communication and exchange between spouses.

We found that spouses' perceptions of the quality of communication in their relationship were themselves affected by unemployment. Unemployed husbands when compared with employed controls reported no differences in the openness of communication in their families right after their job loss. By the fourth month, however, they felt that communication with their wives was significantly less open. Based on scores ranging from 3 to 13 with 13 reflecting less open communication, a mean rating of 5.63 was reported by unemployed husbands, whereas the average rating of both reemployed and employed husbands was 4.75; $F = 3.75, p = .03$. Wives of unemployed workers on the other hand per-

---

were aware that they were participating in a study of the effects of work and unemployment on family life. They were not, however, aware of the specific hypotheses being investigated by the study.

ceived immediate deterioration in the quality of communication with their spouses (5.26 vs. 4.13 for wives of unemployed vs. employed workers; $F = 11.54$, $p = .001$ at the time of the first interview) and continued to perceive communication problems after 4 months of unemployment as well (wives of unemployed workers = 5.48; reemployed workers = 4.83, and employed workers = 4.57, $F = 4.54$, $p = .01$).

One of the most dramatic indications that unemployment is a potent threat to the marital relationship was the 7 to 2 ratio of separations and divorces among the unemployed compared to the employed families in our sample. Although these numbers and the research sample, itself, are too small to provide a reliable estimate of the risk of marital breakdown during unemployment, they strongly suggest that unemployment can be a significant threat to the marital relationship. Others have estimated that marital dissolution is twice as high among families where the husband is unemployed as it is in those experiencing stable employment (Elder & Caspi, 1987; Ross & Sawhill, 1975).

Effects on Family Functioning: Role Definitions. Our data suggest that unemployment has a stronger, more immediate effect on the quality of family interaction than it does on how roles are defined within the family. Studies of unemployment conducted during the Great Depression (e.g., Komarovsky, 1940) often reported a decline in the husband's power and authority relative to his wife's as a result of his unemployment. We found no evidence that unemployment changed the balance of power in the families we studied. Neither spouse reported differences in who had the final say in 10 areas of family decision making as a function of unemployment, nor did interviewers observe differences in who dominated the interview sessions.

Although we found no differences in the balance of power between husbands and wives as a result of unemployment, we did observe differences in the manner in which labor was divided within the home but only after 4 months of unemployment. By the second interview, unemployed husbands were doing significantly more child care and household chores than their employed counterparts (for child care, $F = 11.46$, $p = .0001$; for household chores, $F = 3.00$, $p = .05$) and reported participating more relative to their wives in household activities in total ($F = 4.37$, $p = .01$).

These changes no doubt reflect differences between unemployed and employed husbands in the amount of time they had available to devote to family tasks. It is interesting to note, however, that the failure on the part of some unemployed men to take on additional family responsibilities given the availability of more time was directly related to the degree of family cohesion after 4 months of unemployment. As noted, unemployed families reported significantly less family cohesion at the time of the second interview than employed or reemployed families. Those families in which husbands failed to take on additional family responsibilities while unemployed reported even less cohesion than families in which unemployed husbands did perform more of these activities relative to their wives ($F = 4.88$, $p = .009$).

Having identified the main effects of unemployment on workers and their families, our next objective was to examine the dynamic and structural characteristics of families that condition these effects.

Preunemployment Marital Satisfaction and Structural Family Characteristics That Condition the Effects of Unemployment

We were especially interested in undertaking the present study to determine whether family dynamics prior to unemployment and structural characteristics of the family play a role in shaping the effects of unemployment on individual and family functioning. We assumed that factors such as family's social class or location in the life cycle reflect the family's access to social and economic resources and that families with more resources would be more likely to withstand the negative consequences of unemployment.

We also assumed that the quality of the marital relationship prior to the husband's job loss would be a significant influence on the unemployment experience. Based on Komarovsky's (1940) findings from the Great Depression, we expected unemployment to have fewer negative consequences for individuals who were involved in satisfactory marriages at the time the job loss occurred and more deleterious effects for those who were not.

We examined the combined effects of satisfaction with the marriage prior to unemployment and structural family conditions on individual and family functioning using multiple regression analyses. Difference scores contrasting the individual or family functioning of unemployed versus employed workers are used as the dependent variables in these analyses. A significant relationship between one of the predictor variables and one of the outcome variables, therefore, suggests a conditioning effect of that predictor on the degree of difference in the impact of unemployment on the outcome.

The modifying effects of prior satisfaction and family conditions on the impact of unemployment on the worker after 4 months of unemployment are presented in Table 1; similar effects on spouse and family functioning are presented in Table 2. The same analyses were run on

Table 1. The Conditioning Effects of Prior Satisfaction with the Marriage and Family Characteristics on Husbands' Responses to Unemployment after Four Months

	Multiple R	r^2	Prior satisfaction Beta	Social class Beta	Wife's work status Beta	Life cycle Beta	Family size Beta
Total symptoms	.58**	.34	.58**				
Depression	.50**	.25	.50**				
Anxiety	ns						
Hostility	.37*	.13					.37*
Paranoia	.39*	.16	.39*				
Phobia	ns						
Somatic	.37*	.14					.37*
Sensitivity	.50**	.25	.47**		.32*		
Positive mood	.44*	.19	.44*				
Negative mood	.63***	.39	.63***				
Role 1[a]	.58**	.34	.58**				
Role 2[b]	.69***	.47	.49**			.38*	

[a]Role 1 = the husband's assessment of his family role performance.
[b]Role 2 = the wife's assessment of her husband's family role performance.
*p = .05; **p = .01; ***p = .001.
Note. The coefficients presented are based on stepwise multiple regressions. Variables have been coded so that high scores represent more negative outcomes. For example, a high score on positive mood = less positive mood whereas a high score on negative mood = more negative mood. Positive betas between prior marital satisfaction and the dependent variables indicate that husbands who reported having less satisfactory marriages prior to their unemployment are the ones reporting more psychological symptoms, more negative and less positive moods, and poorer role performance in comparison with their employed controls. The relationship is further illustrated using the mean scores for husbands' total psychological symptoms as the dependent measure. Husbands have been categorized as having had satisfactory marriages prior to unemployment if husbands reported being satisfied or very satisfied with their marriages 6 months before the first interview. They have been categorized as having unsatisfactory marriages if husbands chose ratings of somewhat satisfying or not at all satisfying to characterize their marriages 6 months ago.

	Unemployed	Reemployed	Employed
Satisfactory marriages	.47	.29	.28
Unsatisfactory marriages	.91	.46	.48

data collected at the time of the first interview, after 1 to 2 months of unemployment. The findings at each point in time are much the same. If anything, the modifying effects of prior satisfaction with the marriage appear stronger after more time has transpired between the assessment of marital satisfaction and assessments of individual and family functioning.

Prior Marital Satisfaction. The findings indicate a significant conditioning effect of prior satisfaction with the marriage on the relationship between unemployment and individual and family functioning at both

Table 2. The Conditioning Effects of Prior Satisfaction with the Marriage and Family Characteristics on Spouse and Family Response to Unemployment after Four Months

	Multiple R	r^2	Prior satisfaction Beta	Social class Beta	Wife's work status Beta	Life cycle Beta	Family size Beta
Total symptoms	ns						
Depression	ns						
Anxiety	.34*	.12	.34*				
Hostility	ns						
Paranoia	.37*	.13	.37*				
Phobia	.35*	.12	.35*				
Somatic	ns						
Sensitivity	.39*	.15	.39*				
Positive mood	ns						
Negative mood	ns						
Role 1[a]	.64***	.41	.64***				
Role 2[b]	.48*	.23	.48*				
Family							
Cohesion	.51**	.26	.51**				
Conflict	.43*	.19	.43*				
Organization	.35*	.12			−.35*		
Marital relation-I[c]	ns						
Marital relation-H[c]	.70***	.49	.70***				
Communication-W[c]	ns						

[a]Role 1 = the wife's assessment of her family role performance.
[b]Role 2 = the husband's assessment of his wife's family role performance.
[c]Marital relation-I = the interviewer's assessment of the marital relationship; marital relation-H = the husband's assessment of the marital relationship; and communication-W = the wife's assessment of the quality of communication between spouses.
*p = .05; **p = .01; ***p ≤ .001.
Note. The coefficients presented are based on stepwise multiple regressions.

the first and second interview. Men who reported satisfactory marriages prior to unemployment experienced significantly less depression, interpersonal sensitivity, paranoia, and total psychological symptoms in comparison to their employed counterparts after 2 and 4 months of unemployment than men who described their marriages as unsatisfactory. They also experienced more positive and less negative mood than men who felt their marriages to be unsatisfactory. Their family role performance as judged both by themselves and by their spouses was also more adequate than the performance of men in unsatisfactory marriages, again using comparisons of the performance of unemployed men and their matched controls.

Prior satisfaction with the marriage had a similar ameliorating effect on the relationship between unemployment and individual well-being for the wives of unemployed men. Women who reported being satisfied with their marriages prior to their husband's job loss were less anxious, less paranoid, and experienced less interpersonal sensitivity after 2 and 4 months of their husband's unemployment than women who viewed their marriages prior to their husband's job loss in less positive terms. Their affective state was also more positive, and they were able to perform their family responsibilities more effectively than women in less satisfactory marriages. After 4 months of unemployment women who described their marriages prior to their husband's unemployment in more positive terms were also less phobic than women in less satisfactory marriages.

The effects of unemployment on family cohesion, family conflict, and the ability of spouses to be supportive of one another were also influenced by spouses' preunemployment satisfaction with their marriage. Unemployment diminished cohesion and increased conflict more dramatically in those families that were already experiencing some dissatisfaction with their marital relationship prior to unemployment. It also affected more negatively the ability of spouses to be supportive of one another during the unemployment period.

This effect is seen most clearly in relation to couples who separated or divorced during their unemployment. They were the couples who reported being most dissatisfied with their marriages prior to unemployment. They were also more likely to have been rated by interviewers as having a tense and conflicted relationship at the time of the first interview than other unemployed couples. In one sense, these couples reflect in the extreme what we observed for all our respondents in the analyses involving satisfaction with the marriage prior to unemployment. Those people who experienced dissatisfaction with their relationships encountered the unemployment with greater likelihood of facing both personal and family strains.

The retrospective nature of our measure of prior satisfaction with the marriage argues for caution regarding the interpretation of these results. The fact that there were no significant differences between unemployed and employed families in their assessment of prior satisfaction is encouraging, however. It suggests that spouses' retrospective assessments of their marriages were not unduly influenced by the husband's job loss. The fact that there was considerable agreement between husbands and wives regarding the status of their marriages 6 months before the husband's unemployment also enhances the credibility of the prior satisfaction measure. The stronger conditioning effect of prior marital satisfaction on outcomes at the second rather than the first interview when respondents made their retrospective assessments of the marriage also weakens the response bias argument. We conclude tentatively, therefore, that the quality of the marital relationship prior to unemployment had a significant effect on how unemployed workers and their families responded to the husband's job loss.

Wheaton (Chapter 8 this volume) has observed a similar relationship between the existence of marital problems and increased distress in the face of unemployment for women who have lost their jobs but not for men. He has found somewhat surprisingly that in his sample, men with marital problems experienced less distress in response to unemployment than men who reported no problems with their marriages.

Family Characteristics: Social Class. We were surprised to find that the structural family conditions that we examined, on the other hand, had very little effect on the relationship between unemployment and individual and family functioning. We found no significant differences, for example, between blue-collar and white-collar families in terms of the effects of unemployment on psychological well-being or family functioning, at least not in the first 4 months of unemployment. This does not mean of course that the unemployment experience is necessarily identical for both groups. In fact, it stands in sharp contrast to the observation that six of the seven families who separated or divorced during unemployment were blue-collar families. It may be that the particular losses created by the unemployment and/or the resistance resources available to cope with those losses do differ for blue- and white-collar families but the differences balance out in ways that result in equally negative health consequences.

Analyses reported elsewhere that focus on the actual duration of unemployment rather than a worker's employment status at particular points in time (Atkinson, Liem, & Liem, 1986) indicate that the decline in marital supportiveness follows a somewhat different path in blue- and white-collar families, for example. The decline occurs earlier in the unemployment experience for blue-collar families and remains fairly constant over time. For white-collar families, there is a more gradual decline in marital supportiveness; the quality of the relationship deteriorates steadily as the husband's unemployment persists. When examined in the fourth month of unemployment, however, the significant decline in marital supportiveness observed in unemployed families in comparison to employed families looks no different for blue- and white-collar families. Both groups of unemployed families by this time have marital relationships that are showing the strain from unemployment.

It is clear from our data that unemployment was a source of greater financial hardship for blue- as opposed to white-collar families. Blue-collar workers had lower-paying jobs to begin with, less savings, and fewer alternative sources of income with which to offset the financial losses created by unemployment. On the other hand, blue-collar families described themselves as having significantly more frequent contact with members of their social network than white-collar families and more often received emotional support from friends, relatives, or neighbors when coping with problems (Atkinson, Liem, & Liem, 1986).

It may be that the anxiety and depression experienced by blue-collar men were largely the product of the financial strain unemployment placed on their families that, in turn, was ameliorated somewhat by supportive social relationships outside the workplace. The psychological distress experienced by white-collar men who lost their jobs, on the other hand, may have resulted more from the loss of status and social connectedness provided by their work; losses that took their toll on the family more slowly but were exasperated by the absence of affirming social relationships. The end result, however, was similar increases in levels of emotional distress for both groups of men.

Attempting to specify the full range of losses associated with unemployment as well as the resistance resources available to blue- and white-collar families to cope with those losses is beyond the scope of this study. What is clear from our findings to date is that unemployment has negative effects on individual and family functioning in both blue- and white-collar families, and those effects, at least during the first 4 to 5 months of unemployment, appear to be quite similar in overall intensity.

Family Characteristics: Dual-Career vs. Single-Breadwinner Families. We found only two differences in individual and family responses to unemployment that were influenced significantly by the work statuses of wives. Unemployed husbands whose wives were full-time homemakers experienced greater differences in their levels of interpersonal sensitivity relative to employed husbands than did husbands whose wives worked full-time outside the home. In contrast, however, they experienced their family's routine and organization as less disrupted by their job loss when their wives were full-time homemakers.

We observed no other differences between dual-career versus single-breadwinner families either in terms of the psychological consequences of unemployment for husbands or wives or in terms of family well-being in general. Few differences between these two family types materialized in spite of the presence of significant differences in the financial resources available to them. It appears that the financial advantage of the dual-career families may have been negated by other stresses inherent in the dual-career life-style. Spouses in dual-career families, for example, described their marriages as less supportive and reported having greater difficulty finding time for one another than spouses in single-breadwinner families.

Bolger, DeLongis, Kessler, and Wethington, in another chapter in this volume, look in some detail at the daily stresses and strains that occur in dual-career and single-breadwinner families. They, too, find that the combination of work and family roles has both positive and negative consequences for both wives and husbands. Our findings suggest that the advantages and disadvantages of dual-career versus single-breadwinner family arrangements balance out when families are coping with unemployment.

Family Characteristics: Place in the Life Cycle and Size. The family's place in the life cycle also failed to condition the effects of unemployment on individual and family functioning with one exception. Wives of unemployed husbands in older families observed significantly greater deterioration in their husbands' performance of family responsibilities after 4 months of unemployment than wives in younger families.

Only two differences were apparent in the way unemployed husbands responded to their job loss when they had large as opposed to small families to support. Unemployed husbands with larger families reported greater feelings of hostility and more psychosomatic complaints than unemployed husbands with small families.

Neither set of findings suggest a critical role of place in the life cycle or size in determining the impact of unemployment in this sample. These characteristics were not, however, important in the selection of respondents for this study, and we would not want to rule out their significance based on the findings from this sample alone.

Interrelationships between Individual and Family Functioning

We have seen that unemployment had an immediate, negative effect on the psychological well-being, mood, and role performance of these unemployed workers followed by an increase in personal distress with continuing unemployment. Effects of unemployment on the wives of unemployed workers were similar but did not occur until their husbands had been out of work for at least 4 months. Although some effects of unemployment on the quality of family interaction were apparent 2 months after the husband's job loss, they, too, became more dramatic as unemployment persisted. The delayed response to unemployment on the part of wives and the correspondence between the unemployed worker's increasing personal distress and the deterioration in family functioning suggest that the effects of unemployment on the family may have been mediated at least in part by the husband's reactions to his unemployment. Deterioration in marital supportiveness, the quality of communication between spouses, family cohesion, and the wife's psychological well-being may have resulted from increases in husbands' anxiety, depression, or hostility created by his unemployment. It is also possible that this process of effect may work both ways such that husbands' emotional responses are also influenced over time by direct effects of unemployment on the family.

We tested both possibilities using hierarchical regressions first to compare the relationship between unemployment and spouse and family functioning at 4 months with and without a control for the husband's psychological well-being at 2 months. We then reversed the procedure and examined changes in the relationship between unemployment and husbands' psychological well-being at the fourth month of unemployment controlling for spouse and family functioning 2 months earlier.

We used the psychological symptom measure (Derogatis, 1977) and the role performance measure as our estimates of individual functioning in these analyses. The husband's assessment of the marital relationship, the interviewer's assessment of the marital relationship, the wife's assessment of the quality of communication between spouses, and cohesion in the family (Moos & Insel, 1974) were our measures of family functioning. We assumed that a decline in the observed relationship between unemployment and spouse or family functioning after controlling for the husband's total symptom score at the time of the first interview combined with a significant beta weight for his symptom score would suggest mediation of the relationship by the husband's psychological well-being. Similarly, a decline in the observed relationship between unemployment and the husband's psychological well-being or role performance following controls for the wife's symptom score or measures of family functioning at the time of the first interview combined with significant beta weights for those variables would suggest mediation of the relationship between unemployment and the husband's well-being by these family factors. Findings from these analyses are summarized in Tables 3 and 4.

The findings support our first line of reasoning that the delayed effects of unemployment on spouse and family functioning suggest me-

Table 3. Mediation of Changes in Spouse and Family Functioning by Husband's Psychological Well-Being

Change in	Unemployment without mediator Beta	Unemployment with mediator Beta	Beta for mediator[a] Beta
Wives			
Total symptoms	.22*	.13	.32**
Depression	.30**	.19†	.34**
Anxiety	.19†	.10	.29**
Hostility	.21*	.11	.28**
Paranoia	.21*	.11	.38***
Sensitivity	.19†	.16	.21†
Role 1[b]	.28**	.16	.37***
Role 2[c]	.35***	.23*	.38***
Family			
Marital relation-I	.34**	.23*	.24*
Marital relation-H	.32**	.19†	.44***
Communication-W	.18†	.08	.23**
Family cohesion	.21†	.10	.48***

[a] The mediator employed in these analyses is the husband's psychological symptom total on the Brief Syptom Inventory (Derogatis, 1977).
[b] Role 1 = the wife's assessment of her family role performance.
[c] Role 2 = the husband's assessment of the wife's family role performance.
†p = .10; *p = .05; **p = .01; ***p = .001.

diation of these changes by the effect of unemployment on the psychological well-being of the unemployed worker. The reduction to nonsignificance of 8 out of 12 regression coefficients between unemployment and indexes of spouse and family functioning when the husband's total symptom score at the time of the first interview was entered into the regression as well as substantial decreases in the other four coefficients indicate that the psychological impact of unemployment on these men accounted substantially for the increased distress experienced by wives. Changes in the husbands' well-being were also responsible in large part for the deterioration in wives' role performance and in quality of the marital relationship that accompanied continued unemployment. These findings are consistent with others we have reported showing that changes in marital support are mediated more by the husband's psychological response to unemployment than by the wife's (Atkinson, Liem, & Liem, 1986). They also reflect a similar process of mediation documented by Dew, Bromet, and Schulberg (1987). Elder and Caspi (1988) also found that changes in the unemployed worker's behavior play a key role in mediating the effects of income loss on the marital relationship

Table 4. Mediation of Changes in the Husband's Psychological Well-Being and Role Performance by Spouse and Family Functioning

Mediators	Change in					
	H's total symptoms			H's role performance		
	Un 1[a]	Un 2[b]	Beta[c]	Un 1	Un 2	Beta
Wife's total symptoms	.25*	.19	.34**	.28**	.22*	.39**
Marital relation-I	.25*	.24*	.03	.28**	.21*	.22*
Marital relation-H	.25*	.23*	.33**	.28**	.26**	.59***
Communication-W	.25*	.19	.13	.28**	.09	.47***
Family cohesion	.25*	.23*	.20*	.28**	.28**	.40***

[a]Un 1 = the effects of continuous unemployment without mediators.
[b]Un 2 = the effects of continuous unemployment with mediators.
[c]Beta = beta for mediator.
*p = .05; **p = .01; ***p = .001.

and on parenting behavior that in turn affect the well-being of children in unemployed families.

There is only modest support from the findings reported in Table 4 for the position that changes in the psychological well-being of spouses or in family functioning due to unemployment mediate the psychological effects of unemployment on husbands. There are modest effects of wife's psychological state on the husband's psychological well-being and role performance and similarly modest effects on the quality of the marital relationship as assessed by the interviewer and the quality of communication between spouses as assessed by the wife on the husband's role performance. It appears in general, however, that in the early months of unemployment, the personal distress of the unemployed worker has a far more significant influence on the wife's and family's response to unemployment than do their responses on the husband's reactions. The psychological impact of unemployment on workers appears in the first few months to be associated more with the financial strain created by unemployment (Kessler et al., 1988; Liem & Liem, 1988) and with the loss of intrinsically rewarding work (Liem & Liem, 1988) than it is with changes occurring in the family.

The limited role played by spouse and family functioning in mediating the effects of unemployment on husbands is not altogether surprising given the limited effects of unemployment on spouse and family functioning at the time of the first interview. The pattern over more extended periods of unemployment may well be more reciprocal, however, given the greater change in spouse and family functioning with time. Furthermore, it is apparent that wives' psychological well-being, the quality of the marital relationship, and the family climate have a bearing on husbands' emotional distress as evidenced by the beta weights for those factors presented in Table 4. Therefore, as these conditions change in response to the husband's mood, they may in turn, affect his psychological state at a later time.

CONCLUSION

Much of the psychological research on dislocated workers treats unemployment as a stressful event in the life of an individual. It is clear from the research we have conducted that unemployment affects not only individuals who lose their jobs but their spouses and families as well. The interdependence of workplace and family is attested to by our findings indicating that spouses of unemployed workers like workers themselves experienced increases in depression, anxiety, and other psychological symptoms, as well as diminished role performance, when their husbands remained out of work for an extended period of time. Family strain was also evident in the decreased supportiveness and heightened conflict in the marital relationship as unemployment persisted. Communication between spouses weakened, and families became less cohesive. For some families, stress precipitated by the worker's separation from the workplace was so great that separation or divorce was the final outcome.

A critical factor in the process that produced these effects during the early stages of unemployment appears to have been the husband's reactions to his job loss. The husband's heightened anxiety and depression accounted in large part for his wife's distress. It also influenced the climate within the family and affected the marital relationship in particular. As husbands became more sullen and tense, it became harder for spouses to be supportive, harder for them to talk with their husbands, and harder in general to maintain a sense of cohesiveness within the family.

Gradually a small body of work is beginning to appear (Atkinson, Liem, & Liem, 1986; Dew, Bromet, & Schulberg, 1987; Elder & Caspi, 1988) confirming this pattern of relationships among worker and family responses to unemployment. Piotrkowski (1979) has observed a similar pattern for employment-related stresses. Stresses at work become psychologically salient for the family system via their effects on the emotional and interpersonal availability of the worker. Rather than simply a haven from the workplace, the family is, therefore, structurally bound to it. Through his or her dual occupancy in the workplace and family, the worker serves as a structural link between each system, confirming Kanter's view of them as critical, interacting spheres of influence on people's lives.

We found, furthermore, that the extent to which individual and family effects of unemployment occur was dependent on family dynamics before and early in the unemployment. Men with satisfactory marital relationships experienced significantly less psychological distress in the face of unemployment than those for whom the job loss added stress to existing family strains. For the latter group, problems in the home were compounded by problems initiated in the domain of work resulting in the highest levels of anxiety, depression, and other psychological symptoms.

Researchers studying unemployment during the Great Depression (Angell, 1936; Cavan & Ranck, 1938; Komarovsky, 1940) also observed an important role for the family in conditioning the psychological impact of unemployment. In much of that research, however, conditions like the quality of the marital relationship (i.e., whether it was primarily utilitarian or emotionally supportive) were most often treated as stable, intrinsic characteristics of the family.

Our findings suggest a less static view of the quality of family relationships. For example, not only did we find that the marital relationship was responsive to changes in husbands' mood during the course of unemployment; we also observed a significant relationship between external conditions and the level of marital satisfactions prior to the loss of work. Satisfaction with one's marriage prior to unemployment was significantly and inversely correlated with the number of stressful life events a couple experienced during the preceding year.

This relationship can be seen most clearly among couples who separated or divorced during the study period. As noted earlier, these respondents were least satisfied with their marriages before they encountered unemployment. They also experienced the largest number of negative life events prior to the job loss that helps to account for their greater marital dissatisfaction.

The impact of unemployment on these families was not, therefore, conditioned by fixed or inherent qualities in the relationships between these spouses but rather by vulnerabilities to some extent dependent themselves on the family's history of contact with the outside world. Our research leads us to the conclusion that understanding how a family handles an assault like unemployment requires not so much the correct classification of its relational or coping style. Instead, it entails the concrete exploration of the family's ongoing exchange with the relevant surrounding context whether that be the kin network, neighborhood, or workplace.

We failed by and large to discover overall differences in the impact of unemployment related to the demographic or structural characteristics of these families, for example, social class, place in the life cycle, or distribution of breadwinning roles. We suspect, however, that our developing sense of the family/workplace relationship as one of continuous exchange rather than periodic interaction can provide a more adequate conceptual basis for reexamining differences in the experience of job loss according to one's position in the social structure. Rather than focusing on the overall impact of unemployment, we would emphasize different areas of dependence between the family and related sources of protection from these vulnerabilities. How the struggle with unemployment takes place and over what terrain may very well be the more relevant questions for the study of social class, family structure, and unemployment.

ACKNOWLEDGMENTS

This research was supported in part by NIMH, Grant No. MH 31316. The authors would like to acknowledge the major contributions of Thomas Atkinson, Stephen McElfresh, and Joseph Schipani to the Work and Unemployment Project.

REFERENCES

Angell, R. C. (1936). *The family encounters the Depression*. New York: Charles Scribner's Sons.

Antonovsky, A. (1974). Conceptual and methodological problems in the study of resistance resources and stressful life events. In B. S. Dohrenwend & B. P. Dohrenwend (Eds.), *Stressful life events: Their nature and effects* (pp. 245–258). New York: Wiley.

Atkinson, T., Liem, R., & Liem, J. (1986). The social costs of unemployment: Implications for social support. *Journal of Health and Social Behavior, 27*, 317–331.

Bradburn, N. (1969). *The structure of psychological well-being*. Chicago: Aldine.

Brenner, H. (1973). *Mental illness and the economy*. Cambridge: Harvard University Press.

Cavan, R. S., & Ranck, K. H. (1938). *The family and the Depression*. Chicago: University of Chicago Press.

Cooper, C. L., & Marshall, J. (1976). Occupational sources of stress: A review of the literature related to coronary heart disease and mental ill health. *Journal of Occupational Psychology, 49*, 11–28.

Cooper, C. L., & Smith, M. J. (Eds.), (1985). *Job stress and blue collar work*. Chichester: Wiley.

Dean, A., & Lin, N. (1977). The stress buffering role of social support. *Journal of Nervous and Mental Disease, 165*, 403–417.

Derogatis, L. (1977). *SCL-90 Administration, Scoring, and Procedures Manual for the revised version*. Baltimore: Clinical Psychometrics Research Unit, Johns Hopkins University School of Medicine.

Dew, M., Bromet, E., & Schulberg, H. (1987). A comparative analysis of two community stressors' long term mental health effects. *American Journal of Community Psychology, 15*(2), 167–184.

Dooley, D., & Catalano, R. C. (1980). Economic change as a cause of behavioral disorder. *Psychological Bulletin, 87*, 450–468.

Dooley, D., Catalano, R., & Rook, K. (1988). Personal and aggregate unemployment and psychological symptoms. In D. Dooley & R. Catalano (Eds), *Psychological effects of unemployment. Journal of Social Issues, 44*(4), 107–124.

Elder, G. (1974). *Children of the great depression: Social change in life experience*. Chicago: University of Chicago Press.

Elder, G., & Caspi, A. (1988). Economic stress in lives: Developmental perspectives. In D. Dooley & R. Catalano (Eds.), *Psychological effects of unemployment. Journal of Social Issues, 44*(4), 25–46.

Fryer, D. (1985). Stages in the psychological response to unemployment: (Dis)integrative review article. *Current Psychological Research and Reviews, 4*, 257–273.

Fryer, D., & Payne, R. (1986). Being unemployed: A review of the literature on the psychological experience of unemployment. In C. L. Cooper & I. Robertson (Eds.), *International review of industrial and organizational psychology* (pp. 235–278). New York: Wiley.

Goldstein, M. J. (1984). Family affect and communication related to schizophrenia. *New Directions for Child Development, 24*, 47–62.

Goldstein, M. J. (1985). Family factors that antedate the onset of schizophrenia and related disorders: The results of a 15 year prospective longitudinal study. *Acta Psychiatrica Scandinavica, 71*, 7–18.

Gore, S. (1978). The effects of social support in moderating the health consequences of unemployment. *Journal of Health and Social Behavior, 19*, 157–165.

Horwitz, A. (1984). The economy and social pathology. *Annual Review of Sociology, 10*, 95–119.

Kanter, R. M. (1977). *Work and family in the U.S.: A critical review and agenda for research and policy*. New York: Russell Sage Foundation.

Kessler, R. C., Turner, J. B., & House, J. S. (1988). The effects of unemployment on health in a community survey: Main, modifying, and mediating effects. In D. Dooley & R. Catalano (Eds.), *Psychological effects of unemployment. Journal of Social Issues, 44*(4), 69–86.

Komarovsky, M. (1940). *The unemployed man and his family*. New York: Dryden Press.

Larson, J. H. (1984). The effect of husband's unemployment on marital and family relations in blue collar families. *Family Relations, 33*, 503–511.

Liem, J. H. (1980). Family studies of schizophrenia: An update and commentary. *Schizophrenia Bulletin, 6*(3), 429–455.

Liem, R., & Liem, J. H. (1988). The psychological effects of unemployment on workers and their families. In D. Dooley & R. Catalano (Eds.), *Psychological effects of unemployment. Journal of Social Issues, 44*(4), 87–106.

Liem, R., Atkinson, T., & Liem, J. H. (1982). The work and unemployment project: Personal and family effects of job loss. *Proceedings of the National Conference on Social Stress*. University of New Hampshire.

Liem, R., & Rayman, P. (1982). Health and social costs of unemployment: Research and policy considerations. *American Psychologist, 37*, 1116–1123.

Lin, N., Simeone, R. S., Ensel, W. M., & Kuo, W. (1979). Social support, stressful life events, and illness: A model and an empirical test. *Journal of Health and Social Behavior, 20*, 108–119.

Moos, R., & Insel, P. (1974). *Combined preliminary manual for the family environment scale, work environment scale, and group environment scale.* Palo Alto: Consulting Psychologists Press.

Minuchin, S. (1974). *Families and family therapy.* Cambridge: Harvard University Press.

Minuchin, S., Rosman, B. L., & Baker, L. (1978). *Psychosomatic families: Anorexia nervosa in context.* Cambridge: Harvard University Press.

Pearlin, L. I., Menaghan, E. G., Lieberman, M. A., & Mullan, J. T. (1981). The stress process. *Journal of Health and Social Behavior, 22,* 337–356.

Piotrkowski, C. S. (1979). *Work and the family system.* New York: Macmillan.

Piotrkowski, C. S., Stark, E., & Burbank, M. (1983). Young women at work: Implications for individual and family functioning. *Occupational Health Nursing,* November, pp. 24–29.

Rapoport, R. N., & Rapoport, R. (1977). *Dual-career families re-examined: New integrations of work and family.* New York: Harper & Row.

Rapoport, R., & Rapoport, R. N., with Blumstead, J. (Eds.). (1978). *Working Couples.* New York: Harper & Row.

Ross, H. L., & Sawhill, L. Y. (1975). *Time of transition: The growth of families headed by women.* Washington, DC: The Urban Institute.

Schlozman, K. L., & Verba, S. (1979). *Inquiry into insult: Unemployment, class, and political response.* Cambridge: Harvard University Press.

Voydanoff, P., & Donnelly, B. W. (1985). *Economic distress, coping, and quality of family life.* Paper presented at symposium entitled, "Economic Distress and Families: Coping Strategies and Social Policy." University of Dayton.

Warr, P. (1985). Job loss, unemployment, and psychological well-being. In V. L. Allen & E. Van de Vliert (Eds.), *Role transitions, explorations, and explanations* (pp. 263–285). New York: Plenum Press.

Warr, P., Jackson, P., & Banks, M. (1988). In D. Dooley & R. Catalano (Eds.), *Psychological effects of unemployment. Journal of Social Issues, 44*(4), 47–68.

Wynne, L. (1984). The epigenesis of relational systems: A model for understanding family development. *Family Process, 23*(3), 297–318.

10

Stress between Work and Family
Summary and Conclusions

JOHN ECKENRODE and SUSAN GORE

The contributors of this book have presented data from a variety of research projects that show the many and dynamic ways in which the worlds or work and family are intricately connected. This interconnectedness becomes even more apparent when stressful experiences in the workplace or the family upset the homeostasis that may otherwise have been achieved between these domains. As such, the investigation of chronic stress in the workplace and disruptions such as job loss becomes a potential window investigators can use to explore normative family processes, just as chronic stress and change in the family informs our understanding of the meaning of work roles.

In this concluding chapter, we will attempt to summarize some of the findings of the previous chapters, particularly as they relate to issues raised in the introduction of this book and in places point to areas we believe need further investigation. The reader is encouraged to refer back to the chapters themselves because the authors often provide illuminating comments concerning the theoretical implications of their findings, limitations of their studies, and directions for future research. The diversity of samples, measures, and analytic procedures employed in these studies must be considered a strength in that it provides us with

JOHN ECKENRODE • Department of Human Development and Family Studies, Cornell University, Ithaca, New York 14853.   SUSAN GORE • Department of Sociology, University of Massachusetts–Boston, Boston, Massachusetts 02115.

a multimethod assessment of a broad set of issues; the smaller and more descriptive studies providing insights on microprocesses that in turn inform statistical relationships uncovered in the larger community studies. Such diversity, on the other hand, often precludes a direct comparison of empirical findings across studies, so that the basis for any lack of agreement between authors is difficult to precisely pinpoint. However, we believe that these chapters, rather than providing the material for a meta-analysis of this literature, open the door for new theories, concepts, and approaches to the study of work, family, and their interface.

MECHANISMS IMPLICATED IN THE TRANSMISSION OF STRESS BETWEEN WORK AND FAMILY

It is apparent from these chapters that the spillover of stress from work to family and from family to work is not uncommon, occurs in both directions, and is not restricted to males or females or persons of one social class. The chapter by Bromet, Dew, and Parkinson reports that 56% of these working-class women experience spillover in either direction between work and family. The professional women studied by Emmons and her colleagues have substantially higher incomes, but spillover was also a common theme. For example, one-third of these women thought their careers suffered because of family responsibilities, and there was considerable preoccupation with the negative effects of their work on their children. Because their husbands in general did not see as much family disruption associated with a dual-career household, it will be interesting to see in future analyses with these data who is at risk for poor mental health outcomes. Bromet and her colleagues investigate this issue and report significant effects of spillover on symptoms of depression, even after controlling for other risk factors known to be associated with such symptoms. Bolger and his colleagues also provide direct evidence that specific forms of stress in the home or workplace may carry over as similar types of problems in the other domain. They present evidence at the daily level that arguments at work may in turn lead to an increased likelihood of arguments at home and that task overload at home is in turn related to subsequent job overloads.

In addition to providing further confirmation of the frequency with which negative forms of spillover occur between these domains and the individual psychological effects of perceived spillover, the chapters in this book have explored various mechanisms by which stress is transmitted across the work–family boundary. These transmission processes operate at both the psychological and social levels. Weiss, Pearlin, and Mc-Call, as well as Liem and Liem, provide richly detailed accounts of the how work stress (in these cases for men) enters the home environment through its effects on the worker's self-concept, self-esteem, and emotional states. These chapters suggest potent ways in which failures and setbacks in the workplace threaten not only the financial well-being of individuals and their families but also attack the worker's conception of self as competent, valued, and in control of one's own destiny. These altered conceptions of self in turn may lay the groundwork for altered relationships with a spouse or with children. The analyses by Liem and Liem are particularly noteworthy because they trace through time the influence of job loss and unemployment on individual- and family-level processes. The psychological symptoms experienced by these unemployed men appear to set in motion a process in the family that leads to problems in family functioning and a decline in the well-being of their wives. Interestingly, although Liem and Liem uncover disturbance in the quality of the interaction, they did not find the kinds of changes in family role definition, that is, the balance of power, observed in earlier studies of unemployed males workers and their families. This illustrates the importance of using multiple indicators of the effects of interest, and the need for regular reexamination of well-accepted generalizations about the effects of stress.

These chapters also serve to remind us that spillover processes are by no means mechanistic or automatic even though the methodologies we use often make them appear as such by treating "variables" as invariant over persons and contexts. Indeed, even the language we have employed has tended to reinforce mechanistic conceptions in this area of research. Concepts such as "spillover" and "overload" invoke a visual image of a mechanical device (a washing machine comes to mind in this case) rather than a dynamic, human system involving multiple actors responsible for constructing as well as responding to their environment. This is not to deny that phenomenologically some subjects in these research studies report feeling "overloaded," as do the women in the study by Emmons and her colleagues. Rather, if these are to be useful scientific concepts, we need to more clearly specify the meaning of these terms and require that our studies approximate the realities to which they supposedly refer. Weiss, for example, describes how men experiencing work stress will actively orchestrate the transmission of these experiences into the home environment. Although their plans to regulate their emotions or control the gradual and selective disclosure of work-related information to their wives often go astray, what is represented in these accounts is not an image of work stress automatically and uncontrollably spilling over into the home (as if stress were like water leaking into these men's basements) but rather a process involving active cognitive processing, behavioral sequences, and social transactions. Our methodological tools may presently be inadequate to capture the complexity of such processes and their mental health impact, but even here, studies described in this book, such as the one by Bolger and his colleagues, point the way to more sophisticated approaches to these questions.

Despite specifying several psychological and social pathways through which stress is transmitted between work and family, the studies presented here are at times inconclusive as to the mechanisms that might explain significant associations between work-related variables and individual or family outcomes. For example, Cohen and her colleagues report what is likely to be a controversial finding, the link between mothers' employment and conduct disorders, anxiety, and depression in their children. These investigators explored maternal psychopathology, maternal time with the child, quality of the mother's communication with the child, and autonomy from the mother and found that none of these potential mediating processes explained the maternal employment–child psychopathology relationships. These authors speculate about a number of other possible mediating mechanisms they did not investigate (e.g., peer involvement), and in doing so outline some research needs in the area.

At other times, findings reported in these chapters do not always conform to predictions regarding mediating processes that would be made on the basis of existing theoretical perspectives. For example, Bolger and his colleagues point out that a role stress perspective regarding labor force participation of women would predict that working women should experience more overload in the family area than nonworking women. Their detailed diary data do not support this expectation. Such findings call into question some of the predominant conceptualizations (e.g., role conflict) of how work and family roles can intersect to product negative outcomes for the occupants of these roles. However, these data are in keeping with the general pattern of findings regarding the beneficial health effects of women working outside the home.

STRESS-MODERATING INFLUENCES

Represented in the chapters in this volume are at least four types of variables that may modify stress and its transmission across the work–family boundary, leaving individuals either more or less vulnerable to these work or family stressors. These include (1) individual coping behaviors; (2) social support; (3) background or concurrent levels of stress within one role or between roles; and (4) dispositional characteristics or fixed statuses such as gender.

Emmons and her colleagues have provided us with a detailed description of the ways in which the women in their sample reported coping with the difficulties they encountered combining work and family responsibilities. Persisting feelings of overload in both the family and job areas often resulted in reactive coping behaviors they labeled the *superwoman* strategy. We should add, however, that the causal ordering of these variables may be reversed. That is, women who are predisposed to be "superwoman" types may construct overloaded work and family roles. This would be consistent with their finding that the use of problem-focused coping (Lazarus & Folkman, 1984) showed no consistent benefits with regard to alleviating perceived levels of stress or increasing levels of satisfaction in work or family roles, with the exception of perceptions of parenting. On the other hand, a more proactive strategy involving effective planning showed benefits in both the work and family areas and represented the only coping strategy measured here that showed cross-role effects. Women who reported using planning as a strategy for dealing with demands at home also reported less job stress and more job satisfaction. This provides us with a clear example of how functioning in one role can be fully understood only by reference to stress and coping processes occurring in corresponding roles. This finding is also an instance of a positive form of "spillover," in this case from family to work domains. The precise specification of these cross-role effects noted in this sample, however, must await the longitudinal analyses planned for this study that will enable these researchers to investigate changes in stress or functioning due to the adoption of particular coping behaviors.

Social Support

Several of the chapters presented in this book explored social support as a resource for coping with stress in work and family roles. These chapters add to the growing literature documenting the impact of social integration and social support on mental and physical well-being (e.g., Cohen & Syme, 1985). The contribution of the chapters represented here is not so much in their replicating a "stress-buffering" function of social support (that access to intimate and supportive social ties can reduce the statistical relationship between stressful experiences and measures of functioning and well-being) but in outlining some of the complex psychological and social processes that underlay the offering and receipt of support, particularly among family members. Here the chapters by Pearlin and McCall and by Weiss are noteworthy in providing the field with a guide to issues that should be considered in investigations of marital support and occupational stress.

Many lessons can be learned from these two chapters, only a few of which we summarize here. One is that social support, although many times overt and easily observable (and reportable by respondents), is often of a more subtle nature, being subsumed within the normal interpersonal commerce that occurs in relationships, particularly intimate ones. Current approaches to the measurement of social support in community surveys are unlikely to adequately capture these subtle interpersonal exchanges, especially if they are not consciously labeled as *help* or *support* by the participants. It may be that the most effective forms of support are those that are not solicited by the recipient of the aid but those that flow as part of nonextraordinary interpersonal exchanges. Explicit calls for help may in fact signal more severe levels of subjectively perceived stress, a notion consistent with findings reported by Pearlin and Schooler (1978) that help seeking was associated with higher levels of psychological distress in the face of chronic stressors in the work and family areas.

Clearly, not all forms of support, however well meaning, were found by these authors as helpful to the distressed worker. Advice giving, particularly if given too early in the support process, may be viewed as unhelpful and curtails further supportive transactions by undermining the recipient's sense of competence or control. The issue of timing as well as substance is therefore a likely determinant of the effectiveness of social support in these circumstances and as such should be an additional parameter in future research on social support (Jacobson, 1986).

These chapters often go beyond the question of whether social support functions to buffer stress, to ask how this occurs. Pearlin and Mc-Call, for example, discuss the "meaning-shaping" (or cognitive appraisal) function of social support as well as its role in reinforcing individual attempts at coping. Weiss, in turn, suggests that social support from a spouse may have beneficial effects on a worker experiencing stress by bolstering a sense of security and stability at home. This brings to mind Antonovsky's (1979) notion of a "sense of coherence" as a generalized psychological resource for coping with stress and again serves to remind us that overt helping exchanges may tap only a small portion of social support, particularly when discussing intimate relationships.

We suggested in the introduction to this book that stress research needed to go beyond a view of coping resources as static, unmodifiable features of a person's environment or self. Although not well documented in the research literature, there are likely to be empirical relationships between work or family stressors on the one hand and resources thought to buffer those stressors on the other. That is, the stress–health relationship is likely to be mediated by loss of resources. Indeed, the severity of psychosocial stressors may in part be gauged by their degree of negative effects on psychological resources (e.g., mastery beliefs and self-esteem) and the social support network. The studies represented here reinforce this view by providing concrete evidence for the dynamic relationship between stress and the availability of social support. For example, Liem and Liem document the negative impact of unemployment on the quality of the marital relationship, a particularly profound example of how work-related stress may have an impact on the family. This erosion of an important social support resource represents an additional stress for these workers, also leaving them with diminished capacity to deal with future stressors. The onset of difficulties at the family level is further evidence of the social costs of life stress.

Stress as a Contextual Variable

An important part of the context for understanding variations in the impact of work and family stressors on individuals and their families lies not only in the resources available to assist the coping process but also in the constellation of stressors that serve as a background to the family or work problem in question. This is a third type of conditioning process that is easily overlooked in stress research given the prominent emphasis on the support system and other coping resources.

Several of the chapters in this book explore various ways in which stress in one role may condition the impact of stress in a corresponding role area, or how preexisting levels of stress in a given role may determine the effect of a new difficulty arising in that domain. Together, the findings presented here argue against focusing on a single stressor or even a simple additive conception of how stressful experiences combine to affect individual well-being and role functioning. Such additive models underlay much of the field of stress research, particularly that focused on life events (Thoits, 1983). The chapters represented here offer support for an interactive model involving the stressors themselves, whereby stress in one role or at one time may either potentiate or diminish the effects of stress in another role or at another time in the same role.

The chapter by Wheaton explicitly explores these possibilities. He presents and tests the rather elegant hypothesis that the presence of ongoing stress in a given role will moderate the influence of role loss events occurring in those same roles, such as divorce and unemployment, even to the point where positive effects of such presumed stressors may be detected. In this case, life events are understood to mark a transition out of stressful life conditions. A complementary prediction was made when stressors across roles were considered. Here ongoing stress in the work role was predicted to accentuate the negative psychological impact of divorce, whereas ongoing marital problems were predicted to increase the adverse impact of unemployment.

Partial support for these predictions was obtained, particularly with women in the sample, where evidence was found to suggest that the meaning of stressful life events in any role was contingent upon ongoing conditions both in that role and in other roles. So, for the women, having marital problems decreased the effect of divorce, while increasing the effect of job loss, and work problems reduced the effects of job loss. Women in good marriages actually appeared to benefit from job loss. Perhaps job loss for these women helped resolve work–family conflicts or served as a context of strengthening the marital bond.

Alternatively, we see that for women with marital problems there may be a strong need to find success in a different domain, and when there is not, distress results. This is not to say that job success is not as important for men. Wheaton's findings show that whether job problems are more or less important to women is shaped by the broader marital context. This appears not to be the case for men, although for men job loss was also found to have less impact on them in the context of ongoing work problems. Certain of Wheaton's findings for men also suggest some limitations to the straightforward hypotheses guiding this research and the complexity of cross-role effects. The presence of marital problems among men served to *reduce* the effect of job loss (although not to the point where job loss was having a significant positive impact on well-being; see his Table 4). This is a pattern opposite to the one reported for women and stands in contrast to findings reported by Liem and Liem who report that the impact of job loss for men in their sample was exacerbated in the presence of prior marital problems. There are several methodological differences (samples, measures, research design, etc.) between these two studies, however, that may explain this apparent discrepancy. Clearly Wheaton's findings on these stress–stress interactions beg for replication and further exploration with regard to the mechanisms underlying these effects.

At the more microanalytic level, Bolger and his colleagues explored the possibility of daily stressors in one role combining interactively with daily stressors in another role to affect well-being. They found no evidence that arguments at home or work increased the mental health impact of such arguments in the other role. In fact, they found evidence, for men and women, that arguments at work reduced the impact of subsequent arguments at home on the same day (and vice versa). The possible reasons for such an effect are unclear at this time, as these authors point out, but like the results reported by Wheaton, we see the possibility here of nonadditivity among stressful experiences, even without reference to coping resources. Although we hesitate at this time to endorse a general position that stressful experiences are beneficial (given the abundant evidence to the contrary), these studies do begin to outline some conditions under which a broader contextual analysis of stressful events and conditions may inform us as to the real meaning of these clusters of experiences for individuals.

Gender

The last conditioning variable we consider is gender. In the concluding chapter to their volume, *Gender and Stress*, Barnett, Biener, and Baruch (1987) speak to the differences in the stress process for men and women:

> The lesson of this volume is that gender affects the stress process in many ways and at many points. Being male or female influences both the input side of the process, by determining whether a situation will be perceived as stressful, and the output side, by influencing both choices among coping responses and long-term health implications of stress reactions. (1987, p. 350)

The findings presented in several chapters in this book would equally support such a claim. The psychological and social environments experienced in the workplace or in the home are not equivalent for men and women. The men in Weiss's sample, professionals living in a suburb of Boston, seem to be in families characterized by traditional role segregation between husbands and wives. Here we observe clear gender differences not only in economic and domestic responsibilities but also in the distinctly masculine expression of distress and feminine taking of responsibility for maintaining the home as a supportive environment, features that characterize the emotional, as well as structural, division of labor. Together with the data derived from the interviews done by Pearlin and McCall, a picture emerges of men who are most comfortable withholding information about job stress and who complain about their wives' advice giving, with women trying to be unconditionally supportive of their husbands while finding less legitimization for the stressors they experience on the job or at home.

This would seem to suggest that stress does not flow in the same manner across the work–family boundary for men and women. Although there is ample support for such a conclusion, data presented in this volume also suggest that we have much to learn about the conditions under which such gender differences will be manifested. The detailed daily-level data by Bolger and his colleagues, for example, showed that spillover of problems between work and home was equally prevalent for men and women in their sample and flowed in both directions for each.

Although men and women may both be susceptible to stress crossing the boundaries of work and family, an additional question is whether this stress transmission process is subjectively experienced in the same way between the sexes. Wheaton's chapter, as discussed, suggests that women are more reactive to stress across roles, whereas Weiss's data tend to support a view of men compartmentalizing stress. Of course, this cannot be seen as uniformly true. These are complex relationships that will require replication and extension by other researchers in order to identify the underlying psychological and social processes at work. The structurally different positions that men and women occupy within the workplace or the home will expose them to objectively different stressors, but beyond these more clear-cut determinants of stress exposure, the psychological meaning of the same events or circumstances may also vary between men and women, even in the same marital dyad.

The chapter by Emmons and her colleagues provides some intriguing insights into this type of gender effect. Husbands of these professional women, when asked to report on how they thought their wives' careers affected their marital relationship and their wives' relationship to their children, indicated less negative spillover from work to home than their wives reported. The women also appeared to believe that their husbands had a more negative view of these issues than the husbands in fact report. Disagreement was not pervasive, however, with husbands agreeing with their wives' assessments of the degree to which her career had positive effects on the family and the degree to which these husbands supported their wives' careers. As these authors point out, women in this sample seemed to have higher standards for themselves than their husbands did and had unrealistic perceptions of their husband's expectations of them. Is this foolish guilt, or do men in these relationships behave in ways to reinforce such perceptions among their wives, while professing something quite different? Or do these women, based on longer term and broader based socialization experiences, develop these higher role standards independent of the behavior and beliefs of their husbands? Perhaps the longitudinal analyses with these data will clarify these gender effects and estimate the stability of such divergent perceptions, their sensitivity to family and work events (e.g., promotions or the birth of child), and their relationship to the well-being of these women and their husbands.

IMPLICATIONS FOR STRESS RESEARCH

The motivating principle and main lesson learned from this book is that stress processes are best understood when placed within the context of significant roles that people occupy, in this case work and family. A sensitivity to context is not new to the field of stress research, and the benefits of studying human behavior as embedded in multiple and interacting environments have been eloquently discussed by writers commenting on disciplines such as developmental psychology (e.g., Bronfenbrenner, 1986). These chapters have provided the field of stress research with some specific examples of the benefits that can be derived from engaging in a contextual approach.

One implication is in the area of measurement of stressful experiences, their presumed moderators, and outcomes of stress. A consideration of multiple roles and the various role partners in each domain directs our attention to forms of stress previously neglected when measurement focuses on one person and a role-by-role consideration of stress. For example, several of the chapters point to the viability of the construct of *spillover* (for want of a better term), which, as the chapter by Bromet and her colleagues points out, may help explain variation in psychological distress over and above the effects of stress in one or another of the component roles. Moreover, the study of stress contagion requires attention to multiple units of analysis: the individual, the marital dyad, the children.

The difficult choices inevitably faced by investigators as to the range of experiences to include within a given study can also be informed by reference to the various conceptual model(s) represented in this book. The data presented here suggest that the impact of stressful events on individual well-being must include attention to secondary stressors occurring within the major roles occupied by the person and the actors sharing those roles (e.g., spouses). An explicit consideration of multiple contexts suggests new ways to measure these secondary stressors that may be generated following the occurrence of a major event such as divorce or job loss. For example, the methodologies used in the life events tradition of stress research do not differentiate primary from secondary stressors. We expect that the psychological meaning of primary events such as job loss or divorce for the person is formed in the context of secondary stressors.

The results of these studies also suggest areas of research that have received too little attention, resulting in an inadequate specification of the role of stress in human adaptation. For example, chapters such as the one by Wheaton suggest new ways in which stressful conditions of an ongoing nature may modify the impact of acute life events. This challenges the predominant view that the impact of multiple stressors are cumulative with regard to well-being. Several of the present authors suggest that stress–stress interactions are in fact likely, and that stress in one role may in fact decrease the impact of stress in another role. This calls into question the usual practice of summing stressors across multiple role areas to arrive at overall stress scores. It might be more useful (if the investigator's sample size permits) to stop the aggregation process at the level of major social roles and empirically determine if stress in one role moderates the impact of stress in another. It also seems necessary to extend the measurement of stressors from a reliance on discrete life events to include chronic stressors within the same roles.

As noted, these chapters also call into question the conceptualization of stress buffers as static parts of a person's self or environment. Stressors such as job loss may modify a resource such as spouse support by increasing or decreasing it. Such contingencies create possible problems of interpretation with regard to evidence for stress buffering, particularly in cross-sectional studies, and suggest the need to find alternative analytic ways to document stress buffering that go beyond a stress by resource interaction term (Wheaton, 1985).

We also recognize that these chapters, however informative, did not address a number of issues relevant to stress across the work and family roles. One concerns the precise mechanisms by which individuals maintain the boundary between work and family and the conditions under which these strategies become modified. Some of the strategies persons employ in this regard when stress occurs in one of these roles can be gleaned from the chapter by Emmons and her colleagues, as well as the chapters by Weiss and by Pearlin and McCall. But we know little about how people construct and maintain those boundaries in times that are relatively free of stress. This is a terribly important issue because it reveals a lot about baseline mental well-being, the normal difficulties of the family–work nexus, and the individual's skills in managing the stresses of daily life.

These studies also restricted themselves to an examination of interrelationships among two domains—work and family. Although it can be argued that for adults, these represent the major arenas that structure day-to-day activities and are the major sources of stress and social support; for children, it becomes necessary to add school and the role of student as a major area that may condition the effects of stress arising within the family. As Cohen and her colleagues point out, problems of combining work and family for parents may have important implications for the well-being of the child. A consideration of the school-age child's relationship to the school setting in terms of academic achievement and support from teachers may help explain differences among children in their reactivity to different work/family constellations (Rutter, 1980). Parenthetically, we do not want to overlook the importance of friendships for both adults and children. We tend to view friendships as a type of support resource rather than as a domain of functioning, but we know from studies of adolescents that the latter is perhaps the best perspective.

Finally, many of these chapters set forth a research agenda that takes us closer and closer to the daily lives of the persons we wish to study, for example, by using intensive interviews or daily diary methods. These more intensive, microanalytic approaches to stress research have begun to provide us with partial answers to questions regarding the psychological and social psychological processes that may underlie the effects of stress observed previously in less intensive sample surveys. These approaches also begin to specify the reasons for individual differences in reactivity to what objectively seem to be equivalent stressors. The danger in taking this approach, however, is that we put aside a concern with the more distal, yet powerful, social processes at the institutional and societal levels that may have a profound influence on mental health through these microlevel processes and that may serve as potent leverage points for interventions aimed at reducing stress within the areas of the family and the workplace.

The authors represented here are, of course, not oblivious to these issues, many of them having written about these broader issues in other scholarly contexts. (e.g., Kessler & Neighbors, 1986; Liem & Liem, 1978; Pearlin, 1985). The intent of this book was not to explicitly consider intervention and social policy (although we urged authors to make such connections where they felt justified in doing so), but we also realize that a series of studies that tend to focus on microprocesses also invites speculation about interventions, albeit at the individual and interpersonal levels (stress management techniques, social skills training, etc.). Although clearly useful as part of an overall approach to stress reduction, we would not advocate a reliance on such microlevel solutions to what are essentially societal level problems. Ultimately, broader interventions affecting large numbers of working people in families, such as adequate day care, maternity and paternity leave, raising the minimum wage, prior notice of plant closings, retraining of workers, or generally reducing levels of poverty will ultimately do more to reduce both work and family stress.

REFERENCES

Antonovsky, A. (1979). *Health, stress, and coping.* San Francisco: Jossey-Bass.

Barnett, R. C., Biener, L., & Baruch, G. C. (Eds.). (1987). *Gender and stress.* New York: Free Press.

Bronfenbrenner, U. (1986). Ecology of the family as a context for human development. *Developmental Psychology, 22,* 723–742.

Cohen, S., & Syme, S. L. (Eds.). (1985). *Social support and health.* New York: Academic Press.

Jacobson, D. E. (1986). Types and timing of social support. *Journal of Health and Social Behavior, 27,* 250–264.

Kessler, R. C., & Neighbors, H. W. (1986). A new perspective on the relationships among race, social class, and psychological distress. *Journal of Health and Social Behavior, 27,* 107–115.

Lazarus, R. S., & Folkman, S. (1984). *Stress, appraisal, and coping.* New York: Springer Publishing Co.

Liem, R., & Liem, J. (1978). Social class and mental illness reconsidered: The role of economic stress and social support. *Journal of Health and Social Behavior, 19,* 139–156.

Pearlin, L. I. (1985). Social structure and processes of social support. In S. Cohen & L. Syme (Eds.), *Social support and health* (pp. 43–60). New York: Academic Press.

Pearlin, L. I., & Schooler, C. (1978). The structure of coping. *Journal of Health and Social Behavior, 19,* 2–21.

Rutter, M. (1980). School influences on children's behavior and development. *Pediatrics, 65,* 208–220.

Thoits, P. (1983). Dimensions of life events that influence psychological distress: An evaluation and synthesis of the literature. In H. B. Kaplan (Ed.), *Psychosocial stress: Trends in theory and research* (pp. 33–103). New York: Academic Press.

Wheaton, B. (1985). Models for the stress-buffering functions of coping resources. *Journal of Health and Social Behavior, 26,* 352–364.

Index